INDUSTRIAL DEVELOPMENT
IN COMMUNIST CHINA

INDUSTRIAL
DEVELOPMENT
IN COMMUNIST CHINA

Edited by

CHOH-MING LI

FREDERICK A. PRAEGER, *Publisher*
New York • London

FREDERICK A. PRAEGER, PUBLISHER
111 Fourth Ave., New York 3, N.Y., U.S.A.
77–79 Charlotte Street, London W.1, England

Published in the United States of America in 1964
by Frederick A. Praeger, Inc., Publisher

Published in the United Kingdom in 1964
by Frederick A. Praeger, Inc., Publisher

First published in Great Britain in 1964
as a special issue of *The China Quarterly*

Library of Congress Catalog Card Number 64-21808

This book is Number 150 in the series of
Praeger Publications in Russian History and World Communism

Printed in the United States of America

Contents

INDUSTRIAL DEVELOPMENT
IN COMMUNIST CHINA

China's Industrial Development, 1958-63

By CHOH-MING LI

CHINA had no Second Five-Year Plan (1958–62) only five *ad hoc* annual plans during that period. In basic construction and industrial production a great leap forward did take place in the first three years, only to be followed by collapse and readjustment in the last two years. In agriculture, the period started with an unprecedented bumper crop in the first year, after which there commenced an agricultural crisis that grew in intensity from year to year until 1962 when the output of food grains and green vegetables began to show recovery. This was in sharp contrast to the First Five-Year Plan period which concluded with spectacular achievements in heavy industry, moderate success in light industry and slow but steady improvement in agriculture.

The accomplishments in industry during the Second Five-Year period have been officially assessed in different ways. A general evaluation was given by the chairman of the State Economic Commission.[1]

> We have now built an industrial system of some size . . . Now we have progressed from copying to independent designing . . . We are able to make some big precision equipment . . . We are able to design independently and to build with our own technical forces many important construction projects . . .
>
> During the First Five-Year Plan China could make about 55 per cent. of the machinery and equipment she needed. During the Second Five-Year Plan, this level was raised to about 85 per cent. Our level of self-sufficiency in steel products climbed from about 75 per cent. in the First Five-Year Plan period to around 90 per cent. in the Second Five-Year Plan period . . .
>
> Nowadays, not only has the industry in these coastal cities been greatly expanded but every province and autonomous region in the country has established modern industry to some extent or other. . . . Now we have not only thoroughly built up the [large-scale Anshan iron and steel industrial] base but also constructed new iron and steel bases at Wuhan, Paotow and elsewhere . . . now all the big, small and medium-sized cities and quite a number of villages too have power stations of various sizes . . . now many provinces of the country have established up-to-date textile mills.

[1] Po I-po, " The Socialist Industrialisation of China [written for *Cuba Socialista* of Cuba]," *Peking Review*, No. 41, October 11, 1963.

The National People's Congress in November 1963 was told that " since 1958 China's industry has progressed satisfactorily both in the scale of production and in quantity; there has been a leap forward development especially in the variety and quality of products." [2] In comparing 1962 with 1957, the varieties of steel, rolled steel and non-ferrous metals produced in the country were more than doubled, varieties of petroleum products increased by nearly 200 per cent., and varieties of machine tools grew by nearly 150 per cent. The country was used to importing the great bulk of the petroleum products she needed; now she is in the main self-sufficient.[3]

According to another official evaluation, the readjustment since 1960 had produced a better balance within the industrial structure. From 1953 through 1960 China's metallurgical, chemical and other heavy industries showed tremendous growth, but the mining industries (coal, ferrous and non-ferrous metals)—the foundation of all heavy industries—failed to keep apace. Since 1961, priority has been given to the development of the mining industries, and their growth accelerated accordingly. Likewise petroleum, timber, chemical fertiliser, and special steels—the four weak links in the industrial system—have also been strengthened. All this, together with the establishment of new industries producing synthetic fibre, plastics, synthetic fatty acid, etc., during the Second Five-Year period, lays a basis for further industrial growth.[4]

Finally, it was officially claimed that by the end of 1962 the number of scientific and technical personnel in various fields increased by 70 per cent. when compared with 1957; that they had higher scientific and technical standards. As a result, the number of big and medium-sized industrial projects, designed and equipped with installations made by the Chinese themselves, had increased from 413 in the First Five-Year Plan period to 1,013 in the second.[5] China, therefore, is growing more and more independent in technological matters.[6]

These official claims of accomplishments actually cover up many developments of basic importance to the economy during the last five years.

---

[2] " Continue Striving for the Construction of an Independent, Comprehensive and Modern National Economic System," *People's Daily* editorial, December 4, 1963, p. 2; translated in *Peking Review*, No. 49, December 6, 1963. It is, of course, possible that the country is self-sufficient because of a drastic reduction in consumption.

[3] " Press Communiqué of National People's Congress," *People's Daily*, December 4, 1963 ; translated in *Peking Review*, No. 49, December 6, 1963.

[4] " Situation in Industry—Good," *Peking Review*, No. 31, August 2, 1963.

[5] " Press Communiqué . . .," *op. cit.*

[6] A technical note is in order. The official statistical figures quoted in this paper are taken from Chinese and Russian official publications familiar to all those working in this field of study. They will not be cited in the interest of space. All rouble figures have been converted in terms of the 1961 rouble, which is equivalent to $1·10 or 4·44 roubles of the 1950 variety. The official exchange rate of the yuan is 2·617 to the U.S. dollar, but the market rate in Hong Kong, according to one report, was about 5·5 yuan to the U.S. dollar in 1958, 7·7 in 1959, 7·9 in 1960, and 8·0 in 1961 and 1962.

The following discussion starts by examining the nature of the so-called Second Five-Year Plan and tracing the changes in over-all development policies with particular reference to industry. This is followed by an analysis of the course of industrial development during the period, and the consequent structural changes in industry and in the economy as a whole. Then comes a discussion of the internal factors underlying developments for the period; they include the investment programme, the small-industry experiment decentralisation and planning, industrial management and Soviet aid. This discussion will be concluded with the developments of 1963 and the trends which are emerging.

THE SECOND FIVE-YEAR PLAN AND DEVELOPMENT POLICIES

By the middle of 1956, the fourth year of the First Five-Year Plan, socialisation of the whole economy had practically been achieved without serious resistance from the people. Industrialisation based on the development of heavy industry around a nucleus of Soviet-aid projects was proceeding with satisfactory speed. A major wage reform was introduced at this time and the income of industrial and other urban workers rose on average by 14·5 per cent. Basic-construction planning and control, material balances and allocation, comprehensive planning of state budgets, business finance and bank credit had all been systematised for some years and were being improved with practice. The number of engineers and technicians in industry was increasing rapidly, and as a result of Soviet help the Chinese were able to do more and more surveying, designing and installation by themselves. It was against this background that the Central Committee of the Chinese Communist Party decided in July 1956 to convene the Party's Eighth National Congress that September to discuss, as one of the four major items in the agenda, a proposal concerning the Second Five-Year Plan for national economic development.[7]

The proposal aimed to make China 70 per cent. self-sufficient in machinery and equipment, including some heavy and some precision machines which would be needed for national development plans by 1962, and to ensure that by 1967 China would be transformed from a backward agricultural country into an advanced industrialised nation.[8] According to the resolution passed by the Party Congress, the basic tasks under the Second Five-Year Plan included, among others, " continued development of various industries with heavy industry as the core," and

---

[7] *People's Daily*, July 7, 1956.

[8] Liu Shao-ch'i, " Political Report to the Party's National Congress," *People's Daily*, September 17, 1956, and " The Party's National Congress Approves ' The Proposal Concerning the Second Five-Year Plan (1958–62) for National Development,' " *People's Daily*, September 29, 1956.

" further promotion of industrial, agricultural and handicraft production with concomitant development of transportation and trade." The industries to be given special emphasis were the expanding industries such as metal processing, machine making, electric power, coal and building materials, together with weaker industries such as petroleum and radio, and the yet-to-be-established industries of synthetic chemicals and nuclear power.[9] In comparison with the First Five-Year Plan, the amount of basic investment during the second five years was expected to double, with the share for industry increasing from 58·2 per cent. to about 60 per cent. and that for agriculture, water conservation and forestry from 7·6 per cent. to 10 per cent. Target figures for major commodities and other items of special importance were listed.

In February 1957 the State Council accepted the proposal and instructed the State Planning Commission to work out as soon as possible, with various central ministries and commissions and local governments at the provincial level, a draft of the Second Five-Year Plan to be submitted to the State Council and through it to the National People's Congress for approval. The official record, however, shows that no such draft plan was ever submitted to the State Council let alone the National People's Congress.

The proposed targets for the Second Five-Year Plan, together with later revisions, are presented in Table 1, which also gives the official output data for 1957 through 1959 as part of the statistics with which the planning authorities had been working. Several observations may be made about the table. In the first place, even after endorsement by the Party's National Congress, the proposed 1962 targets were still questioned by some Party Members and government officials on the grounds that they were set too low. To answer these objections an article was published in the official journal of the State Planning Commission in October 1956 which pointed out that the proposed basic investment, already more than twice as much as that for the First Five-Year Plan, was based both on a maximum supply from domestic sources, with China producing as much as 70 per cent. of the heavy machinery and equipment required, and on the half a million new graduates from colleges and universities that the country could possibly produce during the period. Hence, it would be inappropriate either to increase the proposed amount for basic investment or to step up the rate of industrial growth.[10] In fact, at the end of the First Five-Year Plan when the economic shape of 1957

9 Chou En-lai, " Report on the Proposal concerning the Second Five-Year Plan (1958–62) for Economic Development," *People's Daily*, September 19, 1956.

10 Chia Fu, " On the Growth Rates for the Period of the Second Five-Year Plan," *Chi-hua Ching-chi (Planned Economy)*, No. 10, October 23, 1956. Also reprinted in *Hsin-hua Pan-yueh-k'an (New China Semi-Monthly)*, No. 24, December 21, 1956, pp. 40–42.

Table 1

OFFICIAL DATA RELATING TO THE PROPOSED TARGETS FOR THE SECOND FIVE-YEAR PLAN

Item	Unit	Proposed target 1957 (FFYP)	Proposed target 1962 (SFYP) proposed 9/56	1962 target, revised 12/57	Actual output (official) 1957	Actual output (official) 1958	1962 target, revised 8/59	1959 output (official)
A. Heavy industry:								
1. Coal	million tons	113·00	190–210	230·00	130·00	270·00	335·00	347·80
2. Crude Oil	million tons	2.01	5–6	" Less "	1.46	2·26	—	3·68
3. Electric power	bil. kw–hrs	15·90	40–43	—	19·34	27·53	—	41·50
4. Steel	million tons	4.12	10·5–12·0	12·00a	5·35	8·00	12·00b	8·63
5. Aluminium ingot	thous. tons	20·00	100–120	—	—	—	—	—
6. Ch. fertiliser	thous. tons	·58	3·0–3·2	7·00	·63	·81	—	1·30
7. Metallurgical equipment	thous. tons	8·00	30–40	—	—	—	—	205·00
8. Metal-cutting machine tools	thous. units	13·00	60–65	" Less "	28·00	50·00	—	70·00
9. Power generating equipment	million kw s	·16	1·4–1·5	—	·20	·80	—	2·15
10. Cement	million ton.	6·00	12·5–14·5	12·50	6·86	9·30	—	12·27
11. Timber	mil. cub. m	20·00	31–34	—	27·90	35·00	—	41·20
B. Light industry:								
1. Cotton yarn	mil. bales	5·00	8–9	—	4·65	6·10	—	8·20
2. Cotton cloth	bil. metres	5·58	7·25–8·00	—	5·05	5·70	—	7·50
3. Salt	million tons	7·55	10–11	—	8·28	10·40	—	11·04
4. Edible vegetable oil	million tons	1·79	3·1–3·2	—	1·10	1·25	—	1·47
5. Sugar c	million tons	1·10	2·4–2·5	—	·86	·90	—	1·13
6. Machine-made paper	million tons	·66	1·5–1·6	—	·91	1·22	—	1·70
C. Crops								
1. Food grains	million tons	181·60	250·00	240·00	185·00	250·00	275·00	270·00
2. Ginned cotton	million tons	1.64	2.40	2·15	1·64	2·10	2·31	2·41
3. Soybeans	million tons	11·22	12·50	—	10·05	10·50	—	11·50
D. Livestock:								
1. Cattle	million head	73·61	90·00	—	63·62	—	—	—
2. Horses	million head	8·34	11·00	—	7·30	—	—	—
3. Sheep and goats	million head	113·04	170·00	—	95·58	108·86	—	—
4. Pigs	million head	138·34	250·00	220·00	145·90	160·00	—	180·00d

Note: a Presumably both factory-produced and indigenous steel
  b Factory-produced steel only
  c Including both factory-produced and indigenous sugar
  d Preliminary
  — Not available

began to emerge, the chairman of the State Planning Commission announced that " with two more years of experience after the Party's proposal in 1956 for the Second Five-Year Plan, the proposed targets for 1962 had to be readjusted." [11] The few revised figures that were released indicate that except for coal, steel and chemical fertilisers, the proposed targets were scaled down either to the original lower limit, as in the case of cement, or further below it as in all other cases. The reduction in the quota for the critical petroleum industry was explained as a

[11] Li Fu-ch'un, " On the Achievements of China's First Five-Year Plan and the Tasks and Directions of Socialist Construction in the Immediate Future," *People's Daily*, December 8, 1957. This was a speech given at the Eighth National Congress of All-China Labour Unions.

result of limitation of natural resources, and the reduction in metal-cutting machine tools, as a result of limited demand. Significantly, in the same speech where these downward revisions of 1962 targets were made public, the slogan of "surpassing Britain in the output of steel, coal, machine tools, cement and chemical fertilisers by 1972" was advanced. And this was shortly after the release of the revised Draft of the Outline for Agricultural Development from 1956 to 1967.

Secondly, although in the latter half of 1957 the planning authorities began to realise the importance of agriculture to industrial development, and the proposed output of chemical fertilisers for 1962 was substantially raised at the end of 1957, the theme underlying the proposal concerning the Second Five-Year Plan remained unaltered, as was evident in Li Fu-ch'un's statement in December 1957: "Heavy industry should constitute the centre of the plan with priority in development" over all other sectors. It must have also been realised at that time that agricultural output could not increase rapidly without a substantial increase in state investment in agriculture. Hence, the proposed 1962 targets for food grains, raw cotton and pigs were scaled down while the target for chemical fertiliser was raised by over 100 per cent., along with the introduction of farm implements as a major item in the national plan. Since both chemical fertilisers and farm implements come under heavy industry, the attention given to agriculture made the "priority development" of heavy industry all the more inevitable.

Mass mobilisation in the winter of 1957 to launch both the national agricultural development programme and the campaign to surpass Britain in major heavy industrial output probably set off the Great Leap Forward movement in 1958. The objective of the movement was formulated by the Party's Central Committee as the "General Line of going all out and aiming high to achieve greater, quicker, better and more economical results in building socialism." [12] As a result, all the caution that had been taken in setting up the growth rates and targets in the 1956 proposal concerning the Second Five-Year Plan was now swept aside. Politics were in command everywhere. Statistics were reported by the cadres in the field according to their "enthusiasm in socialist revolution" rather than on the basis of fact.[13]

Speaking before a joint meeting sponsored by the Metallurgical Ministry and the Ministry of Finance in July 1958, Li Hsien-nien, the Finance Minister, described succinctly the differences of planning then prevailing: "At present the central authorities are compiling targets for

---

12 Liu Shao-ch'i, "Report on the Work of the Chinese Communist Party's Central Committee to the Second Session of the Party's National Congress," *New China Semi-Monthly*, No. 11, June 10, 1958, pp. 1–11.
13 See my volume, *The Statistical System of Communist China* (Berkeley: University of California Press, 1962), especially Part II.

the Second Five-Year Plan, but have not been able to catch up with the swift changes in practical conditions that require upward revision of the targets almost every day." [14] These difficulties multiplied as long as the Great Leap Forward movement continued.

When the Eighth Plenary Session of the Party's Central Committee came in August 1959 to deflate the earlier fantastic claims of economic accomplishments, it singled out coal and factory-produced steel in industry and food grains and cotton in agriculture as the most important of all items in the Second Five-Year Plan and revised upwards their targets for 1962. Yet, five months later when the annual economic plan for 1960 was submitted, it was discovered that by the end of 1959 two (coal and cotton) out of the four revised targets had already been surpassed, one other (food grains) had almost been reached, and only the item of factory-produced steel trailed behind. Either the statistical information available to the planners in August 1959 was faulty or the statistical reports at the end of the year were false. Planning had clearly become impossible.

Table 1 also shows that by the end of 1959, the quotas for 1962, as originally set forth in September 1956, had been fulfilled in the case of thirteen out of the twenty-four items and not fulfilled in the case of eleven others. This called for a " Supplementary Plan for the Last Three Years of the Second Five-Year Plan," which may have been prepared and submitted by Li Fu-ch'un to the National People's Congress in March 1960, but which has not been published. The report of Li Fu-ch'un that was published at the time, concerned the draft economic plan for 1960, in which the idea of regarding agriculture as the foundation, with industry taking the lead in economic development, was advanced. [15] But no indication was given yet that the basic policy of priority development of heavy industry had been changed.

The change began to develop in the autumn of 1960 when the harvest turned out to be much worse than expected. In late September, a movement of " all people to agriculture and food grains " was brought to a peak by cadres all over the country. [16] This represented a complete turnabout from the nation-wide movement of " all people to iron and steel " that took place in the late summer of 1958. Then, in November 1960, an editorial appeared in the Party's journal *Red Flag* under the title " Simultaneous Development of Industry and Agriculture is an Important Law in China's Socialist Economy," in which Mao was credited with formulation of the policy of placing agriculture at the top

[14] *Ts'ai-cheng (Finance)*, No. 8, August 5, 1958.
[15] *People's Daily*, March 31, 1960, pp. 2-3.
[16] *People's Daily*, September 27, 1960.

position in the economy—a policy, observed the editorial, " not incompatible with that of priority development of heavy industry." The importance of agricultural development was clearly realised, but there was to be no change in priority in terms of resource allocation when compared with heavy industries.

The sharp change occurred in January 1961 when Li Fu-ch'un, in his report to the Eighth Plenum of the Central Committee, admitted that the planned agricultural output for 1960 had not been attained because of " severe natural calamities in 1959 " and " natural calamities in 1960 that were unprecedented in 100 years." This led the Plenum to reaffirm the movement of " all the party and all people to agriculture and food grains." The Plenum decided further that " since there had been tremendous development in heavy industry in the last three years, its output of major products already far in excess of the planned level for 1961 and 1962, the scale of basic construction should therefore be appropriately reduced." As to light industry, in order to ease the severe shortage of supply of consumer goods, assistance was to be given to " further development of light industry, rural and urban handicrafts, family side-line occupations and suburban agriculture, and to the revival of primary markets in rural areas." [17] In spite of this lip service paid to the promotion of light industry, the general industrial policy was known to be that of " readjustment, consolidation, reinforcement and improvement." [18] The Great Leap Forward movement was thus officially brought to an end.

The year 1961 saw the agricultural crisis deepen. China began to import food on a huge scale. From December 1960, when the first shipments arrived, up to the end of 1963, about 16 million metric tons of grain have been purchased largely from Canada and Australia. The total includes 5·6 million tons in 1961 (mainly wheat, flour and barley), 4·7 million tons in 1962 (mainly wheat and corn), and 5·5 million tons (mainly wheat) scheduled for delivery in 1963 (about 3·5 million tons for the first half of the year).[19]

When the autumn harvest of 1961 was no better than that of 1960, it was clear that the mere reduction in the scale of basic construction was not enough. In December 1961 the Party issued secretly to the cadres in the field a document known as " Seventy Articles of Industrial

[17] *People's Daily*, January 21, 1961.
[18] Kung Hsiang-cheng, " Produce More and Better Light Industrial Products for Daily Use," *Red Flag*, No. 89–90, February 10, 1962.
[19] " A Report on World Grain Exports to Red China," *Foreign Agriculture*, I, No. 18, May 6, 1963, and " Australia Sells Communist China more Wheat," *ibid*. No. 26, July 1, 1963. These estimates by the United States Department of Agriculture differ somewhat from other estimates, such as those published in this journal; see Allan J. Barry, " The Chinese Food Purchases," *The China Quarterly*, No. 11.

Policy."[20] In essence, it directed that unless special authority was given, all basic construction should be suspended, all those enterprises that had been operating regularly at a loss be shut down, and the practice of recruiting labour from rural areas be abandoned for at least three years. But at this time warnings were still voiced in the official journal of the Party against one-sided emphasis on agriculture at the expense of the simultaneous advance of industry, transportation, culture and education.[21]

Most probably the "Seventy Articles" furnished the basis for Chou En-lai's formulation of "The Work of Readjusting the National Economy and Our Immediate Tasks," which took a whole section in his report on the work of government to the National People's Congress on March 27, 1962. Here he stressed that "the core of readjustment" consisted in carrying through the policy of readjustment, consolidation, reinforcement and improvement, and entailed ten immediate tasks, three of which were of direct concern to industry.[22]

> Task 3. Contract further the basic construction front, and redirect the materials, equipment and manpower to the most urgent areas.
> Task 4. Properly reduce urban population and workers and functionaries, the first move being to send those workers and functionaries who came from the rural districts back to take part in agricultural production, so as to strengthen the agricultural front.
> Task 10. Improve further the work in planning and try to attain a comprehensive balance among different sectors in the national economy in accordance with the [declining priority] order of agriculture, light industry, and heavy industry.

The extent to which these measures were applied may be gathered from the fact that the sudden exodus of Chinese refugees (which included many unemployed from urban areas) from the mainland to Hong Kong took place in May of that year.

The change from the priority development of heavy industry to "agriculture first" was complete when the Tenth Plenum of the Party's Central Committee, meeting in September 1962, resolved that "as the immediate urgent task of the people, the development of agriculture, itself the foundation of the national economy with industry as the

---

20 It has been widely reported that during this period of economic crisis several other policy documents were also issued, namely, "Thirty-five Articles of Handicraft Policy" issued by the State Council in December 1960, and "Sixty Articles of the By-laws (Draft) for Rural People's Communes" and "Seventy Articles of Cultural and Educational Policy" issued by the Party's central authorities in about May 1961. Copies of these have been smuggled out to Hong Kong. The Union Research Institute, for example, has records of them. Extracts have been published in several issues of the Institute's journal, *China Weekly*.

21 Wen Shih-jun, "Centralise all Effort to Seek Solutions for Industrial Problems," *Red Flag*, No. 24, December 16, 1961.

22 *People's Daily*, April 17, 1962, p. 1. The official translation of the ten immediate tasks in *Peking Review* is too abbreviated to convey the full meaning of the original.

leading factor, must be given the topmost position." The resolution made it clear that what was required under this policy was " to re-locate resolutely our work from the industrial departments to the sphere where agriculture is the foundation." In concrete terms, this called for further readjustment of industry without straining existing resources— through better management, greater variety of products, and higher quality of output—in order to meet the needs of the technological reform of agriculture.

The earlier policy changes in 1961 and 1962 had already necessitated the drafting of an " Adjusted Plan for the Last Two Years of the Second Five-Year Plan," a step approved by the National People's Congress as late as April 1962. This " adjusted plan " has not been made public, although at its meeting in July 1963 the Standing Committee of the National People's Congress gave its approval to Li Fu-ch'un's report on the " adjusted plan " and its results as well as to Li Hsien-nien's report on the final state accounts for 1961 and 1962.[23]

Hence, except for the brief statement of intentions and output targets in September 1956 and a few subsequently revised target figures, there has not been any formulation of a Five-Year Plan for the period from 1958 to 1962. The Great Leap Forward made any long-term planning—or any planning, for that matter—impossible, and the deepening of the agricultural crisis since 1959 has rendered the annual plans for the following three years entirely *ad hoc* affairs. There has never been a Second Five-Year Plan in any real sense of the term. As regards development policies, the first three years of the period continued, rather unswervingly, the policy underlying the First Five-Year Plan of focusing on the rapid growth of heavy industry, while the last two years of the period saw an increasingly severe application (at least up to the second or third quarter of 1962) of the measures of " readjustment, consolidation, reinforcement and improvement " in basic construction and industry, with agriculture finally gaining over-riding priority in " development by modernisation " towards the end of the period.

THE COURSE OF INDUSTRIAL DEVELOPMENT AND STRUCTURAL CHANGES

Given the *ad hoc* policies of the Great Leap and subsequent retrenchment during the period from 1958 to 1962, what was the picture of industrial development? It is not easy to give a satisfactory answer because even the officially finalised statistics are of dubious validity for the first two years and are virtually unavailable for the last three.

---

[23] This seems to imply that official statistics for 1961 and 1962 were not finalised until July 1963.

Serious attempts, however, have been made by several scholars to estimate the development in quantitative terms. The most elaborate is certainly the study of China's national income for 1933 and 1952–59 by T. C. Liu and K. C. Yeh, in which a great deal of attention inevitably was paid to industrial growth.[24] Another scholarly study is Alexander Eckstein's, which, however, is concerned with the national income for 1952 alone.[25] W. W. Hollister's early estimates of China's national income since 1950 are being extensively revised.[26] A study of China's economic potential by Y. L. Wu, F. P. Hoeber and M. M. Rockwell has been published, in which China's national income from 1950 to 1962 was "reappraised."[27] Their estimates, based heavily upon the Liu-Yeh study up to 1958, are noteworthy because the estimates were brought up to 1962. For industrial output alone, Kang Chao's index from 1949 through 1959 merits special mention; it is based primarily on official figures without independent adjustment.[28]

All these estimates are beset with technical difficulties generally known as index-number problems, many of which cannot be avoided; and, because of the very nature of the source material, perhaps it is not unfair to say that all the estimates for the period under discussion cannot claim to be more than "educated guesses."[29] Nevertheless, several of them are of interest to students of China's industrial development and deserve a summary presentation here—without a technical discussion of their difficulties or any critical evaluation of them.

Their comparability need not be seriously questioned, as long as they are compared not in absolute magnitude but in general tendencies. For purpose of comparison, it may be noted that "industry" includes manufacturing, mining and utilities, and that within industry the distinction between modern (factory) industry and handicrafts generally depends on whether mechanical power is used in the main working

24 Ta-chung Liu and Kung-chia Yeh, *The Economy of the Chinese Mainland: National Income and Economic Development, 1933–59* (Santa Monica, California: The RAND Corporation, Memorandum RM-3519-PR, April 1963), two vols.

25 Alexander Eckstein, *The National Income of Communist China* (Glencoe, Illinois: The Free Press, 1961).

26 William W. Hollister, *China's Gross National Product and Social Accounts, 1950–57* (Glencoe, Illinois: The Free Press, 1958); also his " Estimates of the Gross National Product [of China], 1958–59," in Yuan-li Wu, ed., *The Realities of Communist China* (Milwaukee, Wisconsin: Marquette University, October 1960). See also his article below.

27 *The Economic Potential of Communist China* (Menlo Park, California: Stanford Research Institute, Technical Report No. 2, October 1963), two vols. The national income estimates given in this work apparently supersede an earlier estimate by Y. L. Wu which appears in his volume *Economic Development and the Use of Energy Resources in Communist China* (New York: Praeger, 1963).

28 Kang Chao, "Indices of Industrial Output in Communist China," *Review of Economics and Statistics*, XIV, No. 3, August 1963. For an estimate by Hung and Wu according to a short-cut method, see their joint article.

29 Thus Lin and Yeh regarded their estimates for 1958–62 as " conjectural."

process, irrespective of the number of workers employed. These definitions have been used by Peking, and are therefore adopted to facilitate the recalculation of growth by sub-aggregates. Gross value product is generally much larger than net value product because the former takes into account the cost of materials used in production and therefore one is confronted with the problem of double-counting.[30] In all the estimates, either 1952 or 1957, prices were employed in order to compute the value of aggregates at constant prices. Because of differences in price structures between those two years, a given time series would show higher rates of growth when computed at 1952 prices than when computed at 1957 prices.

THE COURSE OF INDUSTRIAL DEVELOPMENT

Table 2 summarises different estimates of the value of output for the whole of industry in relative terms. It will be observed that all the four estimates agree that there was a " great leap forward " in industrial growth from 1957 through 1959 or 1960 when the growth rate for these two or three years is compared with that in the preceding five years. Although the growth rate shown in official statistics for either one of these periods is much higher than that arrived at by any one of the

Table 2

DIFFERENT ESTIMATES OF INCREASES IN INDUSTRIAL VALUE PRODUCT OVER SPECIFIED PERIODS, 1952–60

(In per cent.)

Source of estimate	Nature of value product	Total increase over 1952–57	1957–59	1957–60	Increase in 1958	1959	1960
Liu-Yeh	net (1952 p.)	94·2	51·9		19·6	27·0	
Wu et al.	net (1952 p.)	89·2	58·1	82·9	19·5	32·3	15·7
Chao	net (1952 p.)	85·9	71·3		30·3	31·5	
Official	gross (1952 p.)	128·4					
Official	net (1957 p.)		131·5	177·3	66·3	39·2	29·0

three private studies, the official data and Chao's estimate give a steadily declining annual rate of increase in 1958 and 1959, whereas in the other two studies the growth rate was increasing during these two years. But both official data and private estimates agree that the rate of increase fell in 1960, although the absolute magnitudes still

---

[30] Discussion of this problem can be found in many publications. See, *e.g.*, my volume *Economic Development of Communist China* (Berkeley: University of California Press, 1959), pp. 30–35.

showed an increase. Not given in the table, the complete series of Wu *et al.* further displayed a precipitous decline in absolute magnitudes by 74 per cent. in 1961 and levelled off with a slight further drop of 3 per cent. in 1962. In their joint article below, Hung and Wu have tentatively concluded that the economic downswing of 1961 and 1962 had probably come to an end by the second part of 1962 and that the second half of the year was probably marked by a vigorous rebound in the industrial sector.

Modern Industry vs. Handicrafts

Table 3 presents different estimates of changes in the value output of modern industry and handicrafts in different periods from 1952 to 1960. As expected, modern industry showed a much higher rate of increase than handicrafts, the difference being much more glaring in the private estimates than in official data. All the estimates agree that in the case of modern industry the rate of increase was greater from 1952 to 1957 than from 1957 to 1959, but the disparity between growth rates was much less according to Chao's estimate and the official series than it was according to the other two studies. During the first two years of the Great Leap Forward, official data showed a declining rate of growth in modern industry whereas the study of Wu *et al.* gave an increasing rate. The latter study also painted a picture of a declining rate in 1960, and a sharp drop in absolute terms by 71 per cent. in 1961 and by 4 per cent. in 1962. (Not shown in table).

Table 3

DIFFERENT ESTIMATES OF INCREASES IN THE VALUE OF OUTPUT OF MODERN INDUSTRY AND HANDICRAFTS OVER SELECTED PERIODS, 1952–59

(In per cent.)

Source of estimate	Value product (in 1952 prices)	Increases over 1952–57 Modern	Handicrafts	Increases over 1957–60 Modern	Handicrafts
Liu-Yeh	net	140·2	14·0	60·4	20·4
Wu *et al.*	net	134·1	12·5	71·9	9·3
Chao	net	95·9		89·6	
Official	gross	152·3	85·4	144·8[a]	99·7[a]

[a] My interpolation from the official data in 1957 prices.

For handicrafts, there is a sizable difference between the official and private estimates in regard to the rate of growth. But the Liu-Yeh study agrees with official data in showing that the growth of handicrafts was greater during the first two years of the Great Leap

Forward than it was during the preceding five years. The study of Wu *et al.* arrives at a reverse result, and indicates further that because of the agricultural crisis the handicraft value product actually dropped 8·5 per cent. in 1960 and another 11 per cent. in 1961, with the fall halted in 1962.

STRUCTURAL CHANGE IN INDUSTRY

Table 4, compiled entirely from official data, presents the changing composition of industry according to different criteria, namely, method of production, nature of product, operating organisation and level of control. The figures for 1960 were those of the plan for the year; the gross value of industrial output has since been officially estimated at 195·25 billion yuan, that is, 7 per cent. short of the planned figure,

Table 4

OFFICIAL DATA ON CERTAIN ASPECTS OF INDUSTRIAL STRUCTURE, 1957–1960

(In 1957 prices)

Item	1957	1958	1959	1960 planned
Gross value of all-industry output (in billion yuan)	70·4	117·1	163·0	210·0
Composition:	In per cent.			
A. By production method				
1. Modern	70·6	74·5	74·6	—
2. Handicrafts	29·4	25·5	25·4	—
B. By nature of product				
1. Heavy industry	48·4	57·3	58·7	60·5
2. Light industry	51·6	42·7	41·3	39·5
C. By operating organization				
1. Industrial departments ..	100·0	94·7	92·7	91·0
2. People's communes ..	0	5·3	7·3	9·0
a. Rural	0	5·0	6·1	7·1
b. Urban	0	0·3	1·2	1·9
D. By level of control				
1. Central	46·0	27·0	26·0	—
2. Local	54·0	73·0	74·0	—

but no other details are available. Heavy industry includes, of course, defence industries. Consolidation and retrenchment since 1960 must have eliminated a large number of the workshops operated by the rural and urban communes.

The changes in the proportion between local and central industries did reflect somewhat a wider dispersion of industrial location than ever before, as is well demonstrated in the case of the iron and steel industry by Ronald Hsia's article below; but the main reason was the decentralisation move started in the winter of 1957. On the whole, the central authorities controlled all the large and strategic industries, mostly in the category of heavy industry. It should be pointed out that in 1959, since modern industry produced about three-quarters of industrial output and the centrally controlled sector produced a little over one-quarter of industrial output, about one-half of the modern industrial output must be in the hands of local authorities. By the same reasoning, over a half of the heavy industrial output must be out of the hands of the central authorities.

As expected, heavy industry grew much faster than light industry; this was as true in the first two years of the Great Leap Forward as it was in the preceding five years. It is interesting to find that in both periods heavy industry developed faster than modern industry while light industry fell behind the handicrafts.

According to Wu *et al.* modern industry reached the height of its relative importance in 1960 when it accounted for 88 per cent. of the industrial value product, leaving only 12 per cent. for handicrafts; but the proportion between them changed to 69 per cent. for modern industry and 31 per cent. for handicrafts in 1962.

CHANGES IN THE STRUCTURE OF THE ECONOMY

The rapid growth of industry may be viewed in terms of the change in its relative position in the whole economy. Table 5 summarises two different estimates of the changes in national income and its composition from 1952 to 1962. It should be recalled that Wu and his associates relied heavily in their estimates up to 1957, if not up to 1959, on Liu-Yeh's work. The similarity between the two estimates for 1957 is striking.

According to Liu and Yeh, in the space of three years from 1957 to 1959 modern industry increased substantially its contribution to the net domestic product from 21 per cent. to 25 per cent., while handicrafts' share declined slightly from 6 per cent. to 5 per cent. But as a result of the economic crisis that induced a series of policy shifts since the end of 1960, the share of modern industry dropped drastically and that of handicrafts increased in 1961 and 1962, as shown in the findings of Wu and his associates. Their findings also suggest that the sectoral structure of the economy at the end of 1962 had changed little from that at the end of 1952 (not shown in the table). This, of course, does not represent any basic change in structure, since the decline in the relative importance of modern industry was not due to any significant destruction of productive capacity, but rather to the temporary shutting down of many factories and mines.

Table 5

TWO ESTIMATES (IN 1952 PRICES) OF THE CHANGES IN ECONOMIC STRUCTURE, 1952–62

Item	Liu-Yeh estimate of Net Domestic Product			Wu et al estimate of Gross National Product		
	1952	1957	1959	1957	1959	1962
Aggregate in billion yuan	71·41	95·34	124·52	95·2	110·5	82·7
Composition:	In per cent					
1. Agriculture	47·9	39·0	33·9	39·2	32·2	47·1
2. Modern industry	11·5	20·7	25·0	20·3	29·5	14·5
3. Handicrafts	6·6	5·6	4·8	5·7	5·3	6·4
4. Construction	2·6	4·8	6·5			
5. Others	31·4	29·9	29·8	34·8	33·0	32·0
Total	100·0	100·0	100·0	100·0	100·0	100·0

FACTORS UNDERLYING THE CHANGES IN INDUSTRIAL DEVELOPMENT AND POLICY

Given the policies of the Great Leap Forward, what were the factors within industry that made possible the course of industrial development from 1958 through 1960? What accounted for the momentous change in policy at the end of 1960 from priority to the development of heavy industry to the overriding priority for agriculture?

The agricultural crisis, with growing intensity from 1959 through 1961, must be accorded the most prominent place among all the factors that had shaped the economy during the five-year period from 1958 through 1962. As far as industrial development is concerned, however, the crisis was an external factor. The subject has been commented on earlier in the discussion on general economic policies and need not be taken up here.[31]

The internal factors, however, have to be examined. They include the investment programme, the small-industry experiment, decentralisa-

[31] For more details, see Leslie T. C. Kuo's article below. I have commented on the subject in a chapter entitled " Communist China's Economy and its Impact on Afro-Asia," in Kurt London, ed., *New Nations in a Divided World* (New York: Praeger, 1964); a popular version appears as " What Happened to the Great Leap Forward," *Challenge* (New York University), XI, No. 10 (July 1963).

tion and planning, industrial management, and Soviet aid. Each of these subjects will be discussed in turn.

THE INVESTMENT PROGRAMME

The Great Leap Forward policies of 1958 would not have produced concrete results unless the productive capacity of industry had been expanded accordingly. The plants that were brought into operation for the first time in 1958 accounted heavily for the leap forward in production that year. During the period of the First Five-Year Plan, 537 above-norm industrial projects had been completed. But during that period the heaviest investment was made in the last two years, a time span that was generally required for the completion of one of these projects. Hence, in 1958 alone, 700 industrial projects came to completion and were immediately placed in the production front.

As early as September 1956, in his presentation of the proposals for the Second Five-Year Plan, Chou En-lai estimated that the industrial enterprises newly constructed or reconstructed during the period from 1953 to 1957 would contribute 15 per cent. to the gross industrial value product during the First Five-Year Plan period, and that those built or rebuilt during the period of the first two five-year plans (1953–62) would contribute 50 per cent. By the end of 1957, however, it turned out that the new plants and mines contributed about 30 per cent. to the gross value product of modern and co-operative factories.[32] The increase in new productive capacity in 1958 was given in a study which showed that if the value of industrial output of factories derived from the newly increased productive capacity during the year was 100 in 1954, it would be 103 in 1955, 184 in 1956, 179 in 1957, and 449 in 1958.[33] One may, therefore, surmise that new enterprises accounted for 26 per cent. of factory output in 1954, 25 per cent. in 1955, 34 per cent. in 1956, 30 per cent. in 1957, and 50 per cent. in 1958.

Officially it was claimed that there was an improvement of 8 per cent. in the over-all productivity of industrial labour in 1958. Some such improvement must have taken place because of the sudden large-scale increase in plant capacity. Nevertheless, the other major factor, in addition to the increase in plant capacity, responsible for the great leap in industrial output was doubtless the large expansion of the industrial labour force in 1958 and 1959. Shortage of labour was, in fact, felt from the start of the Great Leap. In July 1958, Li Hsien-nien, Minister of Finance, dwelt at length on the lack of labour for basic investment

[32] Lin I-fu, " Seek all effective Means to Develop fully the Productive Potential in Existing Industrial Enterprises," *Planned Economy*, No. 3, March 9, 1958.
[33] Fang Chung, " High Speed and the Wavy Course," *Chi-hua yü T'ung-chi* (*Planning and Statistics*), No. 10, July 23, 1959.

projects, and stressed the urgency of "liberating" housewives from domestic chores for socialist construction.[34] The development of local and commune industries soon aggravated the labour-supply situation. The result was a heavy drain from the working force in agriculture. The problem was publicly admitted by Chou En-lai in August 1959 before the Standing Committee of National People's Congress.[35] According to an editorial in *Red Flag* in November 1960, much of the increase in the output of local industries at the *hsien* level and above since 1958 had been dependent entirely on a continuous increase in the size of the labour force, and not on any improvement in labour productivity.[36] It was late in 1960 that the communes were required to allocate, as much as possible (over 80 per cent. in most cases), of their manpower to participate in agricultural production—at the expense of all other activities, industry included.[37]

If heavy investment in 1956 and 1957 and substantial increases in the labour force accounted for the great expansion in industrial output from 1958 to 1960, the investment programme during these three years was a major factor bringing about the end of the Great Leap Forward. The 1956 proposal concerning the Second Five-Year Plan called for a doubling of state investment as compared with the first plan; this would mean raising the ratio of state investment from 36·5 per cent. of the state budget to about 40 per cent. During the Great Leap Forward, however, state investment jumped from 12·64 billion yuan (41 per cent. of state budget) in 1957 to 21·4 billion (51·5 per cent.) in 1958 and to 26·7 billion (49·2 per cent.) in 1959. When extra-budgetary investments were included, the total for 1958 and 1959 was 58·4 billion yuan, as compared to a total of 55 billion for the five years from 1953 to 1957. The planned investment for 1960, the latest data available, was 38·5 billion yuan, including 32·5 billion (46·4 per cent. of state budget) from the state and 6 billion from sources outside the budget.

These massive investments resulted in the production of large quantities of capital goods which could not be readily used in the economy for lack of complementary factors. This, of course, differs from the case of producing defective goods. But in both cases national income would be boosted, giving a picture of growth that is entirely illusory. William Hollister, in his article on capital formation below, puts forth the interesting thesis that the sharp increase in investment during the three years of the Great Leap Forward represented a case of "over-investment," defined as the situation where capital goods are

[34] *Finance*, No. 8, August 5, 1958. [35] *People's Daily*, August 29, 1959.
[36] "Simultaneous Development of Industry and Agriculture is an Important Law in China's Socialist Economy," *Red Flag*, No. 22, November 16, 1960.
[37] "Explore the Labor-Supply Potential in the Communes," *People's Daily* editorial, September 27, 1960.

added to the economy more rapidly than can be absorbed into the existing system of production in heavy industry and agriculture.

Borrowing Lord Keynes' concept of a "sudden collapse in the marginal efficiency of capital" at the last stage of the boom in the trade cycle, Hollister postulates that even the Chinese planners, in the grip of the Great Leap psychology, would base, like the entrepreneurs in a market economy, their investment decisions on expectations of an increase in production of capital goods which would offset their growing abundance (and growing quantities of investment goods of poor quality or without a market) and rising real costs involved in diverting labour from other productive sectors to construction activities. These optimistic expectations did not materialise. Substantial parts of the investments from 1958 to 1960, especially those in small-scale heavy industry and in agriculture, were ineffectual, resulting in sheer waste of resources. This alone, according to Hollister, would have induced the Chinese planners to reduce heavily the investment programme in 1960. And when the effects of crop failures in 1959–60 and the Sino-Soviet dispute were added, the decline in the marginal efficiency of capital was very large—probably to the same level as in 1957 before the Great Leap. The policy of consolidation, introduced toward the end of 1960 was, therefore, inevitable. Indeed, according to another study, the rate of investment (the proportion of gross investment to gross national product) rose from 28·8 per cent. in 1958 and 35·9 per cent. in 1959 to 43·7 per cent. in 1960, only to drop sharply to 21·6 per cent. in 1961 and 21·3 per cent. in 1962, a level far below that of 1957 and only comparable to that of 1953.[38]

It will be observed that "over-investment" is not over-abundance of capital or investment funds, but misallocation of investment resources. For example, the small-enterprise experiment, especially in heavy industry, was a disaster. Moreover, there was a clear lack of balance within and between the sectors of the economy.[39] Nevertheless, agricultural crisis and the Soviet withdrawal of assistance aside, the collapse of marginal efficiency of capital in 1960 could have been avoided if there were sound or reasonable planning. In fact, as we have seen, during the Great Leap Forward years, economic planning was decentralised, national plans were based on completely erroneous reports from the field, and local plans ran wild with their extra-budgetary investment funds. The return to professionalism in planning and factory management since the beginning of 1961 was probably as inevitable as was the collapse of the investment programme in 1960.[40]

38 Wu et al., ibid. p. 340, Table 80.
39 See the article by Hung and Wu below.
40 For a discussion of return to professionalism, see a later section in this article and also Franz Schurmann's article below.

THE SMALL-INDUSTRY EXPERIMENT

Among the basic points of the General Line put forward by the Party in May 1958 were, first, " to develop industry and agriculture simultaneously while giving priority to heavy industry " and, second, " to develop, under centralised leadership and with over-all planning, proper division of labour and co-ordination, centrally controlled industries simultaneously with local industries, large enterprises simultaneously with medium-sized and small enterprises," and, as was added later, "foreign methods" of production simultaneously with indigenous methods. Both of these points were said to constitute the whole set of policies for balanced national economic development known as " walking on two legs," which is best explained as follows [41]:

> If there were only one leg, that is heavy industry, without the other leg, that is, agriculture and light industry, or if the other leg is too short, it will be impossible to develop national economy at top speed. For this reason, particular importance must still be attached to agricultural development during the Second Five-Year Plan period.

To implement this policy, all people and all *hsien* in the country were told to build up industries. This was the proper, correct road for China to take in her attempt to bring about a great leap forward in industrial development.[42] Decentralisation of control over finance and enterprises since the end of 1957 gave the local Party authorities the necessary means to carry out this new policy.

As a result, manufacturing plants of all sorts sprang up all over the countryside. Preponderantly, they were small handicraft workshops. A report of Kiangsu province in June 1958 revealed that the so-called new industries in the process of establishment in the province were instituted by the various following ways: (a) completely new investment and construction; (b) independent operation of individual workshops in an existing factory; (c) merging of a handicraft producer co-operative with a locally controlled state enterprise or state-private joint enterprise; (d) expansion of a handicraft producer co-operative or group; (e) transformation of certain service trades; and (f) merging of a handicraft producer co-operative with the by-employment group in an agricultural producer co-operative.[43] By the autumn of 1959, some 700,000 workshops were found in operation among the 26,578 communes.

Table 4 shows that the industrial output of the communes contributed 5·3 per cent. to the national industrial output in 1958 and 7·3 per cent. in 1959. The total share for local industries, of which the commune

---

[41] Hsueh Mu-ch'iao, Su Hsing and Lin Tse-li, *The Socialist Transformation of the National Economy of China* (Peking: FLP, 1960), p. 256.

[42] Liang Ying-yung, " Which is the Correct Road for China's Industrial Leap Forward," *Hsueh-hsi (Study)*, No. 8, April 18, 1958.

[43] Yen Chuan and Chiang Chieh, " Certain Views on Statistical Work for Newly Developed Industries," *T'ung-chi Yen-chiu (Statistical Research)*, No. 6, June 23, 1958.

workshops formed a part, however, did not show any important advance. This does not mean that the development of local industries was arrested, but rather that local industries were growing apace with centrally controlled industries. State investment funds were allocated to local as well as to centrally controlled industries. It has been reported that state investment in 1959 represented an increase of 16 per cent. over the preceding year in the case of local industries against an increase of 39 per cent. in the case of centrally controlled industries.

The best proof that this expansion of local industries had gone too far, involving great waste of manpower and materials, can be found in the disastrous so-called " backyard furnace " movement to produce iron and steel toward the end of 1958. This " small-industry " sector has since been reorganised and much reduced, with reasonable cost and profit as the acid test of continued operation. Moreover, as the economic crisis in the country deepened, the resilience of handicraft production became more and more appreciated by the planners. As recently as March 1962, the Party authorities made clear that in the handicraft sector private ownership would be allowed and expected to co-exist with state and co-operative ownership for a long period to come.[44] And for the first time the supply of major raw materials for handicraft production was incorporated into the state plan for 1962.[45] It has also been reported that about one-quarter of the volume of handicraft production, covering the output of a small number of important products, were now under the direct control of central authorities, leaving the other three-quarters in the control of local governments.[46]

Different interpretations may be given to this experiment of " walking on two legs." Peter Schran maintains in his article that the encouragement given to handicrafts in economic development might result from the realisation that handicraft as a traditional sector should generate a surplus to support industrialisation. Another interesting interpretation has been advanced by Shigeru Ishikawa of Hitotsubashi University (Tokyo). He regards China's effort in this area as a novel undertaking to decide to choose to allocate resources between establishments using different techniques (capital intensity) and of differing scales of production (size)—and, one may add, geographical dispersion—instead of only between different sectors or industries, as is generally the case.[47] To him

---

44 " Carry out Correctly the Party's Policy and Develop Handicraft Production," *People's Daily*, March 2, 1963.
45 Chi Lung, " Use the Raw Materials for Light Industry and Handicrafts Properly," *People's Daily*, February 21, 1962.
46 Chen Hung-yung, " Planning and Flexibility in Handicraft Production," *Ta Kung Pao*, March 23, 1962.
47 Shigeru Ishikawa, " Choice of Techniques in Mainland China," *The Developing Economics*, Preliminary Issue No. 2 (September–December 1962), pp. 23–56. This is a publication of the Institute of Asian Economic Affairs in Tokyo, Japan.

the failure of the Chinese experiment seemed to indicate that the most effective way to maximise the rate of economic growth is still the application of the large-scale production method.

DECENTRALISATION AND PLANNING

Decentralisation of control over industry, trade and taxation, initiated in the winter of 1957, enhanced immeasurably the authority of Party committees and secretaries at the local and enterprise levels. As shown in Table 4, the share of the locally controlled enterprises was promptly raised from 54 per cent. of the industrial value produce in 1957 to 73 per cent. in 1958, with the share of the centrally controlled enterprises declining correspondingly from 46 per cent. to 27 per cent. Decentralisation was one of the several strategic developments that made the Great Leap Forward possible.

The effect of decentralisation on planning was profound, not to mention the fact that planning itself was also decentralised. The subject is taken up by Audrey Donnithorne in her article, which is primarily concerned with the mechanism and mechanics of planning. Up to the drafting of the 1959 plan, the process of drafting annual plans was known as the " single track " system, which was, in essence, a scheme of centralised planning mainly for the benefit of the centrally controlled state enterprises—in virtually complete neglect of the interests of the locally controlled state enterprises and other local enterprises.[48] The " double track " system devolved upon the local authorities to draw up a co-ordinated plan for all the enterprises in their locale. As Donnithorne points out, the local plan, depending on the level of government, would have to tackle the problems of balancing needs between different enterprises, different economic sectors, and different areas, of defining targets and scopes of planning, and of maintaining proportionate development between different sectors. Plans were controlled and supervised by various government agencies and committees (many coming into existence in 1958 for the first time) and the People's Bank. The whole system was described as " centralised planning and decentralised control."

Under this system the planning unit was a geographical area—a *hsien*, a special administrative district, a city, a province or even an economic region; and every unit aspired to become as self-sufficient as possible and thus tended to ignore the needs of other units. The resulting disruption of the regular flow of supplies between areas or regions was extremely serious for a long while.[49] This kind of development of localism and " base-ism " was not unanticipated, but, according

---

[48] Liao Chi-li, " The Double Track System," *Planned Economy*, No. 8, August 1958.
[49] Wu Hsia, " Enhance the Nature of Organisation and Planning for Inter-Provincial Economic Co-operation," *Planning and Statistics*, No. 6, April 8, 1959.

to a member of the State Planning Commission, this tendency could be overcome by "strengthening the Party's leadership." [50]

But decentralisation could easily be carried, as it was, to a point where even any pretence of unity in national planning and national economic development was destroyed. This danger was real during the years of the Great Leap, when extra-budgetary funds became significant for the first time. They were derived chiefly from a part of the profits retained by different enterprises, major repair reserve funds, supplemental wage funds, and local surtaxes. Whereas the investment funds outside the state plan totalled 5·73 billion yuan from 1953 to 1957, they amounted to 5·26 billion in 1958, 5·00 billion in 1959 and 6·00 billion expected for 1960. And they were invested in new projects without prior central approval, and, worse still, in keen competition with the state's vital basic construction projects for bank credit, materials and manpower. Hence, a return to central control over fiscal and financial plans was ordered by the State Council as early as January 1960. Later it was realised that the financial control system, which dealt, among other things, with extra-budgetary funds, circulating capital and short-term loans of various enterprises, had to be more centralised than the system of fiscal control.[51]

Hence, the slogan of "the whole nation as one chess game," introduced as early as January 1959, has since been re-emphasised from time to time throughout the rest of the period under discussion.[52] The establishment of six regional "central bureaux" in the country to exercise control on behalf of the Party's Central Committee in January 1961 may well be regarded as a move towards centralising control once more. But co-operation between economic regions (mainly provinces) continued.[53]

INDUSTRIAL MANAGEMENT

It was pointed out above that at the beginning of the decentralisation move in late 1957 and early 1958 the tendency on the part of local governments and enterprises towards localism and base-ism was not unforeseen but the strengthening of Party control at these various primary levels was counted upon to overcome it successfully. Basic organisations of the Party have long been established in all industrial

[50] Liao Chi-li, *ibid*. " *Base-ism* " (" *Pen-wei chu-i* ") refers to the principle of putting the interests of one's own base (workshop, factory, production team, commune, department, *hsien*, or any other) ahead of and giving them priority over the interests of all others, the national or collective interests in particular.

[51] Ko Chih-ta and Wang Cho, " Several Problems of Relationship in Fiscal and Financial Work," *Ta Kung Pao*, November 17, 1961.

[52] See, *e.g.*, Yang Ch'un-hsu, " The Problem of Centralisation in Socialist Economic Control," *Ta Kung Pao*, April 11, 1962.

[53] See Franz Schurmann's article, especially the section on the rise of regional economies.

enterprises. Decentralisation provided the Party committees in enterprises with the opportunity to take over management by shoving the professionals aside—with disastrous results.

Back in 1950 when the Party had to rely on the industrial workers for uninterrupted operation of factories and mines and for fighting the enemies of the state, a system of democratic management was instituted whereby workers' representative conferences, establishd in all state enterprises, were consulted on all major issues. Trade union organisations, also set up in these enterprises, served as the permanent secretariat for these conferences.

This close relationship between management and workers gradually gave way to centralised control. Complaints about authoritarianism were often voiced by workers. In 1956 the Party's Central Committee decided to adopt, as the basic form of industrial management for the country, a system whereby the manager assumes full responsibility for carrying out all production and management functions under the leadership of the enterprise's Party committee, which would consider and decide on all major policies. This in effect upheld the authority of management. In the meantime the workers' representative conference was reorganised into what is known as the workers' representative general conference with standing representatives in between conferences. The conference was given the authority to receive and discuss reports from the management concerning the various plans of the enterprise (production, finance, technology, wages, etc.) and the disposal of its welfare funds, and to recommend to higher authorities the discipline or dismissal of personnel in the enterprise's leadership if necessary. The trade union organisation in the enterprise continued to be responsible for preparing (by way of agitation, for instance) for the conferences and for seeing to it that resolutions adopted were carried out by management.[54]

Its authority thus defined, management began to exert itself, with the acquiescence of the enterprise's Party committee. As a matter of administration, various rules and regulations were introduced, setting forth for each category of workers duties, work norms, pay scales, promotions, penalties, etc. In the course of time these rules and regulations tended to grow and became the centre of workers' grievances.[55] The relationship between worker and management grew more formal and distant. The workers' representative general conference was reduced to " a mere vehicle for management and the Party committee

---

[54] Teng Hsiao-p'ing, " Report on the Rectification Movement," *People's Daily*, October 19, 1957.
[55] According to a report published in the *People's Daily*, September 27, 1958, a diesel-engine factory in Shanghai had been operating with 133 sets of rules and regulations up to the early part of the year.

to make speeches." [56] The *raison d'être* of trade union organisations was seriously questioned.

The situation changed radically in 1958 when the decentralisation programme enhanced the authority of Party committees at the local and enterprise levels. Mass enthusiasm, whipped up by the Party cadres for the Great Leap, let off a severe attack on commandism and bureaucratism of management in general. As a result, three reforms of the management system were instituted in 1958. First, the various sets of rules and regulations were to be extensively revised to take into account "the interests of the masses." Second, workers were to be organised to participate in management at different levels of the enterprise, while management was required to join the workers in physical labour. Third, a system of "close co-ordination among management, workers, technical personnel and administrative staff under the leadership of the enterprise's Party committee" was inaugurated. [57] The secretary of the committee, for all intents and purposes, became the chief executive of the enterprise. The workers' representative general conference, together with the trade union organisation, was revitalised under his direction.

That was the development in 1958. But it was soon apparent that no one in management was willing to assume any responsibility—even on the production and administrative side. In fact, many of the managerial staff preferred to be sent down to work in the workshops than to be responsible for assigning tasks to various units or for fulfilling planned quotas. [58] Moreover, after the old rules and regulations were discarded, no new ones were adopted to take their place. [59] The administrative machinery in enterprises was fast breaking down. If production were to continue, it would have to rely on mass emulation drives which could only result in a one-sided emphasis on quantity of output, to the virtual exclusion of variety and quality which after all were difficult to measure. The situation on a nation-wide scale became so grave that Chou En-lai, in his report in April 1959 on the work of government, warned. [60]

> Every industrial enterprise must carry through the system of the manager's taking up full responsibility under the Party committee's leadership and must abide by the indispensable system of reasonable rules and regulations. It is intolerable to find in production and basic

[56] Li Ch'un, "Why is it Necessary to Broaden Management of Various Enterprises?" *Chung-kuo Kung-jen (Chinese Worker)*, No. 6, March 27, 1957.

[57] Liu Shao-ch'i, "The Triumph of Marxism-Leninism in China," *People's Daily*, October 1, 1959.

[58] Li Pao-k'un, "Problems of Plan Management in Hangchow Machine-Making Factory," *Tsai-cheng Yen-chiu (Financial Research)*, No. 8, November 15, 1958.

[59] Hsu Hsin-hsueh, "Strengthen further the System of Responsibility in Industrial Enterprises," *Red Flag*, No. 20, October 16, 1961.

[60] *People's Daily*, April 19, 1959.

construction that no one takes up any responsibility and that all necessary rules and regulations are being violated.

After this statement, great effort was made to restore the integrity of the administration system in enterprises. What was to be restored was clearly stated by the Party secretary of the Municipality of Shanghai. After stressing that mass movements (like the Great Leap Forward) were not feasible without the Party's centralised leadership, he went on to point out three " questions of principle " in relation to industrial management. First, the system of the manager taking full responsibility entailed not only his being responsible for the enterprise's administration, but also proper division of labour between the Party committee and enterprise administration, and full development of the role of trade union organisations and Communist Youth League in the enterprise. Second, the system of rules and regulations was absolutely necessary, but they should be revised to meet new developments in production. Third, workers should be given explanations of administrative methods and be urged to make recommendations in regard to certain administrative problems.[61]

The struggle between management and the Party committee for authority was not easily resolved. The collapse of the Great Leap Forward toward the end of 1960 had a great deal to do with the re-emergence and recognition of the manager as " head of the enterprise." [62] The development since then is well analysed in Franz Schurmann's article. According to him, it was the severance of Party control over the financial system which contributed one of the most serious blows to Party power during the 1961 reforms. Intellectuals (that is, educated professionals who are graduates from higher middle school on up)—accountants included—were given proper roles to play; and they appeared to be firmly committed to professionalism, expertise and technical knowledge. The Party committee was driven to confine its major interests to ideological work. Schurmann further observed that the tasks of management also changed. The goal had been shifted from production to " accumulation " (in the sense of economy—with profit, cost, and labour productivity as the major targets. This was made possible by the régime's relaxation of control over open market activities and by the growing practice of direct contracting among enterprises themselves.

Like the authority of enterprise managements, incentive policy for industrial workers as well as for members of agricultural producers' co-operatives and the communes was also subject to sharp changes

[61] Tsao T'i-chiu, " Mass Movement and Centralised Leadership in Industry," *People's Daily*, October 24, 1959.
[62] Hsu Hsin-hsueh, *ibid*.

during the period under discussion. This has been documented in Charles Hoffman's article below. The major wage reform in 1956 laid emphasis on material incentives; at that time the piece-rate system had already been applied to between 30 to 40 per cent. of industrial workers in the country. The changes in the " system of wages and welfare " during the Great Leap Forward were well summarised by the chairman of the State Planning Commission as follows: (a) co-ordination of political and ideological education with material incentive with the former playing the predominating role; (b) co-ordination of collective welfare with individual money income, with the former to grow in proportion over time; and (c) adoption of the time-wage rate as the general practice, with piece rates and bonuses as auxiliary methods.[63] This policy of extreme emphasis on non-material incentives was abandoned only in late 1960 when the Great Leap Forward movement came to an end. Since then, the renewed importance of piece-rate systems, renewed emphasis on distribution according to labour, and the playing down of non-material incentives have become widespread.

It may be noted that shifts between material and non-material incentives probably have to coincide with shifts in authority between enterprise managements and Party committees, since only the latter are able to organise, conduct and lead mass movements that make non-material incentives effective. The piece rate is as much a material incentive for industrial workers to increase production as the profit target is for management to increase output, expand sales, improve product quality, multiply variety, and reduce costs.

Thus, in industrial management the turn of events since the end of 1960 has been in favour of the professionals at the expense of the Party committees in enterprises. The impact on the operation of the whole economy has been far-reaching. Hence, the rise of what Schurmann has called the Great Debate, which began late in 1961, and in which one school favoured a return to greater state direction and control of the economy and the other favoured greater autonomy for individual economic units. That such a debate was sanctioned and encouraged by the régime must have been largely due to the fact that its self-confidence had been badly shattered by the collapse of the Great Leap Forward and the deepening of the agricultural crisis. Economic recovery since the autumn of 1962 has rapidly restored its self-confidence. The issues of the debate have not yet been resolved, and discussion is still going on, although much subdued in tone.

[63] Li Fu-ch'un, " Report on the Draft Economic Plan for 1960," *People's Daily*, March 31, 1960.

SOVIET AID

Soviet aid to China has taken many forms. According to official announcements, only two development loans have ever been granted by the Soviet Union to China since 1949; namely, the $300 million in 1950, equivalent to 270·2 million roubles (to be repaid in ten equal annual instalments from the end of 1954 to the end of 1963), and the 117·1 million rouble loan in 1954 (terms unknown). Other long-term debts incurred by China that have been made public include the Soviet shares in four Sino-Soviet joint stock companies and the Soviet military supplies at the Port of Dairen, both of which were transferred to China in 1955; mention should also be made of the Soviet diversion to China in 1961 of 500,000 tons of Cuban sugar as an " interest-free loan " repayable in 1964–67. From various Chinese publications one also gains the impression that Peking's annual debt services have included payments for the supply of Soviet military weapons during the Korean war and probably also thereafter.

The first development loan was used up by 1953, and the second, by 1956—all against Soviet deliveries of industrial equipment and technical assistance. Since 1957 the Soviet supply of capital goods had been largely dependent on China's export availabilities.

Another form of Soviet assistance is the assurance of Soviet supply of complete sets of equipment and technical aid for a number of large industrial projects. From 1950 to 1957, a total of 211 projects had been agreed upon at a cost of 1,824·3 million roubles[64]; the number of projects was subsequently consolidated to 166. This, when added to 47 more projects agreed on in August 1958 (value unknown) and another 78 in February 1959 (at a cost of 1,126·1 million roubles), gives a grand total of 291 Soviet-aid projects since 1950, not including 59 separate workshops and important installations to which Soviet assistance has also been given.[65]

These projects constitute the backbone of China's industrialisation programme. The entire industrial investment plan was built around them during the period of the First Five-Year Plan, and their completion would make a tremendous contribution to the productive potential of the economy.[66] From 1950 through 1957, only 68 had been completed.[67] In 1958 alone, 45 were completed, and their operation accounted

---

[64] I. Andreyev, " Friendship and Co-operation between China and the USSR," *Vneshiaia Torgovlia* (*Foreign Trade*), No. 2, February 1959.

[65] " Soviet Technical Assistance to Foreign Countries," *Foreign Trade*, No. 6, June 1961. Aid has also been extended to China in the form of 60 industrial projects by East Germany (41 projects), Czechoslovakia, Poland, Hungary, Rumania and Bulgaria.

[66] Li, Choh-Ming, *Economic Development of Communist China*, pp. 10–12.

[67] In addition, 33 of the projects aided by the six Eastern European countries had been completed.

significantly for the great leap forward in modern industrial output.[68] At the end of 1960, 41 more projects had been constructed, making a total of 154 projects (and 24 workshops) completed since 1950, with 137 to be finished at the latest by 1967. On July 14, 1963, a Soviet statement published in *Pravda* indicated that 198 industrial enterprises, shops and other projects equipped with up-to-date machinery had been built in China with active Soviet assistance, and that "the Soviet Union continues rendering technical assistance to the Chinese People's Republic in constructing 88 industrial enterprises and projects."[69] Apparently, therefore, 44 more projects were completed in 1961 and 1962 (if not up to the middle of 1963), and the total number of projects had again been consolidated from 298 to 286.

It is important to note the difference in the nature of Soviet aid between the projects built during the period from 1950 to 1957 and those built ever since. In the earlier period all the projects were dependent on the Soviet Union for supply of complete sets of equipment and on Soviet specialists for surveying, designing, installation and first-stage operation. In the latter period, except for a few ultra-modern projects for which Soviet aid had to be as thoroughgoing as before, the Chinese undertook the surveying and designing by themselves, relying on the Soviet Union for principal equipment instead of complete sets and for the supply of the most up-to-date design and product blueprints and other technical materials. The Soviet Union still had to send specialists to help in installation and first-stage operation.[70] It has been reported under these and other arrangements (concluded in October 1954 and January 1958) of Sino-Soviet technical co-operation that the Soviet Union supplied more scientific and technical information in 1958 and 1959 than during the previous five years. In 1960, more than 60 per cent. of all machines and equipment produced in China were based on Soviet blueprints.

Between 1949 and 1958, a total of 10,800 Soviet specialists were in China at one time or another to assist China in economic construction.[71] In the same period the Soviet Union had accepted 14,000 Chinese

68 See *supra*, 23–24.
69 The *Tass* English translation, published in *The New York Times*, Western Edition, July 16, 1963.
70 Sun Hsiang-ch'ing, "Brilliant Achievements and Selfless Assistance," *Economic Research*, No. 11, November 17, 1959.
71 About 1,500 specialists had also come from the six Eastern European countries. The services of Soviet specialists were probably paid for with regular Chinese exports to the Soviet Union. In his *Ocherki ekonomicheskikh otnoshenii SSSR s Kitaem (Essays in Economic Relations of the USSR with China)* (Moscow: Foreign Trade Publishing House, 1957), M. I. Sladkovskii remarked, "China was paying with her commodity exports to the Soviet Union not only for the Soviet exports to China, but also for Soviet technical assistance (survey works, projecting, installation of equipment). This kind of expenses was rapidly increasing, particularly since 1954" (p. 333).

students in Soviet schools and universities, and 38,063 Chinese as apprentices in Soviet factories and plants. At the beginning of 1960, as reported by the Soviet trade journal (February 1960), there were 7,500 Soviet specialists working in China and 6,500 Chinese receiving training in the Soviet Union.

The withdrawal of the Soviet experts in the summer of 1960, who reportedly took with them the industrial blueprints and technical specifications, must have been an important factor in bringing the Great Leap Forward in industrial development to a close at the end of the year. Much speculation has been given to the nature of the agreements and contracts that according to Peking were torn up by the Soviet Government. Clarification has now been given by an editorial in the *People's Daily* on December 4, 1963:

> In July 1960, the Soviet authorities ... suddenly and unilaterally decided on a complete withdrawal of the 1,390 experts who were in China to help in our work, they tore up 343 contracts for experts and the supplements to these contracts and abolished 257 items for scientific and technical co-operation and since then, they have reduced in large numbers the supplies of complete sets of equipment and key sections of various other equipment. This has caused our construction to suffer huge losses, thereby upsetting our original plan for the development of our national economy and greatly aggravating our difficulties.

On another occasion the withdrawal of Soviet aid was described as having " inflicted incalculable difficulties and losses on China's economy, national defence, and scientific research." [72]

The Sino-Soviet dispute has produced another noteworthy development in the economic relations between the two countries. On April 7, 1961, Moscow announced that due to natural calamities that occurred in China in 1960 the Chinese were unable to fulfil their export quota to the Soviet Union in foodstuffs, thereby creating a deficit of 288 million roubles—presumably in their international account with the Soviet Union for 1960.[73] This deficit, continued the announcement, was to be repaid by Chinese exports, apparently without interest charges, in four instalments beginning 1962, namely, 8 million in 1962, 50 million in 1963, and 115 million each in 1964 and 1965. Since at the time Peking had already embarked on a large-scale purchase programme of food on the international market, the arrangement implied that Moscow had no intention of assisting Peking in facilitating the latter's handling of the severe economic crisis at home. Later, when Sino-Soviet trade in 1961

---

[72] Fan Chung, " All-Round Improvement in China's Economy," *Peking Review*, No. 34, August 23, 1963.
[73] Presumably a deficit in China's international balance of payments with the Soviet Union since there was a trade surplus of 27·9 million roubles in China's favour for the year.

netted a surplus of 165·7 million roubles for China, Peking was allowed to repay " part of her debt " ahead of schedule.[74] In a communiqué issued at the close of the National People's Congress in December 1963, Peking announced that all its debts to the Soviet Union, interest included, would be repaid by 1965.

Table 6

COMMUNIST CHINA'S TRADE WITH THE SOVIET UNION, 1958–62

Item	1958	1959	1960	1961	1962
	(in million roubles)				
A. China's imports from USSR ..	571	860	735	331	210
Composition:	(in per cent.)				
1. Complete industrial plants	26	42	46	21	4
2. Other equipment	24	21	16	9	8
3. Petroleum and products ..	14	12	12	33	35
4. Ferrous metals	6	3	5	5	7
5. Others	30	22	21	32	46
Total	100	100	100	100	100
	(in million roubles)				
B. China's exports to USSR ..	792	991	763	496	465
Composition:	(In per cent.)				
1. Agricultural products ..	44	41	31	9	10
(a) Foodstuffs	26	19	15	3	7
(i) Animal origin (meat, fish)	10	5	3	1	a
(ii) Vegetable origin (rice, fruits	16	14	12	2	7
(b) Raw materials	18	22	16	6	3
2. Fabrics, clothing and footwear	25	36	44	58	62
3. Nonferrous metals	14	11	13	15	12
4. Others	17	12	12	18	16
Total	100	100	100	100	100
	(in million roubles)				
C. China's export balance ..	221	131	28	165	255

a Less than one-half of 1 per cent., amounting to 830,000 roubles.

Sino-Soviet trade is a complicated subject to study. The article by Chao and Mah on the rouble-yuan exchange rate below arrives at the conclusion that Peking's official foreign trade returns, while not available since 1958, present a distorted picture because the exchange rate used

74 *Pravda*, April 20, 1963.

is not realistic. If more realistic rates are used, the total volume, regional distribution, and other aspects of the trade picture, would become very different. These same comments apply, if not with equal force, to Soviet trade returns. This is a point worth remembering in discussing the trade picture of any Communist economy.

Table 6 presents the salient changes in Sino-Soviet trade from 1958 through 1962 according to Soviet statistics.[75] The substantial export surplus in China's favour represented Peking's determined effort, especially since 1960, to maintain her export volume to the Soviet Union while reducing her imports from the Soviet Union to less than a quarter of the 1959 level in 1962. The most drastic change in China's imports is found in the sharp drop in both the volume and the relative importance of complete industrial plants and other machinery and equipment in 1961 and 1962; for the first time since 1950 petroleum products topped the import list during those two years. In China's exports the precipitous fall of agricultural products, especially since 1960, mirroring the gravity of the agricultural crisis at home, is as dramatic as the phenomenal rise in textile manufactures and clothing, which Peking in all likelihood would have found it difficult to sell at reasonable prices in comparable quantities in other world markets.

In his interesting study of the terms of trade between China and the Soviet Union, based on trade for the period from 1955 through 1959, F. H. Mah reaches the conclusion that Communist China could realise some economic gains by shifting from the Soviet Union to free and closer markets.[76] It would be interesting to find out whether the conclusion applies equally to the trade in 1960 and 1962 in view of the radical changes in trade composition.

CONCLUSIONS

What will be the economic and industrial policy during the period of the Third Five-Year Plan (1963–67)? No information has been made available concerning the outline of the plan, not even a proposal of major targets as was the case with the Second Five-Year Plan. According to a vice-chairman of the State Planning Commission, the " gravitational centre " of policy has been shifted from the development of the metallurgical and machine-making industries in the First Five-Year Plan period to the development of agriculture " at present and for a long time to come." [77]

[75] For a year-to-year discussion, see Oleg Hoeffding, *Sino-Soviet Economic Relations, 1958–1962* (Santa Monica, California: The RAND Corporation, August 1963).

[76] See his article below. The detailed exposition of his study is given in his *Communist China's Foreign Trade: Price Structure and Behavior 1955–1959* (Santa Monica: The RAND Corporation, October 1963).

[77] Yang Ying-chieh, " On the Problem of Comprehensive Balance in National Economic Planning," *Economic Research*, No. 73, November 17, 1962.

The programme for agricultural development has been included under the catchword of "modernisation," to include mechanisation, electrification, chemical fertiliser, and irrigation.[78] Under this reorientation, the overall policy of taking agriculture as the foundation of the national economy with industry as the leading factor actually creates better conditions for the development of heavy industries, for the policy has been authoritatively interpreted as imposing two requirements on the programme of industrial development. First, the size of the labour force needed for industrial development must be basically proportioned to the amount of marketable grains and other means of subsistence that can be provided by agriculture.[79] This is one of the lessons drawn from the Great Leap Forward, since the drain of agricultural labour for industrial construction seriously hampered agricultural production. Second, the state investment plan will have to be readjusted to the new priority scale with agriculture at the top, heavy industry at the bottom, and light industry in the middle. The share of investment going into agriculture will be raised. But the biggest share will doubtless still be spent in the development of heavy industry, inasmuch as investments for effecting technological reform in agriculture have to be made in such fields as agricultural implements, irrigation equipment, chemical fertilisers, electric power, modern transportation facilities, and insecticides—all of which come under the scope of heavy industry. Moreover, to increase their output also requires investment in the coal, non-ferrous metals, iron and steel, and basic chemical industries. What distinguishes this type of investment programme from that in the First Five-Year Plan is that " in the earlier period heavy industry was developed for the sole purpose of serving heavy industry, while now it is developed for the sake of serving agriculture." [80]

This does not mean that no new heavy industries will be built for the sake of developing heavy industry. One of the vice-chairmen of the State Planning Commission has made clear that given the present overall economic policy the direction for the development of heavy industry should be " to make full use of the existing productive capacity, improve product quality, increase product variety and co-ordinate production of parts and equipment [among different plants] so that we will establish new industries not now in existence in the country." [81] Furthermore, another major factor determining the direction of industrial development is the requirements of national defence. From all indications, the priority

78 See Leslie T. C. Kuo's article.
79 Po I-po, *op. cit.*
80 Yang Po, " On the Problem of Accumulation and Consumption," *Red Flag*, No. 21, November 1, 1962.
81 Yang Ying-chieh, *op. cit.*

accorded to national defence must be on parity with agriculture, if not higher. Thus, the growth in heavy industry will not be hampered. This speculation seems to have been substantiated by the 1963 establishment of three more machine-building ministries in the central government in addition to the three already in existence since September 1960. It has been reported that capital construction was on a larger scale in 1963 than in 1962.[82]

The agricultural recovery beginning in late summer, 1962, had progressed to a point in April 1963 that the market supply of consumer goods was substantial enough to result in a gradual fall of commodity prices. On rural organisation the official line still is that the commune system will always remain " the basic social organisation both for the entire historical period of socialism and for the future period of communism." [83] But, of the 74,000 people's communes in the country today, some " are bigger with production brigades and production teams under them, while other smaller ones have only production teams." [84] That many communes have existed with only production teams under them is a significant piece of information, for it signifies that the organisational retreat from the original commune system has been much greater than expected.

The basic issues of the great debate, however, between a return to Party control over economic and industrial management and the maintenance of professional independence and open-market activities is still unresolved. Significantly, in planning mechanism a nation-wide machinery known as National Commodity-Price Commission was created in September 1963, with Hsueh Mu-ch'iao as chairman. As may be recalled, Hsueh was the founding director of the State Statistical Bureau, created in 1952, but was dismissed from the directorship at the height of the Great Leap Forward in 1959 for his staunch defence of the professional character of statistical and planning work. The establishment of the new machinery under his leadership seems to augur for a much more flexible state pricing policy than before, which would take into account the effects of prices in both the state trading channels and the uncontrolled rural markets on production and market supply.[85]

The cleavage between Peking and Moscow seems beyond rapprochement within the foreseeable future. Peking has disclosed that during the period of her severe economic difficulties China not only did not borrow

---

[82] " Press Communiqué of National People's Congress," op. cit.
[83] Liao Lu-yen, " Collectivisation of Agriculture in China [written for Cuba Socialista of Cuba]," Peking Review, No. 44, November 1, 1963.
[84] Ibid.
[85] See Hsueh Mu-ch'iao, " The Law of Value and Our Price Policy," Red Flag, Nos. 7–8, April 16, 1963. His underlying viewpoint was that because pricing policy is subjective and man-made while the law of value is objective, " unchangeable at man's will," the former would have to be adjusted to the latter.

a penny from foreign countries, but had in fact paid off on time most of the debts and the interest owed to the Soviet Union since 1950.[86] At present, trade and economic relations between the two countries are under increasing strain. The British Council for the Promotion of Foreign Trade reported in October 1963 that the Soviet Union had placed an embargo on exports to China of equipment that embodied advanced technique and of petroleum products.[87] Reference has been made earlier here to the fact that at the end of the National People's Congress in early December 1963 Peking declared its firm intention of repaying the whole of the small remaining portion of its debts, plus interest charges, to the Soviet Union by 1965 according to schedule. Thus, with little prospect for any long-term development loan from the Soviet Union, China has turned to the free world in earnest for trade development. The contracts placed by China for a vinylon plant in Japan and for a urea plant in the Netherlands represent the first orders for complete industrial plants by Peking from the non-Communist world since the establishment of the Chinese Communist régime. The wheat-purchase contracts with Canada and Australia have served as an effective introduction of Peking to non-Communist markets.

Peking was probably not entirely unprepared for the adverse effects of such a dispute with Moscow on Chinese economic development. It has been officially reported that the central authorities of the Chinese Communist Party " foresaw that if we criticised the errors of the leaders of the CPSU, they would certainly strike at us vindictively and thus inevitably cause serious damage to China's socialist construction." [88] Now the keynote is self-reliance, adopted as the theme of the National People's Congress that met from November 17 to December 3, 1963. In preparation for this new turn in policy, three mass movements had been initiated in the summer of 1963 to conduct a nationwide re-education on class struggle, a full-fledged deployment of cadres to the production front, and a concerted drive to persuade the intellectuals to go into scientific pursuits and experiments.[89] The first movement, in particular, regarded by the Congress in December 1963 as " of extreme importance," was unfolding " throughout the country on a large scale " at the end of the year.[90]

Effort has been intensified to produce more technical personnel, factory foremen, and managerial staff. For example, according to a report, throughout 1963 more than 10,000 people, chosen from various industrial

[86] Editorial, " Continue Striving . . .," op. cit.
[87] " Far Eastern Round-Up," Far Eastern Economic Review, XIII, No. 42, October 17, 1963.
[88] Editorial Departments of People's Daily and Red Flag, " The Origin and Development of the Differences Between the Leadership of the C.P.S.U. and Ourselves," Peking Review, No. 37, September 13, 1963, p. 20.
[89] People's Daily editorial, June 2, 1963; and Red Flag editorial, July 10, 1963.
[90] " Press Communiqué . . .," op. cit.; and editorial, " Continue Striving . . .," op. cit.

enterprises all over the country, were organised into study groups to visit Shanghai, China's oldest and biggest industrial centre, for the purpose of learning Shanghai experience "to improve production techniques and streamline management."[91]

What with all the internal and external difficulties of the régime, Communist China has not wavered in her determination to industrialise as rapidly as conditions permit. This article may appropriately be concluded with an official restatement of the goal for national economic development—after five years of economic trial[92]:

> The socialist industrialisation of our country entails building an independent, comprehensive and modern industrial system and putting the whole of our national economy, agriculture included, on to a modern technical basis in a comparatively short period of time. In other words, we must ensure that the raw and other materials and all kinds of machinery and equipment produced by our heavy industries are able to meet the needs of socialist expanded reproduction, the needs of the technical transformation of all sectors of the national economy, and of the modernisation of our national defence. We must also see to it that our light industries are able to produce various kinds of consumer goods to satisfy appropriately the requirements of the continuously rising standards of living of the people.

This is a great deal more balanced, more tempered goal than that put forth in 1953, which was to build up within about fifteen years a complete heavy-industrial complex in the country capable of producing virtually all machinery and equipment needed by industry and national defence. The restatement is more balanced, because heavy industry and national defence aside, agriculture, light industry and other sectors are all explicitly included and integrated into the goal. It is more tempered, because the goal is expected to be achieved, not in about fifteen years, but in a comparatively short period of time without specifying how long it is going to be.

Eleven years of planned development, including five years of economic trials, have driven home some valuable lessons. To build up and expand heavy industry for the sake of further expansion of heavy industry has proved to be an unsound development policy. And undue haste in development makes irreparable waste which the country cannot afford, and will only result in increasing the suffering of the people and delaying considerably the time schedule of development.

[91] "Emulating Shanghai," *Peking Review*, No. 48, November 29, 1963.
[92] Po I-po, *op. cit.*

Capital Formation in Communist China[*]

WILLIAM W. HOLLISTER

THE present situation in China's heavy industry is a strange sequel to the programme for rapid industrialisation that took place from 1950 to 1960. Production of steel and other heavy industrial products were once proudly broadcast to show China's progress. Now the Chinese planners stress only the ways in which heavy industry can support agriculture. The priority once given to heavy industry is now a political liability rather than a basis for feelings of national pride. Behind the euphemistic description of present objectives in industry as " work to readjust, consolidate, fill out and raise standards "[1] is a situation where the planners show little interest in maximising production in heavy industry. This serious setback to the programme for rapid industrialisation needs to be interpreted in the light of the trends in capital formation that have occurred since 1950.

The data analysed is limited to estimates of gross domestic fixed investment at current prices. " Fixed " investment is defined to include all additions and major repairs to buildings and productive facilities and excludes changes in inventories and procurement of military equipment. A brief methodological note at the end of this article outlines the basis for the estimates of fixed investment used in the analysis.

THE RATE OF INVESTMENT—1950–59

Between 1950 and 1959 the Chinese Communists rapidly increased the proportion of current output allocated for investment. Fixed investment expenditures increased as shown in Table 1. These figures show that fixed investment more than doubled between 1950 and 1952 and again in the next three years. Investment expenditures in 1957 was half as much again as in 1955, but the " leap forward " effort of 1958–59 carried investment to nearly three times the 1955 level. Nearly 10 per cent. of output in 1952 went into fixed investment; by 1957 the share had increased to 16 per cent.; and the " leap forward "

---

[*] This article presents some preliminary conclusions reached in the course of research under a grant from the Social Science Research Council and with the facilities and assistance of the Center for Chinese Studies, Institute of International Studies, at the University of California, Berkeley.
[1] *People's Daily (Jen-min Jih-pao)*, January 1, 1963.

39

drive carried fixed investment to one-quarter of the gross national product in 1959. The historical experience in most other countries shows a relatively constant share of output for investment over long periods of time.

Table 1

GROSS FIXED INVESTMENT—1950–59

Gross Fixed Investment	1950	1951	1952	1953	1954	1955	1956	1957	1958	1959
Billion yuan	2·4	4·0	6·4	10·5	12·5	13·0	19·1	18·2	33·0	38·5
Per cent. of Gross National Product [2]		5·5	6·4	9·1	12·4	13·9	13·8	17·9	15·9	23·9	25·7

The drive to raise the rate of investment in relation to output is remarkable, but should not be exaggerated. The percentages for investment in Table 1 reflect Chinese prices that overstate the value of investment goods and other producer goods relative to the value placed on consumer goods. Given these prices, the percentage for fixed investment of nine per cent. in 1952 was the result of economic recovery and probably could have been achieved under any system of economic organisation. The 1952 rate for investment was about the same as the ratio that had been achieved in Japan in the period from 1887 up to the First World War.[3]

The First Five-Year Plan (1953–57) led to further increases in the rate of investment, but the drive for rapid industrialisation in China was just gaining momentum. In the first three years of the Chinese First Five-Year Plan the rate for fixed investment was about the same as for Japan before 1930. The proportion of China's gross national product for fixed investment in 1957 (16 per cent.) was roughly the same as for Japan in the 1930s. This was, however, well below the 18–19 per cent. which the Soviet Union had invested in 1928 before the start of its First

---

[2] The percentages given are only rough approximations. The figures for gross national product (GNP) in current prices given in my book (*China's Gross National Product and Social Accounts—1950–57* [Glencoe, Ill.: The Free Press, 1958]) need to be revised primarily because of data indicating a higher level for changes in inventories. In lieu of a revision of the estimates in my book, the percentages given for 1950–57 are based on adding half of the statistical discrepancy in each year to the end-use estimates for GNP. For 1958–59 the preliminary calculations in my article are used with the estimated GNP in 1959 rounded to 150 billion yuan. See "Estimates of the Gross National Product—1958–59," in *Realities of Communist China* (Marquette University: Studies in Business and Economics, October 1960).

[3] Henry Rosovsky, *Capital Formation in Japan—1868–1940* (New York: The Free Press of Glencoe, 1961), Ch. I.

Five-Year Plan.[4] Furthermore, the Chinese rate of investment in 1956–57 reflected a heavy industrial base that had only arrived at this stage of economic development; in contrast, production in Soviet heavy industry in 1928 was not much higher than it had been in the Russia of 1913.[5]

The tremendous jump in investment in China in 1958 and 1959, however, is indeed surprising and with few historical precedents. In the space of two short years the Chinese Communist " leap forward " undertook to push investment as a percentage of output to a level achieved during the Soviet First Five-Year Plan only after considerable difficulties in industrial planning and organisation and not achieved in Japan until after the Second World War. The thesis of this article is that the sharp jump in the rate of investment during China's " leap forward " between 1958 and 1960 represented " over-investment " at that stage of China's economic development. By " over-investment " I mean that, given the Party's objectives, the cost in real resources used for this level of investment and the increases in output that it could actually achieve, much of the fixed investment was a " sheer waste of economic resources." This argument seems paradoxical because the Chinese economy was still underdeveloped in 1958 and 1959 with small amounts of capital relative to the huge supply of manpower, but in any economy new productive facilities must be combined with labour and absorbed into the existing system of production. Capital was being added more rapidly than it could be absorbed into the system of production that existed both in heavy industry and in agriculture.

INVESTMENT IN THE MODERN SECTORS—1950–59

China's investment trends can best be analysed by distinguishing between *traditional* investment in enterprises where production is being carried on essentially in the same manner as it has been for a long period of time and *modern* investment in enterprises where production techniques are more comparable to those used in more developed economies. Traditional production is primarily labour-intensive; modern productive enterprises are relatively capital-intensive using electric power or other mechanical power.[6]

For this analysis the modern sectors are industry excluding individual handicrafts, modern transport and communications, public utilities, military construction, and investment in science, culture, education and health. Military construction is included because it supports a relatively

---

[4] Abram Bergson, *The Real National Income of Soviet Russia since 1928* (Cambridge: Harvard Un. Press, 1961), p. 88.

[5] *Ibid.*, p. 7.

[6] This classification is the same as Rosovsky's distinction between *traditional* investment and *new* investment except that the term " modern " is preferred because of the ambiguity discussed below. Rosovsky, *op. cit.*, pp. 16–18.

modern military establishment although most of this construction work is labour-intensive. Investment in science, culture, education and health are included because they are essential in building up a skilled labour force to support modern techniques of production and because they are associated with a modern society. The estimates for investment in industry include handicraft workshops but investment in these workshops probably includes additions of machinery and equipment to modernise them.

The Chinese Communist programme for economic development was directed toward a modern economy, and in the Communist view a modern economy is an industrialised economy with a highly developed heavy industry. As the following table shows, between 1950 and 1959 fixed investment was concentrated in the modern sectors and the percentage allocated to heavy industry increased very rapidly.

Table 2

GROSS FIXED INVESTMENT IN MODERN SECTORS—1950–1959

Modern Investment	1950	1951	1952	1953	1954	1955	1956	1957	1958	1959
Billion yuan	1·18	2·15	3·61	5·70	6·94	7·48	11·34	11·12	21·24	25·31
Per cent. of Total Fixed Investment	48·8	54·4	56·5	54·5	55·4	57·5	59·3	61·1	64·3	65·7
Of which: Heavy Industry	11·6	12·6	23·4	24·5	27·6	31·9	33·9	36·9	45·1	44·3
Other Sectors*	37·2	41·8	33·1	30·0	27·8	25·6	25·4	24·2	19·2	21·4

* Light industry, modern transportation and communications, public utilities, investment in science, culture, education and health, and military construction.

Modern investment received about 55 per cent. of all investment in the years 1951 to 1954 and increased to nearly two-thirds of all investment in 1959. The share for the modern sectors excluding heavy industry, however, declined to about one-fifth of all investment in 1958–59. The priority for heavy industry is evident with heavy industry investment increasing from one-fourth of all investment in 1952 to about 45 per cent. in 1958–59.

The priority for heavy industry is even greater than these figures suggest. Investment in the modern sectors was of two kinds. One type of investment is concerned with building up and expanding productive capacity in enterprises using relatively modern techniques which were already well-established in China; the other type of investment is largely concerned with establishing new industrial enterprises with new techniques and new products not previously produced in China. State investment in light industry and modern transportation was not directed toward technological innovations. For example, investment in the textile industry between 1950 and 1959 was almost entirely concentrated in cotton textiles, and the cotton textile industry had already been well-established in China before the Communists came to power. No programme was adopted to develop production of synthetic fibres or to develop a whole new range of textile products. In the food-processing industries the data is not sufficient to make firm judgments, but it is likely that except for the sugar industry and a few canneries, there was relatively little investment aimed at replacing food-processing in the handicrafts sector with more modern facilities for vegetable oil extraction or other food processing.

The drive to produce new products and to introduce new industries not before established in China was concentrated in heavy industry and particularly in the machine industries. These new industries were almost entirely dependent on Soviet technical assistance and Soviet deliveries of machinery and equipment. During the First Five-Year Plan about half of investment in heavy industry was in Soviet aid projects.[7] Not all of this investment was for the introduction of new industries, but the new technology to be introduced into large-scale heavy industry was concentrated in these Soviet aid projects. Most of these new industries were scheduled to go into production during the Second Five-Year Plan (1958–62). A cursory glance at production figures in industry [8] shows that China produced its first truck in 1956, its first electric generator in 1957, its first tractor in 1958.

Most of the large increase in the share of investment for heavy industry in 1958 and 1959 is due to the " leap forward " investment in small-scale industrial enterprises. Data does not permit a firm estimate of the size of this investment, but perhaps one-quarter to one-third of investment in heavy industry in 1958 and 1959 was for small-scale projects. The " leap forward " investment in small-scale heavy industry represented a bold attempt to establish a whole range of new industries in China. This investment called for a high rate of technological innovation because these projects used production techniques that in many cases were not used extensively in more developed economies.

[7] *First Five-Year Plan for Development of the National Economy of the People's Republic of China in 1953–57* (Peking: Foreign Languages Press, 1956), p. 39.
[8] State Statistical Bureau, *Ten Great Years* (Peking: Foreign Languages Press, 1960), p. 98.

INVESTMENT IN TRADITIONAL SECTORS—1950–59

The figures for modern investment are equated with empirically observed figures for investment in industry and transportation, and the other modern sectors; and traditional investment is equated with the observed investment figures for agriculture, trade, and non-agricultural investment in housing, communal services, and government. This is possible because investment in handicrafts and native transportation in this period is estimated to have been negligible. It is also possible because the actual nature of state investment in agriculture was in support of traditional forms of agricultural production. Most of state investment and much of self-financed investment in the agricultural sector was concentrated in irrigation projects. State investment in large-scale irrigation projects required relatively modern construction techniques, but from the standpoint of agricultural production these irrigation projects were large-scale versions of irrigation work that had been proceeding in China for centuries. Moreover, the Chinese Communist investment in agriculture included negligible amounts of purchases of tractors and other modern farm equipment. The First Five-Year Plan called for introduction of tractors only on an experimental basis.[9] Even in the " leap forward " years (1958–60) only small beginnings were made toward mechanisation. In the official timetable the drive for mechanisation would take place in the period of the Third Five-Year Plan (1963–67).[10] This policy is quite different from investment in Soviet agriculture during the Russian First Five-Year Plan, when a very large part of agricultural investment was directed toward mechanisation with the avowed purpose of releasing farm manpower for industry.

As shown in Table 3, the proportion of investment in the traditional sectors shows a decline in the period 1950–59 corresponding to the rising share for modern investment, with the decline after 1952 taking place not in agricultural investment but in non-agricultural investment in trade, housing, communal services, and government construction.

This trend does not justify the commonly held view that the industrialisation drive commanded such large amounts of resources that agriculture was starved for investment. In spite of sharp increases in total investment in absolute terms and as a percentage of gross national product, and a rising share for investment in the sectors supporting industrialisation, agricultural investment since 1952 has continued at about one-quarter of total investment. In absolute amounts agricultural

---

[9] *The First Five-Year Plan, op. cit.*, p. 118.
[10] *National Programme for Agricultural Development, 1956–1967* (Peking: Foreign Languages Press, 1960), p. 46.

investment in 1956 was about 4·7 billion yuan, more than twice agricultural investment in 1952; and in 1959 agricultural investment was probably on the order of 10 billion yuan, nearly twice agricultural investment in 1956.

Table 3

GROSS FIXED INVESTMENT IN THE TRADITIONAL SECTORS—1950–59

Traditional Investment	1950	1951	1952	1953	1954	1955	1956	1957	1958	1959
Billion yuan	1·24	1·80	2·78	4·76	5·59	5·52	7·77	7·07	11·79	13·21
Per cent. of Total Fixed Investment	51·2	45·6	43·5	45·5	44·6	42·5	40·7	38·9	35·7	34·3
Of which: Agriculture [a]	45·2	38·7	34·6	26·2	26·6	28·3	24·4	25·2	26·4	26·6
Other sectors [b]	6·0	6·9	8·9	19·3	18·0	14·2	16·3	13·7	9·3	7·7

[a] Agricultural investment includes investments in rural housing and services.
[b] Trade, government construction, and non-agricultural investment in housing and communal services.

There is some evidence that by 1956 agricultural investment was close to the maximum that could be absorbed given the existing system of agricultural production. The official claim is that the irrigated area increased in 1956 by nearly as much as the total in the previous six years. The claim is probably a gross overstatement, but it is likely that the irrigation programme was accelerated in 1956. The 1956 irrigation effort was only one-fourth of the massive effort of 1958,[11] but even the 1956 step-up in investment seems to have involved much digging of wells that went dry thereafter and other waste, indicating that such investment was on a greater scale than could usefully be undertaken. In 1956 the Communist planners also pushed a programme of two-wheeled ploughs, and state trading enterprises found themselves with large stocks of this relatively simple type of farm equipment facing working peasants reluctant to adopt them. The " leap forward " emphasis on new types of farm equipment was on a much larger scale than the 1956 effort and must have faced even greater difficulties in absorbing such equipment into the traditional system of farm production.

The peasants paid a heavy price for the rapid build-up of heavy industry, but the price was not one of insufficient investment in agriculture. First, as a matter of equity, the peasant bore a disproportionate burden in financing the high rate of industrial investment, and farm per

[11] *Ten Great Years, op. cit.*, p. 130.

capita consumption suffered as a result. Second, the concentration of new technology in heavy industry greatly hindered the introduction of new agricultural techniques not because of lack of funds but because of the greater prestige of heavy industry and the diversion of skilled manpower to modern sectors. Third, direct investment in agriculture was limited due to institutional and economic factors, but agriculture could use unlimited amounts of chemical fertiliser, insecticides, and other heavy industry products that were adapted to the traditional methods of cultivation. The Chinese planners did not push investment in chemical fertiliser plants in the early years of their programme, and imports of chemical fertiliser and other inputs for agriculture had a low priority compared to imports of machinery and equipment for heavy industry.

THE COMMUNIST STRATEGY FOR ECONOMIC DEVELOPMENT—1950–59

Trends in capital formation in the period 1950–59 show a programme of economic development where new technology was to be introduced as rapidly as possible in one sector—heavy industry; agriculture was to be developed along traditional lines. The Chinese model of economic development as established during the First Five-Year Plan was a hybrid model. Its central priority to heavy industry and its system of planning and control was modelled on the Soviet system and its chief source of rapid introduction of new technology was from the technical assistance and the machinery and equipment obtained from Russia. On the other hand, the programme of agricultural development if successful would be an accelerated version of agricultural development as it had taken place in Japan. In the 1956–57 period the Chinese planners were facing two central problems if such a model of economic development could be carried out successfully.

The first problem was the successful establishment of the many new industries being constructed in heavy industry under the Soviet aid programme, getting these industries into full production, and making sure that these new products were of good quality. The situation in the period of the Chinese Second Five-Year Plan was analogous to the situation in Soviet Russia during its First Five-Year Plan (1928–32), and the dislocations in Russian industry during this period were enormous. In the period of the Chinese First Five-Year Plan the development of heavy industry had in large part been the expansion of the steel industry and other heavy industries which had already been well established in pre-Communist China. This expansion put strains on China's limited supply of managers and technicians, but there was at least a nucleus of trained people in these industries that could train and provide cadres for additional productive capacity. The new machine industries would have to start from nothing, and their demands for trained manpower would be harder to meet and would have to compete with the ever-increasing demands of the rest of heavy industry. In short, the period of 1958–62 in heavy industry was likely to be a period where the limitation on production was not simply the number of machines that could be installed but the rate at which the labour force could be trained to use these machines. Soviet technicians and technical assistance was crucial in solving this problem, but the programme would require a very rapid increase in China's supply of managers, engineers and technicians.

The second problem facing the Communist planners was the lag in agriculture and the rapid increase in the population. The characteristics of the successful Japanese programme for agricultural development have been described as " new and wider use of fertilisers, including the general adoption of commercial fertilisers, that permitted double and sometimes triple cropping; a large increase in the variety of plants under cultivation; an enormous extension of irrigation and some land reclamation, allowing a shift from dry to more productive paddy rice cultivation; and finally, helping all these developments, the growth of agricultural science." In the Japanese programme " the requirements for investment were relatively small." [12] The Chinese Communists, even in 1956 had pressed irrigation up to the limits of a soundly engineered programme and needed to give highest priority to production and import of chemical fertiliser, and above all to the " growth of agricultural science." Moreover, the Japanese model for agricultural development had depended on traditional methods of farm production that actually increased the per acre demand for labour; and in Japan this increased demand for farm labour was satisfied by putting ever greater burdens for production on the household unit.[13]

In 1956 the Chinese Communists had organised virtually all farm households into collectives. The transition from the household to the collective system of farm production took place in the context of a labour intensive system of crop cultivation and a programme that required increased efforts from each member of the farm labour force. To be successful, this reorganisation of agriculture would have to overcome difficulties not present during Russian collectivisation because Russian agriculture used extensive methods of crop cultivation and machinery was being introduced to lessen the demands made on the Russian farm labour force.

The Chinese leaders had a very different conception of the chief problems being encountered in their programme, and these misconceptions led to the " leap forward " strategy of 1958 and 1959. In their view

---

12 See Rosovsky, op. cit., pp. 61, 85.
13 Ibid., pp. 81–83.

the chief problems were too low a rate of capital formation and under-employment of the rapidly growing labour force. The leadership felt that increased investment depended on still greater expansion of production in heavy industry and the mobilisation of China's surplus manpower. The chief bottlenecks in heavy industry were considered to be the shortage of steel and other raw materials and over-reliance on large-scale heavy industry. In 1957 there did seem to be a shortage of pig iron and steel for blacksmith shops and for the machine and construction industries, and large amounts of steel products were still being imported. But in the five years 1958–62 the real problem would not be more steel but the processing of this steel into usable machinery and equipment. Small-scale enterprises in heavy industry would require relatively more skilled manpower per unit of output than large-scale heavy industry. Small-scale industrial projects could be completed more quickly than large industrial complexes, but this would give the labour force that much less time to receive the training needed to operate these enterprises.

During the First Five-Year Plan the planners followed a policy of holding increases in the labour force in the modern sectors to a minimum. In 1958 this policy was reversed and every effort was made to increase the labour force in construction and heavy industry. One reason for this dramatic shift in policy seems to have been the conviction of the policy-makers that the programme of economic development during the First Five-Year Plan had led to growing underemployment of the labour force. But the programme for agriculture was not labour-displacing in its effect; in fact, it put added demands on the agricultural labour force. Native transport was being used to supplement and to support the modern transport system and the demand for labour in this sector probably increased during the First Five-Year Plan. The handicrafts sector was largely engaged in processing food products or raw materials supplied locally outside the state system for allocating steel and other products, and very little investment had been directed toward displacing this production by enterprises using modern techniques of production. Farm supplementary handicrafts were still an important sector in producing consumer goods. The expansion of state trade did leave many peddlers without employment but rising urbanisation was bound to create increased demand for consumer services in the cities to absorb any displacement of labour in trade. The rapid growth in the labour force, therefore, meant only that underemployment in the Chinese economy that had existed before the programme for rapid industrialisation began would still exist in 1957; it did not mean that the demand for labour was expanding more slowly than the supply.

The " leap forward " strategy adopted in 1958 might have been successful as a marginal effort superimposed on the programme for economic development. Some increases in irrigation and construction and some small-scale production in heavy industry could very well supplement the existing programme. Instead the " leap forward " campaign was considered to be a new strategy and was pressed on a scale that replaced the economic programme established during the period 1950–57.

THE AFTERMATH OF THE LEAP FORWARD—1961–63

It is not yet possible to reach firm conclusions on the situation in China's industry in the period 1961–63, but the hypothesis presented here is that the " leap forward " years (1958–60) represent a boom period followed by a severe depression—a Communist version of the business cycle in market economies. In the last half of 1960 we have what Keynes described as " the phenomenon of the *crisis*—the fact that the substitution of a downward for an upward tendency often takes place suddenly and violently." [14] The 1960 plan [15] announced targets for agriculture, light industry, and trade based on the claimed increases in grain and cotton production in 1959 compared with 1958, and state investment was planned to be 20 per cent. higher than the very high levels in 1959 with the allocation to the various sectors about the same as in 1959. During the last half of 1960 it became obvious even to the most stubborn believers in the " leap forward " strategy that agricultural production in 1959 was well below 1958 and that the country faced a serious food shortage. The year 1959 is now officially the first of three poor crop years. The Sino-Soviet dispute reached a climax and with the withdrawal of Soviet technicians in the summer of 1960, the Soviet aid programme was ended. These two developments contributed to and reinforced a third cause for the crisis. This third development can best be described in terms of Keynes' explanation of the crisis in the business cycle as a " sudden collapse in the marginal efficiency of capital." This collapse is preceded by " the later stages of the boom . . . characterised by optimistic expectations as to the future yield of capital-goods sufficiently strong to offset their growing abundance and their rising costs of production and, probably, a rise in the rate of interest also." [16] We can disregard the rate of interest because whatever criteria for investment are being used in China these criteria have little relation to the profitability of investment in terms of a rate of return on fixed assets. But even Chinese Communist planners, in the grip of a " leap forward " psychology, base their investment decisions on expectations as to additional production

---

[14] John Maynard Keynes, *The General Theory of Employment, Interest, and Money* New York: Harcourt, Brace and World, 1936, p. 314.

[15] Li Fu-ch'un, " Report on the Draft 1960 National Economic Plan," *Peking Review*, April 5, 1960, p. 5 *et seq.*

[16] Keynes, *op. cit.*, p. 315.

to be achieved by investment expenditures and such expectations depend on the abundance of capital relative to other factors of production. The Chinese planners are also forced to deal with the costs of investment expenditures in terms of high prices for investment goods, poor-quality and unusable investment goods, and the real costs involved in diverting labour from other sectors of production to construction activities.

There is some evidence that the new machine industries being constructed in the period 1958–60 were not getting into production smoothly and turning out high-quality equipment, even in the period when Soviet technical assistance was at its peak. When new equipment was produced, no provision seems to have been made to conduct necessary repairs and to produce the necessary spare parts to keep the equipment in operation. The costs of production in new small-scale enterprises were very high compared to large-scale heavy industry, and these enterprises were not finding sources of raw materials without making it increasingly difficult for large-scale industrial enterprises to get the raw materials needed for their operation. The labour needed for small-scale heavy industry and farm manpower directed to irrigation work and to small-scale commune industry was manifestly in excess of whatever under-employment had existed in agriculture and handicrafts. Much of the irrigation work that had been accomplished was openly admitted to have been wasted and the emphasis shifted to efforts to correct previous mistakes in irrigation projects. For these reasons it is likely that even without the agricultural failures of 1959 and 1960 and aside from the withdrawal of Soviet technicians in 1960, at some time in 1960 the planners would have abandoned the investment programme in small-scale heavy industry and would have drastically reduced investment in agriculture because substantial parts of these investments were a sheer waste of resources.

When the effect of crop failures in 1959–60 and the Sino-Soviet dispute are added to this third factor, the decline in the marginal efficiency of capital must have been very large. The following table attempts to give rough magnitudes to the postulated decline in investment demand in 1961 compared to 1959. These figures are presented only as a hypothesis pending further data.

The postulated decline in investment demand after the crisis of 1960 would be at least one-half of the 1959 level for fixed investment and would indicate a demand for investment in 1961 at about the same level as in 1957 before the " leap forward." On the hypothesis, the demand for investment would be unaffected in heavy industry producing for export, for agricultural production, and for light industry not using agricultural raw materials. Production of these commodities would continue to be limited only by the difficulties of producing up to capacity. Considerable investment opportunities remained to be exploited in rural and urban housing, communal services, and public construction. This investment would not require imported investment goods and would have plenty of labour in view of the cutbacks required in investment in other sectors. All things considered, however, the potential for redirecting investment into sectors where demand remained high was not nearly enough to counterbalance the very large decline in investment demand.

Table 4

SECTORS FACING DECLINES IN INVESTMENT DEMAND—1959 and 1961

Sector	*Factors Causing a Decline in Demand*	*Per cent. of Total Fixed Investment in 1959*	*1961 Decline as a per cent. of Total Fixed Investment in 1959*
Agriculture	Over-investment in 1958–60. Investment opportunities limited to about the 1956–57 level	26·6	10–13
Small-scale Heavy Industry	Over-investment in 1959–60, and assuming 20 per cent. of 1959 investment level could be usefully continued	11	9
Light Industry	Considerable excess capacity in light industry processing agricultural products until agricultural output exceeds 1958 level	6·1	4–5
Soviet-aid Heavy Industry	Sino-Soviet dispute and shift to food imports. Withdrawal of Soviet technicians and 1961 imports of Russian machinery and equipment only 20 per cent. of 1959 level	16	10–13
Heavy Industry producing intermediate products for heavy industry itself	Drop in investment demand for above sectors would indicate a drop in demand of about one-fifth for all final products of heavy industry. This would lead to considerable excess capacity in heavy industry producing intermediate products. 40–50 per cent. of this investment has been included in cut-backs for small-scale and Soviet-aid heavy industry	14	7–8
Modern Transport and Communications	This sector operates largely in support of heavy industry and construction and the above-mentioned decline in heavy industry would lead to substantial excess capacity and reduce investment demands by perhaps 50 per cent.	12·9	6
	Total decline in investment demand for these sectors in 1961 compared with 1959.		46–54 per cent.

A cutback in investment in 1961 to a level only half of investment in 1959 would lead to unemployment for half of all workers in construction and substantial unemployment in heavy industry itself. Faced with so large and disruptive a drop in final demand and given Communist objectives, a programme for building large amounts of excess capacity in industry and transport not directly affected by the withdrawal of Soviet technicians and by reduced imports of machinery, and a shift toward greater investment in urban and rural housing and communal services would be indicated.

The Communist planners, however, having been grossly over-optimistic in their investment calculations in the " leap forward " boom, over-reacted in the 1961–62 period in the way that Keynes described for market economies. " When disillusion falls upon an over-optimistic and over-bought market " it falls " with sudden and even catastrophic force." [17] All the workers drawn into non-agricultural employment in the years 1958–60 suddenly found themselves under severe state pressure to return to the agricultural sector. Worthwhile construction projects in housing and public construction were also suspended. Small-scale industrial enterprises just getting into production found themselves without essential raw materials and in effect were expected to close down. New policies to conserve manpower in construction and industry were essential because of the food shortage and the need for additional manpower for agriculture, but the Communist drive in 1961 and 1962 to send millions of workers back to agriculture was a waste of economic resources, was a shameful imposition on the people concerned, and was not useful for increasing agricultural production.

The investment programme in 1963 has probably shown some recovery from its worst declines in 1961. The Communist planners have had three years for redirecting resources and for adjusting psychologically to the new situation in the economy. The policy makers now seem to be aware of the economic problems that must be solved for a successful programme for economic development, but are reacting with a series of improvisations. It has been argued that continued economic growth in the Communist pattern would have to proceed on the strategy of the First Five-Year Plan and not in terms of the " leap forward " strategy adopted in 1958–60. A successful programme will not depend simply on a high rate of capital formation, but must proceed on two parallel lines. On the one hand, China's manpower must be permitted to use the traditional skills developed in agriculture, handicrafts, and trade. At the same time, a large number of experts must be trained in all the fields associated with a modern economy. The greatest single obstacle to such a programme is the Communist determination to socialise the economy and to make sure that managers, scientists, and technicians have the correct Marxist attitudes.

METHODOLOGICAL NOTE

Table 5 presents the estimates for gross domestic fixed investment. The primary data are the figures for state investment within and outside the

[17] *Ibid.*, p. 316.

state plan.[18] The allocations of state investment to the various sectors in 1950 and 1951 were made on the basis of sector allocations in 1952 and budget expenditures for economic construction for 1950–52.[19] The 1959 estimates are based on budgeted state investment expenditures [20] with adjustments for investment outside the state plan compared to estimates in 1958. State investments in industry and other sectors include investment in housing and communal services, and such investment needed to be excluded for purposes of the analysis.

The judgment was made that the state investment figures include all investment in non-agricultural enterprises subsequently socialised and therefore that these figures include virtually all non-agricultural investment. Agricultural investment other than state investment is the only important category of investment not included in the figures for state investment. Estimates for major repairs is a minor category added to complete the estimates for gross fixed investment.

Deficiencies in the data used affect the magnitudes given in the estimates, but would not affect the conclusions reached in this article. The jump in state investment in 1958 and 1959 may be overstated, and the estimates for total agricultural investment are more likely to be too high than too low. But errors in these estimates are not so great that alternative estimates would lead to different conclusions than those presented in the analysis.

[18] *Ten Great Years, op. cit.*, pp. 55–62.
[19] U.S. Joint Publication Research Service No. 1672-N.
[20] Li Fu-ch'un, " Draft Plan for 1960," *op. cit.*, p. 5.

Table 5

GROSS DOMESTIC FIXED INVESTMENT—1950-59

Million Yuan [a]

Sector	1950	1951	1952	1953	1954	1955	1956	1957	1958	1959
Heavy Industry										
State Investment [b]	185	393	1,298	2,336	3,170	3,791	6,037	6,153	14,889	17,074
Major Repairs [c]	96	106	198	230	293	358	449	557		
Light Industry										
State Investment [b]	133	286	368	398	553	461	814	981	2,049	2,358
Major Repairs [c]	82	92	64	50	62	50	72	100		
Modern Transportation and Communications										
State Investment [b]	241	461	710	927	1,293	1,577	2,349	1,844	3,104	4,675
Major Repairs [c]	142	142	118	105	140	167	199	188		
Agriculture										
State Investment [b]	121	266	560	667	362	556	1,071	1,060	2,401	3,412
Supplementary budget expend. [d]	76	165	347	470	965	829	991	1,018	1,170	1,324
Farm purchases [d]	300	400	500	700	1,100	1,300	1,600	1,400	2,900	3,500
Imputed farm [d]	600	700	800	900	900	1,000	1,000	1,100	2,260	2,000
Trade	29	43	112	234	336	322	684	330	520	449
Urban Public Utilities	20	73	159	217	207	197	315	339	530	542
Culture, education, science, health	110	209	318	667	715	627	999	936	648	645
Government	15	19	19	242	181	125	144	160	173	178
Communal services and housing [e]	102	209	438	1,545	1,741	1,393	2,285	2,007	2,366	2,347
Military construction [e]	174	391	378	767	512	251	102	20	20	20
Total Fixed Investment	2,426	3,955	6,387	10,455	12,530	13,004	19,111	18,193	33,030	38,524
State Investment	1,130	2,350	4,360	8,000	9,070	9,300	14,800	13,830	26,700	31,700
Other Agricultural Investment	976	1,265	1,647	2,070	2,965	3,129	3,591	3,518	6,330	6,824
Major Repairs	320	340	380	385	495	575	720	845		

54

a Estimates are significant only to the nearest 10 million yuan, but are unrounded for use in further computations.

b State investment in all sectors include some investment in housing and communal services. Exclusions from the various sectors were made as follows: (1) Total "non-productive" investment was estimated for the years 1952–58 using the proportions for completed new fixed assets [21]; (2) total investment in housing and communal services in productive sectors was estimated as a residual by subtracting from "non-productive" investment, investment in the "non-productive" sectors and the "Other" category; (3) 62 per cent. of investment in housing and communal services in the productive sectors was estimated for industry based on the percentage of industrial assets for productive assets for 1953–57 [22]; (4) subtractions were made from the productive sectors in proportion to total investment in these sectors; and (5) investment in housing and communal services for "non-productive" sectors was estimated to be the same percentage of investment as in the non-industrial productive sectors.

c Major repairs for 1950–57 as estimated in my book [23] are allocated to the three sectors listed in proportion to total state investment. Such expenditures are believed to be included in state investment outside plan in 1958 and 1959.

d Non-state investment expenditures for agriculture in 1950–57 are based on the definitions, procedures and estimates in my book [24] with minor revisions. The 1958–59 estimates are based on budget figures, retail sales figures for producer goods sold to peasants, and estimates of imputed farm investment based on estimates of the increase in irrigation activities.

e The "Other" category is judged to be primarily investment in housing, communal services, and military construction. In the First Five-Year Plan 72 per cent. of all housing investment was to be undertaken under the ministries.[25] This percentage was applied against estimated housing expenditures for each year based on data in the *Ten Great Years*.[26] Investment in communal services under the "Other" category in each year was estimated to be in the same proportion to housing as for the other sectors. This crude procedure furnishes estimates of investment in military construction as a residual.

[21] *Ten Great Years, op. cit.*, p. 64.
[22] *Ibid.*, pp. 64, 93.
[23] Hollister, *op. cit.*, p. 57.
[24] *Ibid.*, pp. 29–33, 57–58.
[25] *The First Five Year Plan, op. cit.*, p. 195f.
[26] *Ten Great Years, op. cit.*, p. 217.

Conceptual Difficulties in Measuring China's Industrial Output

By FRED C. HUNG and YUAN-LI WU

A SHARP contrast stands between the mood of optimism in 1958 and 1959 when official as well as unofficial reports of industrial progress continued to pour out of Communist China and the silence and complete black-out of statistical information which has characterised the Chinese scene since 1960.[1] If the principal landmarks are retraced, the first major sign of a change in official policy appears to have come in early 1961 when the Chinese Communist Party decided to reverse the policies which had characterised the " leap forward " of 1958–59. This was followed by a drastic policy of retrenchment in investment and reorientation of industrial production during the latter part of 1961 as the economic crisis deepened. Since then the new slogan has been " adjustment, consolidation, reinforcement, and improvement "; the new order of priorities is agriculture, light industry and heavy industry; the new approach is to regard agriculture as the economic base and industry as the " leading factor."

To study the dynamic process of industrial development, information on the changes that take place is indispensable. Here, however, we are faced with two types of problems. First, the official statistical series modern industrial output, *i.e.,* excluding that of handicraft production, does not go beyond the year 1957. Also the series of industrial output, including both modern and handicraft production, does not extend beyond 1959. There is, therefore, a lack of information on the changes between 1960 and 1962. On the other hand, since the official statistics are subject to certain criticisms, various statistical series have been constructed in their place. These substitute series, however, are themselves not necessarily free from the same, as well as other, strictures. They, too, are also not long enough in most cases to bridge the most recent period for which information is lacking.

The official series can be criticised on at least two principal counts. First, being a measure of the gross industrial output based on the

---

[1] Since the second half of 1962, much information has been made available by Communist China on cost savings, quality improvement, percentage increase in output over the previous year, and production of new products. However, information on physical output is still rare.

"factory method," there is a certain degree of double counting in the reported output. Increased industrial output may come about merely as a result of increasing frequency of reports following changes in the organisation of production. In the same category we may include distortion of the series due to changes in the coverage of reporting industrial output. Secondly, the official series are subject to exaggeration because after 1952 they included an increasing volume of new products being produced in Communist China. These products were priced at experimental cost levels which are much higher than the normal production costs. This may be described as the "new product effect."

Partly because of these deficiencies in the official series, efforts have been made by Western scholars to reconstruct an industrial output series of Communist China. Among these are the indices drawn up by Chao Kang[2] as well as the earlier work of F. C. Hung.[3] These indices are physical output indices in which a number of commodities are selected and their physical output series are weighted with values. They themselves, however, are again not free from certain biases. Being indices of output weighted by values, these series may be distorted either because of deficiencies in the output series or because of questionable values used as weights. First, the reported output series from official statistics does not take into account changes in quality. This is especially true between 1958 and the institution of the new policy of quality improvement. Where low quality products are included without proper allowance being made, they would tend to exaggerate the growth of the industrial output series. Second, if the value weights consist of commodity prices, the industrial output series would then reflect the relative weights or prices used. If these prices are biased in favour of certain commodities— in the case of Communist China, the prices of the producer goods—the output series would be exaggerated if the component items which have relatively larger weights also happen to be the fast growing sectors. Third, inasmuch as the industrial output series built up in this manner rests upon only a selected number of commodities, it is a true reflection of the general situation only in so far as the sample selected is an accurate reflection of the entire industrial sector. Since the output statistics are confined only to a small number of commodities, primarily those producer's goods which are fast growing, the industrial output series drawn up in this way inherently has an upward bias. On the basis of these comments, it follows that the two industrial output series mentioned earlier would tend to fall below the official gross value output

[2] Chao Kang, "Indices of Industrial Output in Communist China," *Review of Economics and Statistics*, August 1963.
[3] Hung, Fred C., "Rates and Patterns of Industrial Growth in Modern China," paper presented at the annual meeting of the Association for Asian Studies, New York, 1958.

series because of their complete or partial exclusion of the machine industry, the products of which are not standardised and cannot be easily included in output series, and it is the machine products which were subject especially to exaggeration by the new product effect. On the other hand, for the reasons mentioned above, these series are not necessarily free from an upward bias. Lastly, the use of prices as weights does not allow for changes in the cost of production especially if constant prices are used and if performance does not remain at the same level over a period of time. This objection may be partly met by using values added or factor cost as weights. But if these weights refer to values added or factor cost in any one period (1952, for instance), while they would take into account cost differences among individual commodities included in the overall series, they would still not be able to meet the objection of possible changes in efficiency and in production cost over a period of time.

There is, however, a much more fundamental objection to measuring changes in Communist China's industrial output with any one of these composite output series. That is, when we weigh the various component items either by their prices or by their values added or factor cost, we assume that any increase in output would reflect an increase in the amount of goods in the industrial sector that are useful or would help increase the national product or the enjoyment of the goods produced by the population. This assumes that goods produced are always useful and should be better produced than not. However, if production of certain goods increases beyond the point where they can be used immediately or even over a period of time because of the inadequate supply of complementary factors, then to value this excess output at the same weight as before would exaggerate the increase in output in the sense that the increase would in no way measure an improvement either in the amount of useful goods available to the population for consumption or in the volume of producer's goods which can be used in further production. In a society in which production is regulated by the price mechanism and the system of profit and loss, obviously goods will not continue to be produced if their production cannot cover cost. In an economy which is not governed by these considerations, on the other hand, it is not inconceivable that goods will continue to be produced simply because of the emphasis on quantity production and on exceeding production targets set at any time. If these goods are then valued at constant prices which in no way reflect prices that they can command on the market, even if we assume the quality has remained unchanged, it would seem that the increase in industrial output registered by the statistics would not really reflect an increase in well-being or in the amount of goods at the command of the society; rather it would be a reflection of planning errors. It would seem that none of the indices suggested above could clear away this particular difficulty.

ESTIMATED INDUSTRIAL OUTPUT BASED ON INPUT REQUIREMENTS

The last point cannot be easily brought to light without carefully examining the development of certain industries. As a matter of fact, it is through the study of the steel industry that this idea has been brought to our attention.[4] At the same time, the study of individual sectors within industry has also helped in the projection of industrial output as a whole over the period for which output series are insufficient for the construction of a composite index based on the outputs of selected commodities.

In a recent study on the distribution of electric power by use, it has been possible to establish the amount of electricity consumed by modern industry other than by the power plants themselves. When correlated with the output of modern industry which has been discounted for " new product effect " by excluding the machine manufacturing sector, a high coefficient of correlation can be established.[5] This particular relationship between electric power as input and the output of modern industry conforms with the relationship between power consumption and industrial output in other countries such as the United States, the Soviet Union and Japan, to name just a few. Since power consumption by industry can also be established for 1958–60 as well as for 1962, it is now possible to estimate Communist China's modern industrial output for these years. This approach, therefore, offers us a useful by-product which studies on individual industries have made possible. While this extension of the statistical series of modern industrial output does not meet all the criticisms of the output series devised earlier on the basis of individual commodities, inasmuch as it is still based on the price system of the base period, it does have the merit of bridging the information gap of the recent years. It offers us at least a quantitative assessment of the level of current industrial output in mainland China. On the basis of this appraisal as well as of other available information, we are presented with a tentative conclusion that the economic downswing of 1961 to 1962 had probably come to an end by the second part of 1962, and that the second half of the year was probably marked by a vigorous rebound in the industrial sector.

[4] Yuan-li Wu, *Steel: A Study of the Industrialisation of Communist China* (to be published soon).

[5] Yuan-li Wu, *Economic Development and the Use of Energy Resources in Communist China* (New York: Praeger, 1963), and Yuan-li Wu, Francis P. Hoeber and Mabel M. Rockwell, *The Economic Potential of Communist China* (unpublished).

While electricity is a principal input in most other industries, it is also a component of total industrial output, although only a relatively small component. Use of electric power consumed by industry as an independent variable to estimate industrial output suggests that other estimates may also be made on the basis of other component items of modern industry. For instance, it may be possible to estimate industrial output on the basis of the value added of the various metals. This has been done in a recent study on the steel industry cited above. Similarly industrial output projections may be based on finished steel output. This is probably more useful for the purpose of projection than the series of value added for all the metals because of the longer series available in the case of finished steel and the available estimate of its output for 1962. Futhermore, combinations of individual series of estimates based on different component items of modern industry may also be combined to arrive at composite estimates. Some of these possibilities are presented in Table 1 along with the composite commodity series developed by Chao Kang.

As can be seen in Table 1, the projections of the gross value output of modern industry based on a correlation with the logarithm of finished steel production are lower than the other two series of projections based on power consumption. It may be reasonable to assume that the real industrial output during 1958–62 lay between the lower and upper bounds of these three series. A composite series has been given in a Stanford Research Institute report for the years 1958–60, assigning twice as much weight to the exponential series as to each of the other two.[6] The rationale is that industrial output during the period of the " great leap " through 1960 probably increased mostly by an expansion of industry without any large increase in the amount of electricity input per unit of output. On the other hand, for the year 1962, twice as much weight is assigned here to the projection based on finished steel production as to the other two, yielding a lower composite projection. This is based on the reasoning that in a period of " readjustment, consolidation, reinforcement and improvement," more finished steel and electricity might have been used in the process of production in order to keep the quality of products up to a certain standard. This composite series agrees fairly well with Chao's commodity series which terminates in 1959.

IMBALANCE AND POOR PLANNING WITHIN INDUSTRY

One of the results of a recent study on the electric power industry [7] shows that Communist Chinese planners were plagued by the difficult problem

[6] *The Economic Potential of Communist China, op. cit.*
[7] See note 5 above.

TABLE 1

ESTIMATED GROSS VALUES OF OUTPUT OF MODERN INDUSTRY ADJUSTED FOR NEW PRODUCT EFFECT 1952–57 AND PROJECTION TO 1962

Year	Adjusted Official Statistics		Calculation Based on Correlation with Logarithm of Consumption of Electricity in Industry		Calculation Based on an Exponential Function of Consumption of Electricity in Industry		Calculation Based on Correlation with Logarithm of Finished Steel Production		Composite Series [a]		Chao Kang's Estimates
	Billion Yuan	Index 1952–100	Billion Yuan	Index 1952–100	Billion Yuan	Index 1952–100	Billion Yuan	Index 1952–100	Billion Yuan	Index 1952–100	Index 1952–100
(1)	(2)		(3)		(4)		(5)		(6)		(7)
Data Points 1952–57											
1952	22·0	100	21·5	100	22·8	100	22·3	100	22·4	100	100
1953	28·4	129·1	27·8	129·3	27·4	120·2	28·7	128·7	27·8	124·1	124·7
1954	33·0	150·0	33·9	157·7	32·7	143·4	31·3	140·4	32·7	146·0	141·6
1955	35·6	161·8	37·1	172·6	35·9	157·5	36·6	164·1	36·4	162·5	146·9
1956	45·0	204·6	44·1	205·1	44·0	193·0	46·5	208·5	44·7	199·6	182·2
1957	49·7	225·9	49·3	229·3	51·1	224·1	48·3	216·6	50·0	223·2	195·9
Projections 1958–1962											
1958			59·8	278·1	65·1	285·5	53·9	241·7	61·0	272·3	272·6
1959			71·5	332·6	89·8	393·9	65·2	292·4	79·1	353·1	371·4
1960			79·6	370·2	111·6	489·5	75·3	337·7	94·5	421·9	
1962			72·3	336·3	96·5	423·3	59·3	265·9	71·8	320·5	

[a] With the exception of 1962, column (6) = $\frac{1}{4}$ [column (3) + column (5) + 2 × column (4)]. For 1962, column (6) = $\frac{1}{4}$ [column (3) + column (4) + 2 × column (5)].

Sources: For 1952–60, data from *The Economic Potential of Communist China, op. cit.* The 1962 figures are based on estimated output of 7 million tons of finished steel, and 45 billion kwh of electricity by plants of 500 kilowatts and above. For Chao Kang's estimates, see the *Review of Economics and Statistics* article cited above.

of choosing between thermo and hydro electric power plants. While the construction and investment costs of hydro plants were supposed to be considerably higher than the corresponding costs for thermo plants, this relative cost comparison was drastically altered during the period of the " great leap " with the result that the construction policy was changed in favour of the hydro plants. According to the study referred to, it is believed that this change in policy resulted from faulty cost comparisons because construction costs of hydro plants were underestimated. This arose from an incorrect allocation of joint costs in the case of multiple purpose projects in which irrigation, flood control, and hydro power were the combined purposes of major projects. The construction cost of these multiple purpose projects may also have been underestimated because of the failures to account for labour costs—for a large number of unpaid workers were employed. Monetary payments not being made to the conscript labourers, the planners apparently overlooked the existence of opportunity costs and mistook faulty cost accounting for the absence of real costs. It follows, that because of the shift in emphasis from the construction of thermo power plants to that of hydro plants, a very important incentive to the development of coal mining was absent. When this effect was reinforced by the indiscriminate exploitation of existing coal mines regardless of the depletion effect, the existing mines were exhausted more rapidly during the " great leap," the development of a coal shortage following the onset of the industrial crisis became an inevitable consequence. The reported increase in the output of coal as well as that of electric power during the period of 1958–60, therefore, failed to reveal this problem of imbalance within the industry.

On the basis of the study on the steel industry, the imbalance within the industry has also been brought to light. This imbalance appears both in the form of an excessive development of steel-making capacity relatively to that of both the earlier and the later finishing stages and in the development of inadequate capacity for finishing high-quality steel and special steels. One of the results of the imbalance at the finishing stage for the production of good quality steels was the apparent accumulation of steel stocks, especially in semi-finished products. This means that for much of the increase in the output of ferrous metals at the finishing stages, which also carry higher prices, the reported increases in value output and consequently in the gross industrial output may really reflect an increase in stock which cannot be used either because of quality deficiencies or because of the absence of other complementary factors for which no adequate substitutes could be found. This serves to illustrate how a rising industrial output series may simply conceal the effects of erroneous planning.

Of course the continued production of goods which were either useless or cannot be efficiently employed for further production cannot go on indefinitely. Sooner or later, the planners will recognise their mistakes and adjustments would be made in the plans, which would in turn be reflected in a decrease in the overall output of the commodity in question, and possibly a decrease in the overall industrial output. As long as this mistake is not recognised, however, the effect of the accumulation of useless products would be shown both in the continued increase in unplanned inventory accumulation and in a decrease of the incremental output investment ratio. In other words, statistically, this would be seen in a fall in the rate of expansion of the gross national product, especially of the industrial sector. Viewed in this manner, it would seem quite plausible to regard the present policy of consolidation and quality improvement as a belated recognition of this faulty planning.

However, it does not necessarily follow that Communist China is doomed to fail in her effort to industrialise. It does not follow necessarily that the quality improvement and the resolution of bottlenecks that may now exist cannot be carried out within a reasonably short period.

PROSPECTS AND CONCLUSION

As mentioned earlier, quantitative information on Communist China's industrial recovery is still lacking in most cases. But judged from her production of finished steel and electricity, as well as from the frequency of her official reports on cost savings, quality improvement, production of new products, and sometimes relative increase in output over the previous year, it may be safe to conclude that Communist China had passed her lowest point of recession since the " great leap " around the middle of 1962, and that her rate of industrial recovery since then could be fairly rapid.

A rapid industrial recovery in Communist China should not come entirely as a surprise as the removal of bottlenecks under the new policy could result in an improvement of the output-capital ratio. Also, overcompensation on the part of the Communist Chinese leaders could be corrected by putting the " inefficient " plants back to work. In addition, plants which were laid idle because of temporary material or fuel shortage could resume their normal operation once the shortage is over. In this respect, the improvement of agricultural production in 1962 certainly helped. But it must be pointed out that the increase in agricultural output in 1962 was due more to the restoration of incentive through institutional changes then to the " aid agriculture " programme.[8] The latter would take much more time and larger investment than at present to have its impact felt to any significant degree.

In concluding, the following observations may be made: (1) The new policy of "readjustment, consolidation, reinforcement and improvement" represented the belated recognition of imbalance between and within industries on the part of the Chinese Communist leaders and their effort to remedy the situation. (2) A faster rate of industrial recovery is possible at the beginning because of repair and replacement of worn-out equipment and the removal of bottlenecks. Also, a correction of the mistake of overcompensation may speed up recovery at the outset. Once a normal situation has been reached, much more capital would be required to achieve the same rate of growth. (3) The " Aid agriculture " programme, although a step in the right direction, may not have yet exerted any significant influence on the agricultural crop of 1962 as it would take much longer time and more investment to develop such a programme. (4) The assignment of first priority to agriculture does not necessarily mean that production in Communist China is now less capital intensive. Mechanisation, electrification, and the development of the chemical industry all need large amounts of capital investment. What the change in policy means is that there will be less " round-aboutness " in the Communist China's productive system so that the capital is used for more immediate purposes, *i.e.*, to increase agricultural output. (5) If this new policy is successful, Communist China will increase her output in agriculture. But this will not necessarily make her predominantly an agricultural country as the industries could be equally developed with a more sound agricultural foundation. (6) It is difficult to anticipate at the present time whether Communist China will succeed in her new effort and whether with improved economic conditions her leaders will reverse their policy for another great leap to industrialisation. Only time can tell.

---

[8] For discussion, see Yuan-li Wu " Industrial Development in China," *Current History*, September 1963.

China's "New Economic Policy"— Transition or Beginning

By FRANZ SCHURMANN

POVERTY, ISOLATION AND DEFIANCE

UNTIL a short time ago, it appeared that much of what was going on in China could be characterised by the cynical aphorism *plus ça change plus c'est la même chose*. Many things became manifest in the country that were reminiscent of themes centuries old. China had gone through two radical phases, one during the First Five-Year Plan period when the Chinese Communists tried to repeat the Soviet experience of industrialisation, and the second during the Great Leap Forward when they used their own mobilisational means to try to achieve economic breakthrough. The ninth Plenum in January 1961 called a dramatic halt to the extreme policies of the Great Leap Forward, and launched a period that bears strong similarities to the N.E.P. (New Economic Policy) period of the early 1920s in the Soviet Union. Many traditional patterns that were effaced during the years of radicalism began to reappear. There was talk of the need " to study very well traditional economic relationships." [1] It seemed that for a while the leadership had decided that only a truly voluntary response from below, and not coercion of any sort, could rescue China from the morass in which it found itself. But as of the time of the writing of this article, there are ominous signs that China may be approaching another " 1928." The Party drums are rolling once again, and the themes are not those of the N.E.P., but more like those which preceded the great Soviet collectivisation drive of 1928. During the last few years, the leadership made no attempt to hide the facts of China's poverty and isolation. But now a new note of defiance, of toughness has crept out. Where it will lead is hard to say.

There was never any reluctance on the part of China's leaders to admit the country's backwardness, but the attitude toward it has changed over the years. During the period of the First Five-Year Plan, the leaders were confident that they could give China a heavy industrial base equal to that of any modern nation, and in time carry through an economic revolution in agriculture. During the mid-1950s serious doubts began to set in, but there seemed to be a way out. Backwardness was the theme

---

[1] Kuan Ta-t'ung, " Our Country's Socialist, Unified Domestic Market," *Red Flag*, No. 6, 1963, p. 34.

underlying the Great Leap Forward, but also a supreme confidence that with organisation and energy China could overtake England in a short period of time, and within a few more years reach the level of the Soviet Union. Much of the earlier confidence has gone, and the theme of backwardness and hard work, and the admonition that it will take decades before China can escape its traditional curse of poverty, comes out again and again in the statements of its leaders. It is the theme of poverty, and the strength which comes from consciousness of poverty, rather than race or colour, which makes the Chinese sense a common cause with all the poor and oppressed nations of the world. Chinese often say that it is their lot in life to suffer. This is said, not in resignation, but as a spur to work, like the dual implication of suffering and work in the expression *ch'ih-k'u*. Mao Tse-tung once said that " we want to carry out construction on a very vast scale, but we are still a very poor country—this is a contradiction." [2] This sums up the attitude prevailing today in China.

Along with the theme of poverty, there is that of isolation. The bitterness against the Soviet Union runs very deep in China. There has been anger against the Party and its leaders over the fanaticism and failures of the Great Leap Forward, but even greater anger against the Soviet Union for abandoning China during the years of its greatest economic difficulties. China wanted equality among the fraternal socialist nations, but not in terms of Khrushchev's attitude of " prosperity for the Soviet Union—and good luck to the rest of the comrades." [3] While the remainder of the " third world " benefits from foreign economic aid from one side or another or both, China, the largest of the poor countries, must go it alone. One of the taunts most often levelled against India is that India is dependent on assistance from imperialist nations, as well as from the Soviet Union. Though it has never been reported officially, most informed Chinese are aware of the fact that wheat purchased from abroad had to be paid for in hard foreign exchange. [4]

[2] Quoted in an article entitled: " Since You Calculate the Big Account, You Also Have to Calculate the Small Account," *Workers' Daily*, April 13, 1963.

[3] Edward Crankshaw, " The Changing Mask of Marxism," *San Francisco Chronicle*, August 11, 1963.

[4] Note the statement in a recent issue of *Red Flag*:
Everybody knows that our country's socialist capital accumulation, just as Stalin has said, cannot be carried out through methods imperialism uses in robbing colonies, cannot be carried out through methods capitalism uses to carry out foreign aggression and extort reparations, nor can it be realised by methods of relying on enslaving foreign loans. Imperialism will not make us any loans. The running dogs of imperialism and foreign reactionaries will also not make us any loans. We also have no intention of accepting any kind of unequal conditions to obtain loans from imperialists, foreign reactionaries, or anyone else! *Red Flag*, No. 13–14, 1963, p. 11.

Poverty and isolation have gone together to breed defiance and not resignation. The Tenth Plenum in September 1962 came when a campaign had started to rebuild the morale of the Party and restore its image in the eyes of the people. In the late spring of 1963 the leadership launched another campaign to get cadres out of their offices and work alongside the people. Though industry too has been affected by orders to engineers and technicians to move onto the production floor,[5] the main target is agriculture. Cadres from the production brigade level on up to county administrative levels have been told to do physical labour alongside the peasants to assure a good summer harvest. Increase agricultural production and greatly accelerate the speed of socialist capital accumulation—these are the main policy themes of the spring and summer of 1963. The similarities to the kind of talk that went on in the Soviet Union in 1927 and 1928 are striking. Whereas just a short time earlier, the leadership had shown N.E.P.-like tolerance for administrators and technicians, the old anti-bureaucratic hatred has reappeared with vituperations against those who " love idleness and hate work, eat too much and own too much, fight for status, act like officials, put on bureaucratic airs, do not care about the sufferings of the people, do not care about the interests of the country." [6] What makes the present truculence even more ominous is its association with the idea of isolation, of the fatherland in danger. Sense of crisis, national isolation, poverty, the need to secure more savings from agriculture—all these were elements behind the Soviet collectivisation drive of the 1920s. Is it possible that the Chinese have already passed through their N.E.P. period, and are plunging into their own " 1928 "? This article deals with the period which began early in 1961 and lasted through 1962 and early 1963, and one which can roughly be described as a Chinese N.E.P. Whether the Chinese N.E.P. is simply a transition to another " 1928 " or the beginning of a really new and different period of economic development is something which only events will tell.

THE LINKAGE OF INDUSTRY AND AGRICULTURE

One traditional theme that has emerged is the over-riding stress on agriculture. Ever since the Ninth Plenum, the bulk of economic articles in the country's newspapers have been devoted to the subject of agriculture. In ancient China the primacy of agriculture and the derivative nature of commerce were expressed in the phrase: agriculture is the root and commerce the branch. The old saying has been altered to read: agriculture is the root and industry the guide, a phrase which is linguistically awkward, but leaves little doubt as to which of the two is primary.

[5] See, for example, *Workers' Daily*, July 18, 1963.
[6] *Red Flag*, No. 13–14, 1963, p. 11.

Actually, the shift toward agriculture in economic strategy took place in 1957 when the plans for the Great Leap Forward were being drafted.

During the First Five-Year Plan period, agriculture was the ultimate source of savings with which the programme of industrialisation was financed. Savings in tangible form were not directly generated by agriculture, but rather through industrial enterprises which acquired raw materials from the agricultural sector at low prices and produced goods sold at high state-set prices, thus generating a sizeable profit for the state. In contrast to the Soviet Union, enterprise profits have formed the major source of savings in China, so much so that in the 1960 draft budget, 93·4 per cent. of total budgetary revenue was accounted for by profits and taxes from state enterprises (of which profits accounted for 64·7 per cent. of the total).[7] Within the state-owned sector, however, there was an implicit division of labour between the large modern enterprises and smaller regional industries. Whereas the former were allowed to be wasteful with capital and expected to concentrate mainly on output, the main role of the latter was to generate savings for the state. Since light industry in China is 80 per cent. dependent on agriculture for its raw materials, and has played such a major role in generating savings for the state,[8] it is not difficult to see that, in the absence of outright foreign aid, a leap forward in the modern industrial sector would require a concomitant expansion of light industry, which in turn was only possible if there was a sizeable increase in agricultural output. Furthermore, since imports of capital goods from the Soviet Union were to be financed with massive export of food products, agriculture was faced with a double burden: to produce more food and raw materials for urban consumers and industries, and more food and raw materials for export to the Soviet Union. If one looks at the economic statistics for 1957, one sees a uniform pattern: lower rate of industrial output (particularly of consumer goods), lower rate of state revenue (particularly of enterprise profits), and a decline in trade with the Soviet Union.[9]

The Great Leap Forward, with all that it involved, was conceived of as the answer to the problem. There was no change in the view that agriculture still was the basic source of savings for China's programme of industrialisation, but there was a new realisation that " industry and

---

7 *Chukyo no zaisei* (*Chinese Communist Finances*), published by the China section of the Asian Bureau of the Japanese Foreign Office (Tokyo: 1961), p. 44.

8 *Fei-ch'ing Yüeh-pao* (Taipei), May 20, 1962, p. 4. To my knowledge there are no statistical breakdowns for budgetary receipts from different branches of the state-owned industrial sector. Such a breakdown would indicate the extent to which light and regional industry have contributed to the national investment programme.

9 Ta-chung Liu and Kung-chia Yeh, *The Economy of the Chinese Mainland: National Income and Economic Development, 1933–1959* (Santa Monica: Rand Corporation, 1963), Volume I, pp. 160–227; see also Robert F. Dernberger, " Communist China's Foreign Trade, Sources of Investment Funds and Rate of Growth " (unpublished paper), p. 21.

agriculture had to develop simultaneously." This meant in effect that the economic revolution had to take place throughout the economy.

The failure of the Great Leap Forward did not change the view that industry and agriculture were inextricably linked together. The key to China's further development is still seen as lying in agriculture. However, the failure of mobilisation to elicit greater output from the peasants forced the state to revert to different methods. Aside from organisational liberation, the state resolved to provide material incentives for the peasants. This meant not only greater freedom to tend their private plots, but higher prices for farm products, and assurances to the peasant that he could purchase industrial goods with the larger amount of cash in his pockets.

To meet this new source of demand, the government resolved on a far-reaching programme to re-orient industrial production more and more in the direction of satisfying consumer demand, both urban as well as rural. This was not an easy task to accomplish. With the sharp cutbacks in industrial investment carried out since 1961, major industries had fewer resources with which to meet state output targets. But at the same time, they were expected to broaden their assortment of products to meet the new demand for industrial goods coming from the rural areas. Heavy industry, which still remains capital favoured, has had a somewhat easier time than light industry. Many small plants, set up in haste and in defiance of economic rationality during the Great Leap Forward, were closed down altogether, or had to reduce their operations sharply. Those that remained, however, saw themselves faced with new burdens. Not only had they to fulfil plan targets, particularly profit targets, and meet rising consumer demand, but they had to do this under increasingly adverse conditions, foremost among which were shortages of materials and higher prices for agricultural raw materials. In fact, as during the Great Leap Forward, the smaller industries still had to carry the burden of accumulation, except that now Party organisation was no longer able to dictate and control the conditions under which production took place.

W. W. Rostow, in discussing the preconditions for industrialisation, stresses the role of agriculture as a supplier of food and materials, a market for industrial products, and as a source of savings for the modern sector.[10] Communist economic planners have regarded agriculture as a supplier of food and savings for the modern sector. However, as long as agriculture's task was essentially to bear the burden of the costs of industrialisation, it was idle to conceive of it as an expanding market for the products of the modern sector. Rostow argues that rising real

10 W. W. Rostow, *The Stages of Economic Growth* (Cambridge University Press, 1962), pp. 22–24.

incomes in agriculture, rooted in increased productivity, can act as an important stimulus to new modern industrial sectors. Essentially the same argument was made by Bukharin during the industrialisation debates in the Soviet Union during the 1920s. He argued that improving the peasant economy and increasing peasant demand for industrial products could stimulate industrial advance.[11] At a time when the Chinese are in a N.E.P. period of their own it is significant that Chinese theorists are now making the same argument.[12]

If one were simply looking at present reality and for the moment forgetting history and ideology, that seems to be what the Chinese Communists are doing at the moment. Although there are no statistics, official reports and refugee accounts all indicate an upward turn in peasant income, even to the extent of causing considerable worry in official circles. The question is, of course, whether this is only temporary expediency designed to muddle through present difficulties, or whether there has been a real change in economic strategy. Many feel, perhaps rightly, that a Communist system cannot change its spots, like the proverbial leopard. Maybe they are right, in view of the harsher tone that has come out of Peking in the last few months. But one can at least say that individuals in very high places in China have been giving serious thought to a basic approach to economic development that is neither a return to the Soviet model of centralised planning nor a return to the Great Leap Forward approach of guerrilla type mobilisation and production.

The Shift from Production to Accumulation Goals

In 1956 and 1957, Chinese writers began seriously to question the production mania which governed industry, and suggested that the so-called " gross output value " target be scrapped in favour of other targets that would bring about greater efficiency in production. Already at that time it was suggested that profit be made the main success

---

11 Alexander Erlich, *The Soviet Industrialisation Debate*, 1924–28 (Cambridge: Harvard University Press, 1960), pp. 8–23.

12 In presenting the views current in their economic debate, the Chinese usually do it by listing pairs of juxtaposed opinions. Thus the more conservative position argues that low peasant purchasing power must be accepted as a necessary fact, with the state rectifying inequity through financial credit and price policies. What might be called the Bukharinite position argues that industrial support of agriculture must take the form of commodity exchange, which means that the size of peasant purchasing power is the main factor determining the saleability of industrial goods in the rural market. " Summary of the Main Problems Discussed by Shanghai Economists During the Year 1962," *Ching-chi Yen-chiu* (*Economic Research*), No. 4, 1963, p. 64. Another significant similarity between arguments advanced now by the Chinese and earlier by Soviet N.E.P. economists is the acceptance of a priority sequence of agriculture-light industry-heavy industry. *Ibid.*, p. 63; Ehrlich, *op. cit.*, pp. 25–26.

indicator of enterprise operations.[13] During the entire period of the First Five-Year Plan, as is the case now, the current slogan had been: increase production and economise. However, as many Chinese writers have more or less openly acknowledged, these two aims are a bit contradictory, for the nation as a whole as for the individual factory manager. If one looks at economic statistics and political documents for the years of the First Five-Year Plan, it is clear that in years when waste was fought and cost-cutting emphasised, production rose at a slower rate. When production soared, as during the 1955 and early 1956 period, savings increased, but at a much slower rate.[14] In modern state-owned enterprises, managers did not worry much about costs, concentrating entirely on meeting their output figures, as has been the case with their Soviet colleagues. Managers of light industry were in a more precarious position. Having fewer investment resources to rely on than their colleagues in heavy industry, they had to struggle constantly to keep output up while at the same time keep costs down to the barest minimum in order to meet the financial targets of the plan.[15]

During the Great Leap Forward the leadership decided that it needed and desired both maximisation of output and of profits. However, in its formulation of the famous decentralisation decisions of November 1957, it demoted the " gross output value " target from its " commanding " position, and in effect substituted profit.[16] As is obvious, this by no means implied a slackening of the state's interest in maximising output, but it removed something which often was as much a restrictive

[13] Sun Yeh-fang, " Speaking of ' Gross Output Value '," *T'ung-chi Kung-tso* (*Statistical Work*), No. 13, 1957, p. 11; Yü I-ch'ien, " Can One Substitute ' Profit ' for ' Output Value '," *Statistical Work*, No. 5, 1957, p. 16.

[14] This can be seen in the following table:

Percentage increases of profits and output over preceding year

	1952	1953	1954	1955	1956	1957
State enterprise profits	0	34·0	29·0	12·4	19·0	5·9
Gross value product	0	32·0	17·0	4·7	38·2	6·9
Producers' goods	0	39·9	21·0	19·5	48·6	18·0
Consumers' goods	0	28·8	15·0	−3·0	31·5	−1·2

Based on T. C. Liu and K. C. Yeh, *op. cit.*, pp. 160–227.
During the years 1953–54, the leadership laid great stress on combating waste and keeping costs down, and so the figures for 1954 and 1955 show a higher savings than output rate. This is even more the case if we compare figures for state enterprise profits as a whole and consumer goods output, in view of the fact that light industry provided a disproportionately high share of national savings. In 1955 the leadership launched its great production drive, and so the figures for 1956 show a reverse picture: output, even for consumer goods, climbs at a faster rate than profits.

[15] On tendencies to beat the output plan without regard to costs in capital-favoured modern industries, see Sun Yeh-fang, *op. cit.*, pp. 8–9. Sun admits quite openly that " light industry must bear the burden of accumulation whereas heavy industry does not " (p. 12).

[16] See *People's Handbook 1958*, pp. 461–462; see also Ishikawa Shigeru, *The Structure of Capital Accumulation in China* (Tokyo: 1960), pp. 72–73.

as a stimulative factor guiding managerial decisions. In the spirit of decentralisation, factory managers (which at that time meant Party secretaries) were given broad discretion to set their own commodity mixes, responding to the changing kaleidoscope of national and local needs. There was no doubt in the mind of the government that all the conditions were present for a production craze, for the Party apparatus, which was now in solid control of the factories, always favoured output over money. Production had a Socialist ring to it, while money seemed to be a capitalist remnant which, in any case, would disappear with the imminent advent of Communism. Profit targets would be assured by maximisation and acceleration of turnover.

The more one looks at the details of the failure of the Great Leap Forward, the more it has the appearance of a depression, such as in the capitalist world: overproduction, underconsumption, drying up of savings, unemployment, decline in business morale, disruption of the market, etc. It is clear from the whole literature of the past few years that, aside from insufficiency in agricultural production, the leadership regards the savings picture as the most serious problem it faces. There has been a continuing emphasis on the need for economy, to meet financial targets, for a correct price policy, for a thorough-going reform of the banking system, for financial authority and responsibility in enterprises and in the country as a whole. The counterpart of the drastic cutback in industrial investment was a campaign launched to create new sources of investment funds. The discussion on how to do this has ranged over the whole framework of the economy. There has been discussion on how to set prices in order to satisfy interests on all sides, how to make commodity turnover more efficient, how to accelerate the circulation of capital, how to increase labour productivity, how to save on this and that. But in all this, one thing has become clear. The main targets that are given by the state to enterprises to meet are not output targets but profit targets. There have been Chinese Libermans arguing for the acceptance of profit as the one main goal for state enterprises to meet.

Early in 1962, some orthodox economists were still arguing for comprehensive fulfilment of plan targets, including both physical and value targets, but by the summer of 1962 the leadership had apparently come around to the view that the main targets had to be financial: costs and profits.[17] The acceptance of the cost and profit targets as primary has

[17] On July 19, 1962, the *People's Daily* published a theoretical article by two economists who are generally identified with the less liberal wing of the economic debate in which the following statement occurs:

We feel that cost targets and profit targets are the main indicators for evaluating the economic effectiveness of an enterprise.

However, it is hardly necessary to cite a theoretical article to show that the

not meant a complete conversion of the leadership to the profit principle. More conservative voices still argue that the main concern of a factory manager should be cutting of intra-enterprise costs with the implication that factory managers should continue to be restricted in their scope for selection and preference. Nevertheless, whatever the real situation—and all signs indicate that it fluctuates—the leadership has inaugurated a sharp change through its clear de-emphasis of output targets. This does not mean that production is being discouraged, although there was a real decline in production during the years of severe crisis, but rather that the leadership attaches paramount importance to accumulation, with which to finance its future programmes of expansion.

The Rise of Regional Economics

When the Chinese Communists first came to power, they had to admit what was obvious fact: the country did not constitute an economic entity. For five years, the country was administered as seven large regions. By 1954, the political difficulties obstructing complete unification (notably in Manchuria) had been overcome, and China, for the first time in decades, became truly unified. Political unification was an indispensable prerequisite for carrying out the First Five-Year Plan, which envisaged a steadily expanding modern sector cutting across regional lines and directly administered by the central authorities. The far-reaching decentralisation put through in November 1957 was a tacit recognition of the fact that the Chinese economy could not be directed as a single entity, that regional planning and co-operation would play a vital part in propelling the economy forward. This gave rise to the ideas of " economic co-operation zones " discussed in the literature during 1958.[18]

Regional economic co-operation meant that industries should rely mainly on materials deriving from the given administrative region rather than on materials that had to be transported from some distant source. If the needed materials were not available, they were to be developed or substitutes found. Under the earlier régime of centralised administration, regional economic co-operation would have encountered great administrative difficulties, but with new power and authority vested in the provincial authorities, intra-region allocation of materials could be greatly

leadership has come around to accepting cost and profit targets as the main success indicators of enterprises. The press has been full of articles urging an all-out effort on the part of factory employees to meet cost and profit targets, with only secondary mention of output targets.

[18] Liu Tsai-hsing, " On Problems in Establishing Complete Industrial Systems in Economic Co-operation Zones," *Hsin Chien-she (New Construction)*, No. 10, 1958, pp. 45–57; Wang Shou-li, " Consideration of the Principles in Outlining Economic Zones Within Provinces," *Economic Research*, No. 1, 1958, pp. 18–21.

simplified. What precisely an " economic co-operation zone " was supposed to be was a matter of dispute. Some of the articles revived the old idea of seven major regions. The decentralisation measures did not provide for any administrative mechanism between centre and provinces, and handed decision-making authority over to provincial governments, thus laying the groundwork for making the provinces the units of economic co-operation. The idea of a regional autarky reached its extreme and most absurd point with the formation of the communes. But by late 1958 it was amply clear to the planners that decentralisation had gone too far, and a swing of the pendulum backward was demanded. In the following year the planners called for a renewed emphasis on national co-operation in the programme metaphorically called : " all the country is a single chessboard." The 1959 attempt to counteract the adverse effects of excessive decentralisation did not work. When the leadership decided to reverse the policies of the Great Leap, it did not call for a massive effort at recentralisation, but changed the conditions which had been largely responsible for the mess : excessive Party control of the production apparatus.

Since January 1961 the leadership had made efforts to reorganise the whole system of economic administration. This has been particularly true of the financial and statistical systems. The banks, which had been under excessive local Party control, have once again acquired authority over financial transactions, as have financial officers in enterprises and state organs. Although one hears little about it, there must be considerable improvement in ministerial work at all levels. However, while there has been a definite recentralisation of financial functions, there is as yet no clear-cut evidence that production administration has been recentralised. Factory managers apparently still have a fairly wide range of discretion in determining concrete production policies at the enterprise levels, and are essentially only held to fulfilment of their financial targets and delivering to the state a particular line of products which the state has ordered from them. During the Great Leap Forward management at the factory level had a similar range of discretion, except that everything was run by the Party cadres, in close liaison with Party cadres who dominated the various levels of local government. It is apparent from a number of indicators that, while some recentralisation has gone on, in other areas the leadership has continued the decentralisation policies introduced in 1957.

One of the emphases that continues is that on regional co-operation. Enterprises have been told that they must try to purchase their materials and equipment within the given administrative area and wherever possible sell their products in the same area. To facilitate this type of local exchange, the government has even suggested that exchanges take place directly between sellers and buyers, bypassing the state-controlled commercial network. Despite the recent expansion of the use of advertising media to find more distant markets for inventories (and also to solicit orders for goods), enterprises have been urged to try to confine their economic relationships as much as possible within the given region, " not to go outside the area to seek objects for economic co-operation." [19] The fostering of direct exchange relationships between economic units means that the state, in regard to a very broad line of goods, has surrendered one important means of control over allocation, namely, the requirement that all factory products be turned over to the state purchase and procurement agencies. It is not uncommon to find references in the literature to " historical " or " traditional " economic relationships, which often is another way of stressing the importance of the regional as opposed to the national economy.

One of the persistent complaints against the idea of regional economies was that it would lead to inequities and gaps. The advanced regions would move ahead faster, while the backward regions would remain behind. The Great Leap Forward policy of the simultaneous development of the entire economy was, among other things, designed to overcome the inequities that had arisen during the First Five-Year Plan period as a result of the favoured treatment of the modern sector. However, the Ninth Plenum ended the levelling tendencies of the Great Leap Forward. The existence of inequity has not only been admitted, but actively encouraged. In fact, regional differences are now regarded as a spur to the less advanced regions to catch up with the more advanced. As in so many other cases, a policy once applied in one sector sooner or later becomes generalised for the system as a whole. Thus the recognition of inequity can be found in agriculture as well. Advanced production brigades are no longer penalised by levelling as they were during the Great Leap Forward. With the stress on material incentives, productive workers are once again regarded as models for their less productive brethren to follow—and are duly rewarded in material terms. As refugees will testify, the standard of living varies sharply from one area to another in China, it generally being highest in the cities, and among the cities highest in Shanghai—as it always has been. The effect of the present policy of encouraging regional co-operation must be to further widen the gap between the advanced and the backward areas. However, at a time when the leadership is deeply concerned with getting the economy moving again, it cannot afford to overlook the fact that the advanced regions add proportionately more new value to the country's economy than the poor regions.

[19] *People's Daily,* April 2, 1963.

INDEPENDENT MANAGERIAL AUTHORITY

One of the complaints that was already made in 1956 against the Soviet system of centralised planning and control was that it left too little room for flexibility at lower echelons of the system. The factory manager was hamstrung by a web of bureaucratic controls which often left him with little choice other than trying to beat the output plan, with all the obvious consequences of waste, inefficiency, and poor product quality. The decentralisation measures of 1957 were designed to change this situation, and give managers much more flexibility in making economic decisions. The principle was fine, but the question was: who actually made the decisions at the enterprise level? During the three years of the Great Leap Forward there was little doubt that it was the Party committee. Given official encouragement to leap forward in production, factory Party cadres started on a production craze that turned out to be one of the causes of the economic crisis of 1960–61. The decisions of the Ninth Plenum changed that, and as became apparent from subsequent publications, authority returned to the hands of the administrators. One might think that Party and management had fairly well coalesced by this time, but judging from repeated attacks levelled against management cadres during the Great Leap Forward, it appears that this was not the case. But in returning authority to administrators and technicians, the leadership could not afford to go back to the practices of bureaucratic centralisation that had prevailed during the First Five-Year period. What this meant was that factory managers for the first time were in a position to exercise the flexibility which the 1957 decisions had granted them.

In both the Soviet and Chinese literature on the subject of " economic accounting," it was always pointed out that enterprise management had the right to make autonomous use of the capital furnished it by the state, as long as the requirements of the plan were fulfilled. In Russia as the forces of centralism grew stronger during the 1930s, such autonomy became increasingly meaningless, as more and more real decisions were made by the *glavks*, the local arms of the state ministries. However, since 1961, the Chinese have once again stressed the aspects of " independent managerial authority " that are inherent in the concept of " economic accounting," and have made it clear that it is up to the enterprise manager to make the correct economic decisions with the capital furnished him and the tasks which the state assigns him.[20]

What are the tasks enterprise management must fulfil today? It is probably impossible to generalise inasmuch as the situation differs from

[20] Chin Li, " Discussions in the Very Recent Period by Our Country's Economists on Problems of Socialist Economic Accounting," *Ching-chi Yen-chiu* (*Economic Research*), No. 11, 1962, pp. 66–67.

industry to industry. Yet, judging from consistent lines of discussion in the official literature, it seems that his main tasks are to meet the financial targets given him by the authorities. He must periodically remit to the state the profit targets set. He is enjoined to repay on time and with interest loans that he has received from the state banks. Furthermore, inasmuch as all investment quotas are now furnished in the form of bank loans, he must be able to generate sufficient profit to pay back on time what he has " borrowed." Furthermore, given the present stress on material incentives, he must also generate enough of an above-target profit from which his premium and reward funds derive. In addition to the profit targets, he must satisfy the state in regard to cost-cutting and productivity targets. In the last few months, there has been considerable stress on these intra-enterprise targets, the implication being that the manager should not rely on a favourable price situation to generate his profits, but rather on " subjective efforts " to improve the performance of the firm. However, what goes on within the enterprise is much harder to check on than the size of the profit remittance. He is also obligated to furnish the state a set volume of goods which the state has ordered from him, and which he must deliver on time. But inasmuch as the state no longer sets a high " gross output " target, there is a considerable gap between the large volume he must produce in order to get a satisfying profit, and the smaller volume of output which the state has ordered from him.

For the rest, he is allowed a considerable range of discretion in determining what the enterprise shall produce. He is urged to accept orders from other factories, retail agencies, and from communes and production brigades. Such ordering is nowadays widely solicited through the medium of advertising. Once an order is placed, it is put in the form of an " order agreement." Agreements or contracts, *ho-t'ung*, have played an important role in the workings of the economy in China ever since the early days of the Liberation in Manchuria.[21]

As in Russia, they were regarded as devices for overcoming defects in the planning system, by allowing firms to conclude agreements with each other, and then working the agreements into the over-all planning system. Whereas in Russia, the contract system was taken over by the *glavks* in the form of what was called " general contracts " for a range of industries, in China the planning mechanism never worked well enough completely to replace relatively autonomous contracting by individual firms. Since 1961 the emphasis on " direct contracting " has grown. What this means in effect is that two economic units agree on the exchange of goods for such and such a price at such and such a date,

---

[21] See Kao Kang's speech to the first congress of the CCP Manchurian region, *People's Daily*, June 5, 1950.

much in the manner of capitalistic enterprises. All this, of course, is supposed to take place within the framework of the plan and according to prices set by the state. However, at this point it is hard to say what the state of planning is, how much in the way of real production, materials, and commodities the plan actually covers. And furthermore, given the continuing discussion of price policy, the least one can say is that there is considerable fluctuation in the price picture. There are even some indications that factory managers have some initiative in setting prices for their products.[22]

What this means is that the factory manager must hunt up customers, find out what they want, and then try to produce what he has agreed to produce for them. But isn't he hampered in determining his assortment by state control over supply and materials allocation? There are many indications that the state has surrendered allocational controls over many goods, more or less allowing them to change hands through the market.[23] It must be recalled that it was already in the decentralisation decisions of 1957 that the government surrendered many of its allocational powers to provincial governments. Since then there are indications that these powers have lessened even further, obviously not in

---

[22] This is, of course, a very delicate area inasmuch as all prices are supposedly subject to one or another form of state control. The following story, however, seems to indicate that factory managers, upon pressure from their customers, were able to lower their ex-factory prices:

... last year, the Tientsin Machine Casting Plant cast some sewing machine frames for the North China Sewing Machine Plant. Because casting costs were high the latter lost money on its sewing machines. Subsequently, the workers of the Tientsin Plant tried hard to raise quality and productivity, and cut down on the wastage rate. Three months later, costs for casting sewing machine frames were greatly cut, and they were able on their own to reduce the unit price. This way the North China Plant was able to save about 20,000 yuan each month, and solve the problem of losing money on its sewing machines.

People's Daily, April 2, 1963. One can only conjecture at what lies behind this story, but it is reasonable to reconstruct it as follows. The North China Sewing Machine Company refused to renew its contract with the Tientsin plant unless they could reduce their unit price. Since the authorities could not be persuaded to make the North China " take " the goods nor presumably lower their financial targets, the only way out was to cut costs. That this is the procedure is indicated by a remark in the same article that a Kweichow factory sent its representatives to Tientsin, found the price right, and concluded an ordering agreement. See also Yang Fang-hsun, " Consider Price on the Basis of Quality—the Better the Quality the Better the Price," *Ta Kung Pao*, July 16, 1962.

[23] It is hard to find any hard and fast statements on what types of goods are still subject to strict state allocational controls, and what types can be freely exchanged. Writers stress that the state maintains unified allocational controls over all " major " and " important " agricultural and industrial goods, but allows " a certain number of secondary goods to be freely produced and freely sold." Current policy on commodity exchange is described as a combination of " planned allocation " and " selective buying." See Kuan Ta-t'ung, " Our Country's Socialist Unified Domestic Market," *Red Flag*, No. 6, 1963, pp. 33, 35. However, already in 1957, Hsueh Mu-ch'iao admitted that of the thousands and tens of thousands of goods on the market only a few hundred were " plan (controlled) commodities "; " Some Preliminary Opinions on Carrying Out the System of Plan Administration," *Economic Research*, No. 9, 1957, p. 23.

regard to materials that are regarded as critical, but over a range of materials that are generally called " secondary." Once he has produced a line of goods, the manager often still faces the problem of disposal. I gather from refugees that contracts are frequently broken, leaving the manager with undisposed inventories. State purchase and procurement agencies no longer automatically take over inventories, which earlier meant simply transferring the burden of storage from the factory to the commercial warehouse. Again advertising is resorted to, as well as the traditional device of sending out " representatives," *ch'u-ch'ai*, as they are called in China (somewhat like the Russian *tolkachi*), to various places, to secure takers.

The scope of " independent managerial authority " for the factory manager is real only to the extent that the planning mechanism does not function well, and there is nothing to indicate that it does now, or ever has, in China. The financial side of things is apparently still rigorously controlled by the state banks through the system of " current accounts " (the equivalent of the Soviet *rasschëtnyi schët*), and neither money nor credit is supposed to move directly between economic units. But in regard to purchase-sales and production agreements, the manager appears to enjoy considerable autonomy. What, one may ask, is then the incentive for the manager to produce? Here the answer seems to be simple. He must meet the high and stringent financial targets which the state sets for him. He can argue with the authorities about prices, argue out contracts with other units, press for greater savings within his factory, but when the time comes he must pay over the set profit sum to the state. But there is also a material incentive element. Another aspect of the decentralisation policies of 1957 was the so-called profit sharing system. Earlier, all above-target profit was taken by the state, but a portion of it was returned to the enterprise to use for premiums. However, under the profit sharing system, the enterprise was allowed to retain a fixed percentage share of all above-target profit. Obviously, the more profit it could generate, the greater its absolute share. That this proved to be a great boon to the enterprises is already attested to by outcries from the planners as early as the end of 1958 that enterprises were wasting their new source of income on irrational construction projects and workers' welfare.[24] Though there has apparently been some reduction in the size of the enterprises' profit share, the system remains very much in effect. Ever since early 1961 enterprises were ordered to cut down employment, keeping only the best of their workers. There also has been a return to a system of individual material incentives. Thus the premium fund is of great importance to the manager in giving him a

[24] T'ao Sheng-yü, Tan Ya-sheng, " Revised Opinions on the Enterprise Profit Sharing System," *Ts'ai-chang (Finance)*, No. 15, 1959, pp. 13–14.

source of rewards for his workers, now fewer in number than before, but who can thus expect a more substantial " bonus," or *fen-hung* as it is called in Chinese.

IS THERE A CHINESE N.E.P.?

When war Communism failed in Russia, the Soviets started their New Economic Policy which turned out to be a temporary return to market mechanisms in order to get the economy on its feet once again. When the Russians started criticising the Chinese communes, they said sarcastically that they had already tried something similar during the War Communism period. Perhaps they were right and the Chinese are repeating history by moving from War Communism to their own version of the N.E.P.

There are plenty of grounds on which one can argue from internal evidence that the Chinese are indeed in a N.E.P. period, but there are some scriptural references from the Chinese side that indicate that the Chinese see it that way themselves. The most frequently quoted saying of Lenin applicable to the economy today is a statement he made in 1922: " I think that trusts and enterprises have been put on a basis of economic accounting precisely so that they themselves be responsible, and furthermore completely responsible that their enterprises not incur losses." [25] Chinese know their Soviet history well and are not unaware of when Lenin made this statement and in what context.

The main question, from an economic point of view, is to what extent the open market functions in China today. Professor C. M. Li has indicated that an open market of one sort or another existed throughout the period of the First Five-Year Plan.[26] There are indications that the open market was broadened during the Great Leap Forward because of reduced state control over commodities. However, the power and arbitrariness of Party control interfered greatly with the free working of the market mechanism. Since 1961 the leadership has made a number of significant concessions to the open market. Open markets for agricultural products, the so-called *chi-shih*, started to develop, supported by growing amounts of garden crops brought by the peasants to market.

[25] One of the earliest references to this quotation from Lenin that I have come across is in an article entitled " All Enterprises Must Strengthen Economic Accounting." *People's Daily*, December 24, 1961. It is significant that it was just around that time that the economic debates started. It would appear, therefore, that it was around the end of 1961 that the Chinese began to see themselves as in a new N.E.P. period. The passage is from a short memorandum, dated February 1, 1922, which Lenin sent to the Commisariat of Finance urging severe judicial action against enterprises that constantly incur losses. Lenin adds: " if we can't assure our own interests in full in a business-like, merchant-like manner, then we are complete fools! "; Lenin, *Sochineniia*, XXXV (Moscow: 1951), p. 468.

[26] Choh-ming Li, *Economic Development of Communist China* (Berkeley: University of California Press, 1959), pp. 19–24.

Judging from the weakening of state control over a wide range of manufactured commodities and the present emphasis on producing consumer goods, it can be surmised that the open market for manufactured goods has been considerably broadened over preceding years. There is no doubt that the leaders are disturbed by the extent of open market phenomena. Hsueh Mu-ch'iao, recently published an article in Red Flag calling for more stringent measures to keep open market prices in line. However, what is significant is that Hsueh Mu-ch'iao admits that the open market exists alongside the planned market as a valid mechanism of exchange. Though he calls for greater price controls, he is against " simple administrative measures to freeze prices." [27]

The price picture is immensely complex in China today, among other reasons, because the state is using its price powers to spur on this or that area of the economy. For example, as one writer admits openly, if factories manage to improve the quality of their output, " they are rewarded price-wise." But is it always the authorities who have the final say on prices? The same writer implies indirectly that ex-factory price changes are often simply authorised in an *ex post facto* way by the state agencies.[28] I get the impression that the Chinese have come up with another of their famous contradictions, this time one between the planned market and the open market. The problem is how to find some kind of Hegelian resolution between the two.

It is quite clear that if the state does not move in with new controls, open market phenomena will continue to grow. Judging from refugee reports, the release of a range of " top class goods " to retail outlets unleashed a buying spree somewhat reminiscent of the one that followed the German currency reform in the summer of 1948. More consumer goods came on to market with the explicit approval of the state, thus strengthening open market tendencies. There is clear awareness of strong inflationary pressures, and much discussion has been published on ways to combat inflation. The state presumably could move on to the open market in two ways. It could either re-institute the whole planning system and try to do what it did during the First Five-Year Plan period, or it could accept the workings of market mechanisms, ranging from completely tolerated functioning of the open market to discreet tolerance of market mechanisms within the so-called planned market, and try to use its enormous administrative and financial powers to obtain leverage over the workings of the price system. I see no indication that the leadership has as yet opted for the first course, and at present seems to

[27] Hsueh Mu-ch'iao, " The Law of Value and Our Price Policy," *Red Flag*, No. 7–8, 1963, pp. 1–9.
[28] Yang Fang-hsün, " Consider Price on the Basis of Quality—the Better the Quality the Better the Price," *Ta Kung Pao*, July 16, 1962.

be trying to muddle through in the manner suggested by Hsueh Mu-ch'iao, *i.e.*, somewhere between the two extremes of using administrative power to fix prices and of completely allowing supply and demand to determine prices.

What the Chinese N.E.P. suggests is that internal conditions have been more similar to what exists in the country of their arch-enemy, Yugoslavia, than their anti-Yugoslav vituperations would let one think. In September 1962, when the Tenth Plenum was meeting, *Red Flag* published an article excoriating the Yugoslavs for their return to capitalism.[29] However, since then, the Chinese Communists have preferred to republish attacks on the Yugoslav economy originally published in some of the fraternal newspapers, e.g., Albania, North Korea, North Vietnam. The reason is quite obvious. There is already too much in the September article which must have set Chinese minds to wondering how different Yugoslav " capitalism " was in fact from some of the things going on in China. The Tenth Plenum was devoted to the problem of the Party. The rectification campaign waged against the Party during much of 1961 had gravely weakened Party control in some areas and had resulted in a lowering of Party morale, quite understandable considering the sudden comedown from the Great Leap Forward period. Since September 1962, there has been a gradual re-emphasis on the Party, on the collective economy, on the role of the Party in the life of the country. But the course launched in 1961 still appears to be the dominant line in the country. Despite the September 1962 communiqué, only a few months later the government issued new regulations on the position of accountants, which gave accountants far-reaching financial authority in enterprises and agencies. The accountants were the arch-enemies of the Party cadres during the Great Leap Forward, for the accountants, like most financial people everywhere, were appalled by the free-spending tendencies of the Party cadres. It was the severance of Party control over the financial system which constituted one of the most serious blows to Party power during the 1961 reforms. Given the continuing pervasive emphasis on accumulation goals, it was hardly likely that the leadership could once again be persuaded to open the doors of the nation's coffers to the Party cadres.

In early 1963 the N.E.P. policy was still in effect. A third five-year plan period has begun, yet little has been said about it beyond that it has begun. Economic conditions have been improving, so the sting of severe crisis has passed. The leadership, for the last few years, had been following Bukharin's famous slogan, " enrichissez-vous," and there has been a payoff in improved living conditions. But microeconomic getting

29 Ch'en Mao-i, " Let Us Talk About the Worsening of Economic Conditions in Yugoslavia," *Red Flag*, No. 17, 1962, pp. 24–31.

rich does not make sense in the face of macroeconomic poverty, and the leadership may be contemplating a change. There have been recent rumours of a 10–20 per cent. wage cut in the cities, which may presage a new wave of austerity. The accent on accumulation is still strong but the N.E.P. approach may not provide dividends fast enough. If China is going to industrialise fast, as Russia did under Stalin, the peasant and the worker will have to bear the burden of sacrifice.

THE RE-EMERGENCE OF THE PROFESSIONAL INTELLECTUALS

As in the Soviet Union, intellectuals in China constitute a social stratum, not quite a class and not just an occupational group. If it is difficult to define precisely what an intellectual is in Marxian class categories, there seems to be little doubt in the minds of the Chinese, judging from the copious literature on the subject and refugee statements, that the intellectuals are the educated professionals of the country. The status of intellectual is acquired through education, graduation from higher middle school on up. In a country in which education continues to act as an important (perhaps the most important) criterion of status, being an intellectual more or less puts one in the ranks of the elite. Although the academic intellectuals are most prominent because of their verbal expressiveness, most of the country's intellectuals are found, not in the universities, but at the management level of organisations. They are the engineers, technicians, administrators, researchers, doctors and teachers of the country. In a factory, though they are to be found at the management level, they do not constitute all of management. Again as in the Soviet Union, lower level management employees, the so-called functionaries, are not accorded the status of intellectuals.[30] They are the true social élite of the country, and are jealous of any encroachments on their hard-earned status, as can be seen in their resistance to admitting skilled workers to the job category of technician, which normally requires a higher educational degree.[31]

The attitude of the Chinese Communists toward the country's intellectuals has fluctuated from time to time. Although the top leadership of the Chinese Communist Party can validly consider itself intellectual, the farther down one goes in Party ranks, the stronger the worker and peasant component. At the factory level, worker membership in the Party predominates, even though most of the top management

---

[30] The conception of what an intellectual is appears to be much the same in both the Soviet Union and Communist China. In the Soviet Union, too, ordinary white collar employees, the so-called *sluzhashchie*, are not considered intellectuals. See Alex Inkeles and Raymond Bauer, *The Soviet Citizen* (Cambridge: Harvard University Press, 1959), pp. 72–73.

[31] K'o Pai, "Preliminary Discussion of the Salary System of Leadership Personnel, Engineers and Technicians, and Functionaries in Industrial Enterprises," *Chung-kuo Kung-yeh* (*China's Industry*), No. 2, 1956, pp. 6–7.

cadres are at least formally within the Party. There can be little doubt, judging from the accounts of refugees who have worked in factories, that there are sharp cleavages between intellectuals and workers. The management-worker gap or the white-collar blue-collar antagonism is well known from just about every country that has gone through a process of industrialisation. It is even more serious during the early stages of industrialisation and perhaps more serious in countries outside the Western world, where cultural and social distance add to the gap. The gap was there in pre-1949 China and has remained to the present time. Whether one can meaningfully speak of a class conflict between intellectuals and workers in Chinese industry prior to 1949 is hard to say. But the constant preaching of the doctrines of class conflict by the Chinese Communists have served, in the end, not to eliminate the gap and assuage the conflict, but to intensify it. Upon Liberation, workers were told that they were now the masters of the factory. This was not empty talk, for large numbers of workers were promoted to leadership positions, some even to positions of factory manager. Top factory cadres, from the earliest days on, were often of worker origin. But it was impossible to proletarianise management, for the simple reason that workers lacked the skills and education necessary to run a factory. The leadership has made continuing efforts to bridge the gap between intellectuals and the workers, by drawing the intellectuals into the Party and mass organisations, by raising the educational level of workers, by trying to create a worker-peasant intelligentsia. But all indications are that this attempt has failed. A goodly number of the country's intellectuals are still of " bourgeois " origin, and the effort to forcibly " reduce the gap between mental and physical labour " has only intensified the antagonism.

During the early 1950s, the leadership was forced by circumstances to make fullest use of the professional intellectuals: managers, technicians, specialists. However, with the intensified production drive and Party recruitment campaign that arose in 1955, the pendulum swung against the intellectuals. But the swing was temporary, and with the " hundred flowers " period, a new period of tolerance set in, that lasted until the abrupt switch in the summer of 1957. By the summer of 1957 the juxtaposition of intellectuals and masses had assumed sharp form, more specifically in the form of conflicts between Party and management, workers and technicians, generalists and specialists. Though the anti-rightist campaign started with denunciations of academic intellectuals, it soon spread throughout the country. In the factories, it took the form of greater Party control over management, of the so-called " send them down " (hsia-fang) movement, through which thousands of intellectuals were sent down to the front line of production, of denunciations of managers for demonstrating "conservative tendencies" in the period of the Great Leap Forward, of levelling tendencies between workers and intellectuals with greater equality in pay, of managers and technicians being made to carry out physical labour along with workers, and with workers urged to participate in management (a slogan which was by no means empty, for many crucial economic decisions were "transferred downward" to the production teams). In general, it was a period when the leadership tried to create a single amalgam of cadres, intellectuals, and workers. Force, short of complete extirpation, has never succeeded in reducing status differences that are based on values universally accepted by a population. As long as higher education is still valued in the country (as it is), and as long as higher education remains a scarce commodity, the status of the intellectual is secure. The levelling attempts of the Great Leap Forward failed, and the gap between intellectuals and masses remains.

In the old days, the Chinese scholar-bureaucrat was an amateur, a man of many talents, solidly grounded in the orthodox ideology. Though he had to rely on specialists to conduct his bureaucratic affairs, he despised the status of professional.[32] One of the human reasons for the failure of government-directed early industrialisation in China was the inability for the long-gowned factory administrator to understand the need for expertise; for that, he felt, one could rely on foreign experts. I seem to remember that someone once suggested that one of the results of great social revolutions is that the new ruling class tends to take on the values of the class it has overthrown. There are grounds for arguing that China's present élite of Party cadres is suspiciously like its scholar-bureaucratic predecessors in many respects. The Party cadre is schooled in Marxism-Leninism, he is a man of many talents, rather than a professional (usually a reflection of the type of political education a Party cadre undergoes, with its short courses in economics, politics, theory, technology), and, as became amply evident during the Great Leap Forward, contemptuous of professional expertise. The typical local Party cadre is also a worker (or a peasant if in the villages). On the other hand, China's intellectuals today appear to be firmly committed to professionalism, to expertise, to technical knowledge. All intellectuals I have talked to are admiring of the advanced countries, Russia as well as the United States. They are firmly convinced that only expertise, not political direction, will modernise the country. Expertise is after all their one possession that the Party cannot take away from them, even if it sends them out into the fields to work. The more the Party has tried to convince them of the greatness of improvisation, of

---

[32] See Joseph R. Levenson, *Confucian China and Its Modern Fate* (Berkeley: University of California Press, 1958), pp. 15–43.

native over foreign methods, of politics over techniques, the more stubborn the resistance. I have found a strong nationalistic streak in the young intellectuals, but no obscurantism, no desire to return to the roots of the past, no love of populism. All these tendencies are what they accuse the Party of wanting to do.

When the Ninth Plenum decided on a radical reversal in economic policy and launched a campaign to pry the Party loose from its totalistic control of the economy, it had to take a further consequent step: once again seek the aid of the country's intellectuals. Factory managers reacquired power. Engineers were once again given control over the production process. Technicians were once again favoured, and their educational status assured. Technical education was once again stressed over political education.[33] Technical accountants were once again given far-reaching powers over an enterprise's finances.[34] Rationality, rather than the mass movement, became the dominant theme of industrial management. The mass movement, in fact, has disappeared as a mechanism of production organisation. Bureaucratic management has superseded worker participation in management. Factory administration has been recentralised, with major decisions once again being made at the executive level, rather than on the production floor. Money is stressed over production. Concern over money somehow seems to be a conservative attitude in almost any society, and much of the talk about economising could come from the mouths of good Republicans in the United States. Concern over money also implies an orientation to some kind of professional or technical élite (bankers, executives, etc.), and so it is not surprising that the present turn toward accumulation goals has gone hand in hand with a return of authority to the country's professional intellectuals. Even the remnant bourgeoisie has benefited from the new atmosphere through promise of continued " fixed interest " payments.

If the Party were suddenly to disappear from the country, and given all the other tendencies we have already described, it is not hard to imagine that China would revert to a kind of state capitalism, politically based on a ruling class of professional intellectuals. But the Party remains with a membership of something around 17,000,000. The communiqué of the Tenth Plenum made amply clear that the leadership was by no means ready to let the Party wither away. On the contrary, there has been a growing campaign to rebuild the image (and power) of

---

33 See, for example, Shih K'o-chien, " Sufficiently Develop the Capacities of Technical Personnel," Red Flag, No. 8–8, 1962, pp. 42–45. There is also now renewed emphasis on the need for Party cadres to have administrative and technical competence; see Chao Han, " Some Questions Concerning Party Cadre Policy," Red Flag, No. 12, 1962, pp. 1–13.

34 " The State Council Publishes Tentative Regulations on the Authority of Accounting Personnel," People's Daily, December 14, 1962.

the Party in the eyes of the people. Once again, during the summer of 1963, there was a campaign underway to get cadres and intellectuals to work alongside the people. The primary importance of political leadership in the armed forces is once again stressed. There has been a slow toning down of the 100 flowers spirit which, among other things, produced the remarkable economic debates of 1962. Nevertheless, there has been no real attempt on the part of the leadership to subvert the renewed authority that the professional intellectuals gained in 1961. There is no indication that the Party is once again moving into managerial councils, the way it happened earlier. As long as the N.E.P. situation lasts, it is almost impossible for the leadership to let the Party take over the economy once again. All signs indicate that this is a period of tense contraposition of Party and intellectuals, not unlike that which prevailed in 1956 and 1957.

THE PARTY AND THE IDEOLOGY

Of all the organisations that make up the body politic of Communist China, none is in as indecisive a position as the Communist Party. During the early 1950s, the Party was told to stay out of production and let the managers run their factories. However, this was simply a transitional policy. Starting from the great recruitment drive of 1955 (if not earlier), the Party began gradually to expand its leadership functions in industry, as well as in the remainder of society. The Great Leap Forward was the great period of Party leadership. Everywhere Party cadres were in command. Party cadres were young, they were workers and peasants, they were members of a superbly disciplined organisation whose channels of command and communication cut across bureaucratic jurisdictions. It seemed as if the Chinese Communist Party had found the organisational key to social engineering on a scale never before known in the world. Through the cadre-led production team, any problem could be solved. Moral fervour, enthusiasm, the use of group dynamics (to use an American term), leadership which could activate and unite all elements in the society—all this would consumate the economic revolution and push China to the brink of take-off.

When the decisions of the Ninth Plenum gave the order to the Party apparatus to release its hold on the economy, a rectification movement had already started in some parts of the country. Though the leadership was careful not to make the movement too well known, popular resentment against the Party was openly expressed in many areas of the country. There can be little doubt that there was a serious drop in Party morale in 1961 and early in 1962. By the summer of 1962 the leadership decided that Party morale and organisation must once again be strengthened. The Sino-Soviet dispute provided an occasion for intensifying the ideological campaign. The cult of personality, which had been constantly growing, has been more than ever emphasised. The more Mao has retreated from public view, the greater the adulation. The Party held China together in its moments of greatest crisis, and there is no indication that the extraordinary unity and strength of this great organisation has been impaired. However, the Party was taught to lead and not simply to control. Stalin ruled Russia through the secret police, but the whole outlook of the Chinese Communist Party has been opposed to its simply acting as the police guardian of society. All the recent changes in economic policy have put the Party in a difficult position.[35]

Ever since January 1961 management has resumed its old authority in the enterprise. Expertness, not redness, is stressed in the making of economic decisions. Management discussions now deal with technical production and marketing problems, rather than Party policy. Enterprise accountants have complete control over the factory's purse strings. Staff work is once again being emphasised, and the intellectuals who were earlier sent down to the production floor are back in their offices. Within government, there is apparently less to administer than before, with the encouragement of direct relationships between economic units, bypassing state agencies. What is the Party organisation to do under such conditions? Already by the mid-1950s, in some factories as much as 20 per cent. of the total number of employees were Party members. What are all these leaders to do in the absence of mass movements to lead? What does the Party secretary now do in Party committee meetings in enterprises and state agencies? All that can be said is that the situation is very complicated and difficult. In dynastic China, the magistrate usually let his functionaries, who were local experts, run the routine business of the yamen, intervening only if some extraordinary situation demanded his personal decision. Perhaps the same thing goes on today, except that the magistrate was quite content with his role, whereas such a role is something new for the contemporary Party cadre. During the early 1950s, when the Party was instructed not to interfere with production, it was told to concentrate on ideological work and help the unions organise the workers. By now the country is, if anything, over-organised, so not much remains to be done in that area. But it is in the field of ideology that the Party appears to be active today. Without Confucianism, the traditional scholar-bureaucrat was nothing. So today, apparently, the Party holds on to the ideology as its main

---

[35] The situation in China appears to be the opposite of that in the USSR, where since the death of Stalin, there has been a consistent effort to make the Party into an active organisational instrument and give it greater power for making economic decisions at all levels of the system.

weapon in the struggle to maintain the country's unity. Ideology has played a major part in holding China together as a political entity since pre-Christian times, and when the monarchical system collapsed, political failure and ideological erosion went hand in hand. In this context, it may be easier to understand the seriousness of China's charge that the Russians have been guilty of ideological heresy.

But the Chinese Communists have been trained to see ideology and organisation going hand in hand. Today there is a gap. While the ideology remains orthodox, the country as a working system of organisation seems at times suspiciously similar to Yugoslavia. The gap between ideology and organisation existed in Russia during the N.E.P., but at that time Russia was involved in a power struggle. China's leadership and its Party remain, at least on the surface, solidary. Within the country the many gaps that Party leadership was supposed to narrow continue to grow. There are regional gaps, status gaps, economic gaps. The gulf between rich and poor, advanced and backward has not been bridged. The N.E.P. policy has paid off in small but real dividends, but the dividends have been earned by managers, skilled workers, productive peasants without benefit of direct Party leadership. What is the Party to do under these circumstances?

THE GREAT DEBATE ON THE ECONOMY

Before concluding this article, it is well to say a few words about one of the more extraordinary phenomena of recent times in China. This has been the great debate on the economy which began late in 1961 and has continued down to the present time. We have already pointed out that there are interesting parallels between this debate and that which went on in the Soviet Union during the N.E.P. period. Discussions on the economy were held throughout the country in all major academic centres. It is perhaps significant that the local discussions often had as their direct concern economic problems within their own general region. Articles and summaries of the discussions were published in major newspapers and journals, and continue to appear. All the discussants appear to be economists, and only rarely has a person of official prominence, such as Hsueh Mu-ch'iao, entered the debate. The problems discussed have immediate relevance for the course of the economy, but are also problems of a type that would be discussed in any academic circles, east or west. Publications on the discussions which appeared in the spring of 1962 seemed sometimes to reflect a spectrum of views, but by the end of the year, it was clear that there were two main streams of thought. One favoured a return to greater state direction and control of the economy. The other argued for greater autonomy for the individual economic units. It is incorrect, though tempting, to label the former " orthodox " and the latter " liberal," the former proponents of state planning and the latter proponents of a market economy. One must remember that it was the group of political radicals who argued against the planners for decentralisation and greater autonomy at lower levels (of course, under Party leadership). It is hard to say what today constitutes an " orthodox " view in China, inasmuch as the Stalinist approach to economic administration was already attacked during the Eighth Party Congress and scrapped with the decentralisation decisions of 1957.[36]

The debates probably have little relevance for the ordinary factory manager who struggles with day-to-day problems. But they do reflect a similar debate that must be going on in the highest councils of the leadership. Western observers have termed an earlier debate as one between the planners and the sloganeers, the proponents of a centralised planning system and the advocates of a guerrilla approach to economic revolution. The sloganeers won out, as is well known. However, all the articles on the debate point out that issues discussed earlier are not so much discussed now, and that new issues have arisen. Thus, no one seems to question the crucial importance of profit targets as enterprise success indicators, but the question is: what kind of profit target? Should estimation of enterprise success be based on cost-profit ratios or on capital-profit ratios? Should cost targets be emphasised as well as profit targets? What about productivity targets? If the debate is indeed a reflection of a much more significant debate higher up, then it is likely that the issues of the debate are no longer quite the same as they were a few years ago. My own guess is that the two main streams of argument within the leadership are the same as in the economists' debate: should the role of the state be enlarged or should autonomy be further broadened? In their extreme form these arguments could

---

[36] So far four articles have appeared summarising the issues in what might be called the nation-wide debate (there have been several articles summarising the regional debates). All are signed by a man writing under the *nom de plume* of Chin Li. Of these, the third of those listed recapitulates more or less the same issues discussed in the first, indicating some significant changes in views. It would be extremely desirable that a careful analysis of these debates be undertaken, somewhat like Alexander Erlich has done for the Soviet debates in the 1920s.

(1) " Short Presentation of Dissimilar Viewpoints in the Discussion of Problems of Economic Accounting Under a Socialist System," *Ching-chi Yen-chiu*, No. 3, 1962, pp. 61–67.

(2) " Dissimilar Viewpoints in the Discussion of Price Problems Under a Socialist System by Our Country's Economists," *Ching-chi Yen-chiu*, No. 6, 1962, pp. 63–69.

(3) " Discussions in the Very Recent Period by Our Country's Economists on Problems of Socialist Economic Accounting," *Ching-chi Yen-chiu*, No. 11, 1962, pp. 66–67.

(4) " Discussion in Recent Years of Problems of Socialist Economic Effectiveness by Our Country's Economists," *Ching-chi Yen-chiu*, No. 1, 1963, pp. 60–65.

probably be qualified as Stalinist or revisionist respectively. It is hardly likely that anyone is arguing for either of these extreme positions. One would mean going back to a centralised bureaucratic system; the other going all the way over to the Yugoslav system with its implications for Party control. The argument is one about direction: whereto now?

Heinrich Cünow, a German Socialist commentator on Marx, writes that Marx conceived of state and society as two separate, juxtaposed entities. For Marx, society meant essentially the economy, and state the political community. Whereas the early Marx felt that revolution would arise out of the transformation of society and thereby overcome the state, the later Marx began to assign greater importance to political revolution, *i.e.*, the forcible overthrow of the state, as a means for revolutionising society.[37] One can probably say that the economy in China today is functioning along N.E.P. lines with a broad range of autonomous market tendencies. But the state is governed by different rules deriving from the ideology. Which will transform which? Will the social and economic patterns that now prevail transform the political system, or will the political system once again assert itself and try to fashion society in its own image? China seems to be standing at a kind of crossroad. What it will do internally will probably ultimately be of much greater significance than the role it decides to play on the international scene.

---

[37] Heinrich Cünow, *Die Marxsche Geschichs-, Gesellschafts-, und Staatstheorie* (Berlin: 1923), pp. 252–255, 310–314.

Work incentive Policy in Communist China*

BY CHARLES HOFFMANN

IN their concerted and ardent efforts to industrialise and develop the economy rapidly, the leaders of the Chinese Communist Party have given work incentives an important role—a role which operates narrowly within the limits set by economic necessity and ideology.[1] The pendulum has swung from an emphasis on material incentives (First Five-Year Plan, 1953–57) to a stress on non-material incentives (1957–60) and back again (1960 on). These major changes in incentive policy have reflected the significant turns in the grand socio-economic strategy of the Chinese Communist Party.

It would seem that the régime cannot just mandate any desired level of output. It aims, therefore, at maximising output with a minimum of labour input (and consumer goods) within the limits of the incentives prescribed by Marxism. Where the leaders are unable to exact what they want they must vary their technique and even yield ideological ground; where they see a possibility of exacting more than they had hoped they push ahead extending material and ideological goals.

INCENTIVE POLICY, 1953–57

Between 1953 and 1957, the task was to " lay a sound preliminary groundwork for [China's] socialist construction and socialist transformation." The planning of the economy was to be implemented on the Soviet model as part of the transition to a socialist economy with special emphasis on heavy industry. " More rational use of labour " was to parallel a " continuous increase in production and labour productivity." The task of " gradually " improving the wage system by eliminating

* The author is grateful to the Joint Committee on Contemporary China of the Social Science Research Council and the American Council of Learned Societies for its research grant for 1961–62 and to the Chairman, Center for Chinese Studies, University of California, Berkeley, Professor Choh-ming Li, and his staff, who extended generous assistance while the author was visiting research fellow at the University and the Center. Professors Walter Galenson and Li generously made helpful suggestions on an earlier draft.
1 See Charles Hoffmann, " The Basis of Communist China's Incentive Policy," *Asian Survey*, III, No. 5 (May 1963), pp. 245–257, for a discussion of the ideological and economic framework of incentive policy.

egalitarian and irrational elements in favour of piece-rates was emphasised as a paragon of rational payment according to productivity.[2]

Applying this principle of distribution according to labour to the
Chinese peasant was more complex since individual ownership of
agricultural capital was expected to exist for some time. The goal was
gradually to transform agricultural cooperatives into collective farms
where peasants would be paid only for their labour in the hope that this
would increase production.[3]

Industry.

During the First Five-Year Plan both the Party and the Government [4]
gave considerable attention to the many problems impeding workers'
efficiency and productivity. The most important of these were: insufficient stimulation to technical innovation and invention; and irrational and egalitarian elements in wage scales, which made for some
sharp disparities between increases in labour productivity and wages.
The attempts to cope with these questions involved primarily both
sharpening material incentives by reordering wage and bonus mechanisms and eliminating certain non-monetary payment schemes.[5]

It was not until May 1954 that the Government set forth a uniform
incentive scheme for inventions, technical improvements, and rationalisation proposals which succeeded in reducing production costs. Both the
innovators and those who assisted in putting the idea into practice were
to receive monetary awards. The awards were paid over three to five
years in the case of inventions and for one year in the case of technical
improvements and proposals for rationalising production. The value
varied with the amount of money saved by the innovation. The origina-
tor was to receive a percentage of that amount, ranging from 30 per cent.
for inventions saving less than 100 yuan a year to 2 per cent. of those
saving over 100,000 yuan. A similar scale operated for technical
improvements and proposals rationalising production, ranging from 20
per cent. to ·5 per cent. for the former and 10 per cent. to ·25 per cent.
for the latter. The maximum award for any one person was 50,000 yuan
and the minimum 5 yuan. Those assisting with the innovations could
receive separate awards of up to 25 per cent. of the main award.[6]

---

[2] *First Five-Year Plan . . . 1953–1957* (Peking: Foreign Languages Press, 1956),
pp. 3, 192–193.

[3] *Ibid.*, p. 194.

[4] See Charles Hoffmann, "Industrial Work-Incentives in Communist China," *Current
Scene*, II, No. 13 (May 1, 1963), for a review of incentives in industry.

[5] See Peter Schran, *The Structure of Income in Communist China* (Ph.D. dissertation)
(Berkeley: University of California, 1961), *passim.*

[6] NCNA, *Daily News Report* 1723, August 30, 1954, pp. 329–330, and *Labour Laws
and Regulations of the People's Republic of China* (Peking: Foreign Languages
Press, 1956), pp. 54–64.

To encourage scientists to make practical contributions to research, the State Council, in August 1955, provided for awards and prizes to outstanding Chinese scientists. These awards, which were first made in January 1957, are made every two years by the Academy of Sciences. Three grades of awards and medals are given—10,000 yuan; 5,000 yuan; 2,000 yuan.[7]

The lack of a clear-cut relationship between reward and performance dampened workers' enthusiasm and held back productivity. Systems of payment in kind and wage points tended to obscure the relationship between output and reward that money payments make crystal clear. Operating alongside wage systems they were an obvious anachronism.[8] In August 1955, the State Council replaced the supply system for government employees with a wage system on the ground that the former contradicted the socialist principle of distribution according to labour. It published a pay scale for its employees and price subsidy tables for certain localities; and it specified unusual conditions under which the supply system might be retained.[9]

The transformation of the supply system into a wage system foreshadowed the end of the wage-point system in industry in the major wage reform of June 1956. Direct money subsidies to compensate for regional variations in staple commodity prices were also abolished.[10]

The irrational and egalitarian features in the wage system also raised barriers to increasing production. Among the irrational elements were such anomalies as different wage scales for the same type of enterprise and wage differentials unrelated to differences in skill. Traditional gratuities and allowances unrelated to quantity and quality of performance, bonuses for good attendance, and other compensations listed under the heading of welfare payments made up an uncoordinated patch-work of payments that were a major reason for the wage reform. Complaints against egalitarianism were aimed at all those practices which eliminated

---

7 NCNA, September 1, 1955, in *Survey of China Mainland Press* (SCMP) (Hong Kong: U.S. Consulate-General), No. 1122, pp. 10–11. The author has checked original Chinese sources in certain instances; for convenience and uniformity, however, he cites both original and translation. See also Leo Orleans, *Professional Manpower and Education in Communist China* (Washington: National Science Foundation, 1961), pp. 122–123.

8 Tu Shao-po and Wang I-cheng, " Why the Changeover from Supply System to Wage System," *Shih-shih Shou-ts'e* (*Current Events*), No. 18, September 25, 1955, in *Extracts from China Mainland Magazines* (ECMM) (Hong Kong: U.S. Consulate-General), No. 19; L. Lavallée, P. Noirot and V. Dominique, *Economie de la Chine Socialiste* (Geneva: Librairie Rousseau, 1957), pp. 415–416; and Chao Kuo-chün, *Economic Planning and Organization in Mainland China* (Cambridge: Harvard Un., 1960), II, 71.

9 Tu Shao-po, *op. cit.*

10 *Ibid.* and Ma Wen-jui, " Report to the Third Session of the First National People's Congress . . . ," in *Current Background* (CB) (Hong Kong: U.S. Consulate-General), No. 405.

or minimised considerations of skill and performance in determining wages and bonuses.[11]

In many situations, wages did not act as a proper stimulant to improvement of skills and increased productivity. The wide variety of wage-grade systems led to inconsistent wage policies in the same industry and types of enterprise. This difficulty was met in the wage reform through unification of wage standards and the coefficient of wage grades for each industry and a more rational set of differentials according to trades and districts. The eight-grade wage system was more widely implemented with the ratios of the first (lowest) to the eighth (highest) grade raised appropriately so that the differentials between grades would act as incentives.[12] Differences between more and less skilled workers could be rewarded and the less-skilled motivated to develop their abilities; heavy labour, underground jobs, work at high temperatures could be more generously rewarded. The authorities looked on wages as "important economic tools . . . in stimulating development of production" and they felt that "owing to the errors made in wage work . . . situations incompatible with production . . . must in a certain degree affect the labour enthusiasm of the workers and office employees."[13]

Some of the wage increases given in June 1956 were aimed at widening skill differentials and making readjustments for groups whose activities were important to society. Greater wage increases were given to workers in heavy industry, in production departments, and senior technicians, widening the differential between them and those at the lower end of the grade scale. Pay to management, engineering, and technical personnel was increased more than that for administrative personnel of the same grade. Increases for professors, higher level scientific personnel and other intellectuals were sharp; for example, in Peking such individuals had their wages raised by 36 per cent.[14]

The significance of the piece-rate system was acknowledged in a *People's Daily* editorial: "The piece-rate system of wages is the system that will most easily realise the socialist principle of payment according to work. . . . Accordingly, during and after the current wage reform . . . [that system] must be consolidated and expanded." Higher standard

---

11 Tso Chun-t'ai, "Several Questions Concerning Reform of the Wage System," *Cheng-chih Hsueh-hsi (Political Study)*, No. 6, 1956, in ECMM, No. 47; Schran, *op. cit.*, pp. 249–252; Ma Wen-jui, *op. cit.*; and *People's Daily* editorial, May 3, 1956, in SCMP, No. 1287.
12 For example the ratio of 1 to 2·87 for metallurgical workers was raised to 3·2. See Ma Wen-jui, *op. cit.*
13 Schran, *op. cit.*, pp. 285–286; Chin Li, "Certain Problems Concerning Betterment of the Current Wage Grading System." *Labor* (Lao-tung), No. 3, 1956, in ECMM, No. 35; and *Ta-Kung Pao*, editorial, May 22, 1956, in SCMP, No. 1314.
14 Ma Wen-jui, *op. cit.*

payments were set up for piece-rate systems and extension of such schemes, where technically possible, to replace the time-rate plus bonus system was urged. In the two years 1956 and 1957 piece-rate systems were developed very widely, a peak of about 42 per cent. of all workers in state-operated factories and mines being covered by some sort of piece-rate system.[15]

The irrational and egalitarian features of the wage system were further reduced by eliminating such anomalies as double pay at the end of the year and awards for good attendance.[16] Promotion procedures and policies were revised to " stimulate workers to study politics, technique, and culture, and master professional skills, strengthening their sense of responsibility, and thereby raising labour productivity and increasing output." [17]

Finally, there was the pressing problem of workers sharing in the fruits of increased productivity. Official policy was committed to wages rising at about half the rate of productivity increases. Since productivity was increasing faster than planned and since a certain caution marked decisions raising wages, the disparity between the two in certain years was quite wide and, therefore, the goal of gradually improving the workers' level of living was threatened.[18] Li Fu-ch'un, chairman of the State Planning Commission, characterised this as a " one-sided " tendency and a " mistake." He held that " in 1955 in particular, the adjustment of wages and the construction of living quarters were ignored to some extent, *thereby preventing workers and staff* from showing more enthusiasm for work." [19]

In both 1954 and 1955 wages were raised proportionately much less than the 1:2 ratio between wages and productivity. In the earlier year, money wages went up 2·3 per cent. while productivity was up 15 per cent.; in the latter year, the comparison was ·6 per cent. to 10 per cent. Thus, in 1955 wages were only 13·7 per cent. above those of 1952, while productivity had risen 41·5 per cent. The ·6 per cent. rise of money wages in 1955 meant that for many workers real wages declined.[20]

To rectify this situation, wages in general were raised 14·5 per cent. above the 1955 level by the June 1956 wage reform; the average increase

15 July 6, 1956, in SCMP, No. 1331. See Sun Shang-ch'ing, " On the Nature and Destiny of our Current Piece-rate Wage System," *Ching-chi Yen-chiu (Economic Research)*, No. 4, 1959, in ECMM, No. 180.

16 It was estimated that the former cost 7 per cent. of average wages; the latter 2–4 per cent. See Ma Wen-jui, *loc. cit.*

17 *People's Daily*, editorial, July 6, 1956, in SCMP, No. 1331.

18 Existence of strikes in 1956 suggests that workers may have been reacting to unfavourable wages. See Mao Tse-tung, *On the Correct Handling of Contradictions Among the People* (Peking: FLP, 1960), p. 59.

19 *New China Advances to Socialism* (Peking: FLP, 1956), pp. 86–87. Emphasis added.

20 Ma Wen-jui, *loc. cit.* and Tso Chun-t'ai, *loc. cit.*

per person was 80 yuan. As indicated above, wage increases for specific groups varied. The increases were expected to " consolidate the enthusiasm of the workers and *to further manifest the stimulating effects of material interests for individuals in the form of wages . . .*".[21]

Agriculture.

While efforts were being pushed to rationalise the battery of material incentives in industry, a more gradual parallel development was being fostered in agriculture. Material incentives were an important feature of the movement, though they were shaped by the very different conditions in agriculture where private ownership and non-labour income existed. The emphasis on material incentives was reflected in the goal of putting as many peasants as possible on piece-work rates. In the phased transition from individual peasant ownership to the advanced cooperatives (collectives) in which payment was based on labour alone, material incentives were used both to soften the impact of eliminating the most capitalistic forms of agriculture and to stimulate production in collectives.[22]

The rapid growth of cooperatives was facilitated by recognising the peasant's deep attachment to his land and equipment and rewarding him for pooling this capital in the lower level cooperatives. The elementary agricultural producers' cooperative was set up as a semi-socialist, transitional form of organisation with land and equipment pooled and members compensated both for their labour and capital contributions. So long as private ownership of even a part of the means of production persisted the socialist principle of compensation according to labour could only be partially implemented. The incentive system, therefore, contributed both to the establishment of the agricultural producers' cooperatives and to the encouragement of efficient combination of the various factors of production. With the advent of the advanced agricultural producers' cooperatives, or collectives, incentives could be geared more closely to the principle of reward according to labour since each member's contribution was in labour alone.[23]

The transitional nature of the elementary agricultural producers cooperative was reflected in the mechanism of payments for land and

---

[21] Ma Wen-jui, *loc. cit.* and *Ta Kung Pao (Tientsin)*, May 22, 1956, *loc. cit.*

[22] See Government of India, *Report of the Indian Delegation to China on Agricultural Planning and Techniques* (New Delhi: 1956), p. 117. The report stressed what was the official Chinese view at the time, that " a cooperative cannot function efficiently without a piece-work system."

[23] See *First Five Year Plan . . .*, pp. 119–120 and *Decisions on Agricultural Co-operation* (Peking: FLP, 1956), pp. 14–15. Capitalistic forms existed even after the collective emerged in the form of private plots tilled for the peasant's own use. These plots were limited to 5 per cent. of the village's land holdings.

equipment pooled by members. The peasant received a dividend payment for the land he contributed based on the amount and quality pooled. The dividend was gradually reduced until eventually income would be for labour input alone. Less substantial payments were also made for use of means of production other than land. The total income return for means of production was not to be as great as that paid for agricultural labour.[24]

During the First Five-Year Plan, as party leaders were implementing the socialist principle of remuneration according to labour in agriculture, they were confronted with the same kinds of problems as in industry—a growing disparity between worker and peasant income. Egalitarian tendencies in agriculture, as in industry, carried over from earlier periods, taking the form, primarily, of food grain distribution on grounds mainly unrelated to either work input or output. In some cooperatives, grain distribution was based on the number of people in each family; in others, distribution was according to status: a standard amount for children, more for working members, still more for those doing heavy work. In many instances, cooperatives did not pay for work on capital construction, afforestation, and land reclamation without even making such work part of a voluntary emulative campaign.[25]

In the period under review, irrational features of payment systems constantly appeared and were officially rejected as inimical to important economic and political goals. In many cooperatives standards used in crediting work-points for specific tasks were not the same for all work brigades; workers doing the same jobs in different brigades received different rewards. Another irrational mechanism was greater payment for work on the cooperative than for work on sideline production; the result was that the less highly rewarded activity was neglected to the general detriment of over-all economic activity. Paying women less than men for the same kind of work was another incentive problem.[26]

Although official policy on such irrationalities was unequivocally for their elimination, many of them persist even today in the communes. The mandate of " more work, more pay " was reiterated and cadres were under great pressure to carry out this rule. Not only were payment systems expected to reflect the quantity and quality of work performed in daily stints but, as in industry, the inventing and innovating efforts of individuals were rewarded. The different quantities and qualities of

[24] For one method of payment for use of animals, see *Socialist Upsurge in China's Countryside* (Peking: FLP, 1957), pp. 98–100. See also *Model Regulations for an Agricultural Producers' Co-operative* (Peking: FLP, 1956), pp. 14–15.

[25] See Robert Carin, *China's Land Problem Series: Agricultural Cooperativization Movement* (Hong Kong: 1960), II, pp. 421–23, 500–502 and *Socialist Upsurge . . .* , p. 88.

[26] Carin, *op. cit.*, pp. 23, 239–245, 259.

performance were scaled in a multi-grade payment system with the top grade two to three times that of the lowest one.[27]

Given the very low level of peasant income in general, sharp disparity between peasant and worker incomes was an especially troublesome problem. By the middle of 1956, the discontentment of many peasants was recognised by Party leaders. Teng Tzu-hui, Vice-Premier, admitted that a "too rapid and too great increase in public [accumulation] funds, disregarding the . . . present living conditions of [cooperative] members, and at the expense of the members' income, would necessarily undermine the community of interests of the individual and the collective." He reiterated the need to raise incomes for 90 per cent. of the members and stated that it was "imperative to maintain the principle of 'less deduction, more distribution.'"[28]

Even though easing the peasants' situation by reducing relatively the amount of agricultural output going into accumulation was a further concession to the policy of spurring on work effort through material incentives, this did not appease the peasant so long as the disparity between his income and that of workers remained the same or widened. In 1957, Mao Tse-tung acknowledged this problem when he pointed out that "the wages of a small number of workers and some government personnel are rather too high, [and] the peasants have reason to be dissatisfied with this, so it is necessary to make certain appropriate readjustments. . . ."[29]

The action taken in 1957 to rectify this situation was hardly more than a partial attempt to ease the peasant's biggest grumble on this score —the higher income of *unskilled* workers in rural areas. The provisional regulations on wages for unskilled workers in enterprises, business units, and state organs adopted in November 1957 tried to rectify the situation. In general, these regulations set wages for unskilled workers in the lowest three wage grades at about the level similar to that of an average peasant doing full-time work in a medium-sized cooperative, with adjustments for the higher cost of living in cities.[30]

This concession of reduced income disparity between peasants and workers conformed to broad incentive policy. And yet, the enormity of the task of effecting a rational pattern of peasant-worker income differentials when capital accumulation was being stressed seems self-evident. The extreme difficulty of achieving a rational economic solution to this

---

[27] *Decisions on Agricultural Co-operation*, pp. 23–24; *Model Regulations* . . . , pp. 33–39; and *Model Regulations for Advanced Agricultural Producers' Co-operatives* (Peking: FLP, 1956), pp. 18–22.

[28] See Teng Tzu-hui's report in *New China Advances to Socialism*, pp. 130–131 and Schran, *op. cit.*, p. 246.

[29] *Op. cit.*, p. 38.

[30] See Chao Kuo-chün, *op. cit.*, II, 108–109.

vexatious problem was probably a major factor determining the great leap forward strategy.

Non-material Incentives.

Though we have focused attention on the major theme of stressing material incentives in the period 1953–57, it is important not to lose sight of the minor theme of non-material incentives. The operation of both types at the same time, though with different degrees of emphasis, is rooted in the Party's doctrinal outlook. In the First Five-Year Plan, though much detail is devoted to various aspects of material incentive policy and goals, there is brief allusion to non-material incentives.[81]

In the years 1953–55 development of emulation and mass participation campaigns and cultivation of model and outstanding workers and groups did not occur rapidly, probably for organisational reasons. In 1956 and 1957 the tempo was stepped up considerably. These patterns are seen in the statistics on outstanding groups and workers. From 1953 to 1955 the growth in numbers from 15,000 groups and 155,000 individuals to 21,000 and 316,000, respectively, was at a greater growth rate than the increase in workers. In both 1956 and 1957 over a million outstanding workers and 100,000 outstanding groups were honoured.[82]

INCENTIVE POLICY, 1957–1960

By late 1957, the policy of emphasising material incentives had run its course and the grand strategy of the party in the " great leap forward " veered sharply from the Soviet model. This did not mean that material incentives were abandoned but rather that they were, for a time, soft-pedalled. From the end of 1957 to the end of 1960 the policy of " politics in command " was reflected in organisational decentralisation, in the great leap forward, in the revolutionary innovation of people's communes, as well as in changed incentive policy.

In retrospect, the first clear-cut signs of an impending change in policy date from a *People's Daily* editorial of November 21, 1957, in which a review of labour achievements was qualified with the lament that, " We have also over-emphasised the importance of material encouragement, while inadvisably relaxing our political and ideological work. . . ." Such a lapse in correct behaviour was held responsible for the " growth of individualism, egoism, and the equal-treatment ideology among the working masses." In May 1958, Liu Shao-ch'i put the great

---

81 *First Five Year Plan* . . . , pp. 172, 195.
82 Chen Po-wei, " Labour Emulations Supply Huge Power . . . ," *Political Study*, No. 5, 1956, in ECMM, No. 47. For implementation of such techniques see *Socialist Upsurge* . . . , pp. 300, 324, 354–355. Statistics are from *Ten Great Years* (Peking: FLP, 1960), p. 186.

leap forward in its proper political context. Major economic goals were to be attained mainly through mass movements in which the usual motivational instruments were to be subordinated to ideological and political techniques; they were to be the " soul and guide for every kind of work." Such practice was " to raise the level of communist consciousness of the masses " in order that they might " meet the needs of consolidating the socialist system and further expanding the productive forces." Liu maintained that " a communist ideological emancipation movement" was occurring among the people and that it had " brought about a new upsurge in production and construction . . . The political consciousness and socialist initiative of the masses . . . have been greatly enhanced . . . As a result, all sorts of negative trends reflecting surviving bourgeois ideas . . . have been greatly reduced and the just spirit of communism is in the ascendant." These significant changes reflected the " revolutionary tasks before the Party and the people "; Liu was expounding the basis for the " uninterrupted revolution." [33] This delineation of changed conditions and the more advanced outlook of the masses was a prelude to the dramatic and revolutionary innovation of people's communes.

Industry.

In state-operated industry, where Party and Government directives were easily and expeditiously executed, carrying out the new incentive policy involved changes in tempo and emphasis. Innovations of new techniques were advanced in the intensive application of non-material incentives—particularly emulation. Piece-rate wages were cut back over a wide area of economic activity and monetary prizes, while still offered, were overshadowed by the greater emphasis placed on the social status attaching to awards for outstanding achievements. No significant broad raises in wages occurred, though there were some variations calculated to reduce disparities between different classes of workers and workers and peasants and some changes were made in benefits of workers leaving jobs.[34]

The piece-rate system—symbol *par excellence* of emphasis on material incentives—was widely eliminated in the great leap forward. Although there were major complaints against the system on technical and equity grounds, its general, though not complete, abolition was

---

[33] Editorial in SCMP, No. 1667. See " Report on the Work of the Central Committee . . . ," *Second Session of the Eighth National Congress of the Communist Party of China* (Peking: FLP, 1958), pp. 20–21, 24–25, 39–40, 62.

[34] The reaction against material incentives included the notion that social welfare and insurance ought to be reduced. For such a view, see Wei Li, " The System of Wage Allowances Should be Radically Reformed," *Chi-hua Ching-chi (Planned Economy)*, No. 5, 1958, in ECMM, No. 135.

related to the exigencies of the great leap forward. In many factories, workers frequently increased output norms in their frenzied drive to achieve the fantastic goals set by the party leaders. The piece-rate system lost its *raison d'être* and non-material and more conventional material incentives took over.[35]

Though no quantitative measure of the extent to which the system was abolished is available, the degree of abolition or reduction in its operation was probably great since scattered evidence indicates that in industrially concentrated areas the cut-back was sharp: before the end of 1958 state-operated machine and power plants, iron and steel units, and shipbuilding establishments in Shanghai had completely eliminated the system. The Wuhan Tool Plant, Shanghai Diesel Engine Plant, and Chiangnan Docks also abolished the piece-rate system in 1958.[36]

Although official encouragement was given to a general diminution of piece-rate schemes, some restraint was shown and there were experiments in modifying the system to reflect emphasis on group and social incentives. A similar aim was outlined for the hourly wage system which had a progressive aspect—bonuses for outstanding performance. The new principle was that: "Bonuses should be granted with honorary awards as the main thing and with material awards included; they should be granted mainly to collective bodies. . . ."[37] One measure of the stepped-up pace of non-material incentives was the number of outstanding groups and workers. For the year 1958 the numbers were roughly 200,000 and 2·4 million respectively, a doubling of the numbers in 1957.[38]

Starting with the notion that "political leadership means first of all the awakening of enthusiasm," the party policy-makers drew up a series of competitive and group schemes to channel enthusiasm into productive outlets. Emulation campaigns were carried out on various levels. Emphasis was put on the co-operative aspects of contests in order to develop collectivist attitudes and habits. Competition was held on various bases depending upon the nature and function of the particular campaign: family, *hsien* (county), within plants, between plants, industry-wide, and nation-wide competitions. Different contests were held, often resulting from challenges hurled forth by a plant or industrial complex, with the

[35] See *Labour*, No. 10, 1958, pp. 28–29, in U.S. Joint Publications Research Service (JPRS), No. 878; No. 3, 1958, in JPRS, No. 760; and No. 9, 1958, pp. 11–13, in JPRS, No. 760. See also Liu Ch'eng-jui *et al*, " Contradiction in the Piece-Wage System . . . ," *Chiao-hsüeh yü Yen-chiu (Teaching and Research)*, No. 9, 1958, in ECMM, No. 153.

[36] Liu Ch'eng-jui *et al.*, *loc. cit.*, and Sun Shang-ch'ing, *loc. cit.* See also " A Study of the System of Piece-work . . . ," *Labour*, No. 23, 1959, pp. 24–27, in JPRS, No. 2640, and *People's Daily*, September 25, 1958, in SCMP, No. 1875.

[37] Lui Ch'eng-jui *et al.*, *loc. cit.*, p. 17, and Chao Te-huan *et al.*, " How Do We Rouse the Masses to Cancel the Piece Wage System?" *Kung-jen Jih-pao (Workers' Daily)*, August 29, 1958, in SCMP, No. 1862.

[38] *Ten Great Years*, p. 186.

victor receiving the " red flag," symbolising the excellence of its team. National records were set only to be toppled in short order by either the defending holder of the " red flag " or one of its close competitors. Vying teams were expected to assist one another on technical matters; victory or defeat was to reflect greater ingenuity and energy, not guile or secrecy. In this atmosphere of a perpetual athletic league competition in which the spectators became the players as emulations turned into mass movements and every unit had something to contribute, tremendous amounts of labour power were unleashed.[39]

While mass movements and emulation campaigns became a major device for harnessing productive energies, mechanisms for spurring individuals and groups on without calculated competitions with other individuals and groups were also developed further. In all such incentive schemes, whether or not they were combined with built-in material incentives, the greatest emphasis was placed on the prestige or status aspect of the award. Such awards as distinguished titles—labour hero, model, or outstanding worker—and banners and citations paralleled publicity on wall newspapers or in the more prestigious newspapers and journals, admission to advanced educational institutions and research institutes, election as representative to conferences, selection to meet Mao Tse-tung in a small group, and admission to the Communist Party. While none of these techniques was new in itself, they were all employed to a significantly greater degree and with greater intensity than in the period before the great leap forward.[40]

Agriculture.

In the agricultural sector, the reversal in incentive policy was most drastic as the people's communes took shape. Yet in many communes the new incentive policy did not mark so sharp a reversal since earlier incentive schemes, such as existed, had advanced little beyond crude averaging of grain distribution. In other communes, which had more sophisticated incentive methods, the new policy represented some reversal, but the cadres proceeded cautiously and never approached the extremes that have become the basis for characterising the commune as a completely " communist " unit with distribution according to need as the main operating principle.

With the advent of the communes in 1958, the income and material incentives of the peasants were affected by the supply and wage system

---

[39] See, *e.g.*, " 100 per cent. Quota, 120 per cent. Measures, 240 per cent. Enthusiasm," *Red Flag*, No. 3, 1959, pp. 17–19, in JPRS, No. 648D, and Li Po, " Keen Competition and Close Co-operation," *Red Flag*, No. 8, 1958, pp. 39–41, in JPRS, No. 9181.

[40] See Ronald Hsia, " Labour Incentives in China," *Far Eastern Economic Review*, January 7, 1960, pp. 10–11.

and the severe restrictions placed upon individual economic activity outside the control of the commune. The basic assumptions about the readiness of the peasants to endure the hardships of the great leap forward and the new commune system implied major reliance on non-material incentives. As time passed and the difficulties occasioned both by natural calamities and the dislocation and inefficiency attendant upon commune operation, the more extreme implementation of the reversed incentive policy gave way gradually to dependence on material incentives.

The resolution of the Central Committee announcing the communes in August 1958 stated that the system of distribution in the communes was to be " to each according to his work," but pointed out that the communes were " the best form of organisation for the attainment of socialism and gradual transition to communism " which " is no longer a remote future event." The Central Committee made clear its intention to transform the peasant almost completely into a farm labourer : " Generally speaking, reserved private plots of land may perhaps be turned over to collective management in the course of the merger of [agricultural] cooperatives; scattered fruit-trees, *for the time being*, may remain privately owned and *be dealt with some time later*." [41]

In the Central Committee's resolution of December 10, 1958 on commune problems, policies playing down material incentives were reiterated. While the peasants were reassured that their personal property would remain inviolate, no mention was made of private plots, marked for oblivion in the August resolution. Until late in 1960, private plots were generally withdrawn. On the question of wages, the December resolution ritualistically announced " continued adherence " to the principle of distribution according to labour and then approved the new supply-wage method of payment, suggesting the need for caution in fixing the ratio of supply to wages. The importance of the principle of " politics in command " and the need for the Party to lead in mass-line techniques was emphasised. [42]

In its very nature the part-supply part-wage system dulled material incentive since distributing supplies collectively (anything from meals alone to meals, some clothing, some fuel, etc., varying according to commune) was a form of " averaging " and meant that smaller and more efficient households got less than under any graded wage system. The degree to which this levelled incomes depended, of course, on how large a proportion supply was. In the extreme, the supply portion reached as

---

41 " Resolution . . . on the Establishment of People's Communes . . . ," *op. cit.*, pp. 6, 8. Emphasis added.
42 " Resolution on Some Questions Concerning the People's Communes," *Sixth Plenary Session of the Eighth Central Committee* (Peking: FLP, 1958), pp. 32, 34, 44–45.

high as 80 to 90 per cent. with the slim remainder being distributed as money wages sometimes under a graded wage system with the more efficient receiving higher wages.[43]

Under pressures from discontented peasants, not only was the proportion of supply to total income sharply reduced, but even within the supply portion itself greater flexibility and choice were allowed. For example, peasants were allowed either to eat in the commune mess halls or take their food rations and prepare them at home. The ideal ratio of supplies to wages was set in 1960 at " three to seven " or 30 per cent. supply and 70 per cent. wages. And yet, even at that late date critics of the principle of distribution according to labour were given space in important media to press their line, maintaining that " emphasis on material incentives would adversely affect the activism of the section of the people who had a more difficult life in the building of Socialism." [44]

While material incentives in communes were being dulled by the supply-wage system, expansion of non-material incentives and political indoctrination were pressed. With the twin goals of spurring labour productivity and cultivating the communist spirit, the new incentive methods in the rural communes contained heavy doses of political and ideological medicine. Political incentives included a wide range of devices—based on emulation and mass-indoctrination. Emulation involved both individuals and groups who received honorary awards in addition to pecuniary reward. Involvement of peasants in mass activities ranged widely with mass discussion meetings, often very long, a customary and onerous aspect of life. Group decision-making at such meetings was a very important feature of this phase of spurring peasants on through identification and commitment rather than through increasing amounts of consumer goods—a material spur costly in terms of planned high levels of investment.[45]

Incentive Policy, 1960 on

By late 1960, the policy of extreme emphasis upon non-material incentives had been abandoned. Although such incentives were still to play an important role, as they always have, material incentives were to be extended and refined to help prod workers and peasants to greater

---

[43] For analysis of the implications of the supply-wages system and its levelling effect, see Schran, *op. cit.*, p. 211 *et seq.*, and especially Table 4.49, p. 224.

[44] See " The Ratio of Three to Seven," *Nan-fang Daily*, November 12, 1960, in SCMP, No. 2405, and Wu Chih-pu, " Consolidation and Development of People's Communes," *Red Flag*, No. 1, 1960, cited in Carin, *op. cit.* IV, 740.

[45] For evidence of non-material incentive indoctrination, see Li Po, *op. cit.*; " 100 per cent. Quota, 120 per cent. Measures, 240 per cent. Enthusiasm," *op. cit.*; " Motivation in the Great Leap Forward," *Political Study*, No. 1, 1959, pp. 1–4, in JPRS, No. 1512; and Shu T'ung, " Expand the Mass Line and Exalt Realistic Spirit," *Red Flag*, No. 3, 1959, in JPRS, No. 648D.

effort. A key to the major change in economic strategy and incentive policy was the assigning of the highest priority to the agricultural sector of the economy and a retreat from the classic Soviet policy of forced heavy industrialisation. The new strategy stressed the fundamental importance of grain and agriculture for economic development and held that " only through the solving of the grain problem can a greater and better leap forward of the entire national economy be guaranteed." This policy was endorsed in January 1961, at the Ninth Plenary Session of the Eighth Central Committee of the Chinese Communist Party.[46]

After urging reforms that called for raising peasant and consumer enthusiasm through better price and supply conditions, at the expense of heavy industry, if necessary, the Party leaders implied the great importance of material incentives by attacking those who were " misapplying " the socialist principle of distribution and dulling workers' and peasants' enthusiasm. Apparently policy based upon the assumption of a high level of political awareness and widespread communist spirit, supported by the Party starting in 1958, was being abandoned.

Industry.

The change in incentive policy in industry did not become clear until 1961 when the renewed importance of piece-rate systems, emphasis again on distribution according to labour, and de-emphasis of non-material incentives became widespread. The change in policy emerged first and more unambiguously in agriculture because it was there that earlier policy, emphasising non-material incentives, was pushed to its extreme and had its most disruptive effects. In industry, the new policy in force between 1958 and 1960 was never developed to the same extent nor with as disruptive results as in the communes.

Late in 1960, in a drive to raise the quality of industrial work effort, Party cadres took recourse both to non-material and material incentives. There was an awareness of the problem of work enthusiasm after the impact of reversing material work incentives was fully assessed. Lamenting that " some [mine] workers began to think that how much they worked made no real difference and relaxed their effort gradually," a group of reporters deplored a decline in work-discipline as attendance fell off. The favourable results achieved when a more rational system of rewards was set up on an individual basis were acclaimed and explained by the " logical " reward scheme. A greater concern for the livelihood and living conditions of miners was counted a major factor in decreasing absenteeism and raising work enthusiasm generally.[47]

[46] Peking Review, No. 4, 1961, pp. 5–7.
[47] Wang Yu-ch'ang et al., " Attend to the Livelihood of Workers Report No. 1 . . ." People's Daily, May 19, 1961, in SCMP, No. 2507.

As 1961 progressed, the renewed importance of piece-rate systems signalled that the role of material incentives was again in full swing. Refinements were made so that wherever feasible, wages would be based upon team piece-work rates—a felicitous ideological combination of collective and individual interests. Where this was not technically possible the unadorned individual piece-rate system was reinstated. Perfection of wage-grade systems, bonuses, etc. in line with the principle of distribution according to labour was fostered. Allusion to " politics in command " was still made, but seemed mainly ritualistic.[48]

By late 1961 the overwhelming proportion of state-operated enterprises was under either the hourly-wage-plus-reward system or some form of piece-rate system; the straight hourly wage system was seldom adopted because it did not reflect accurately a man's actual output. Party leaders admitted that maximum labour stimulation depended upon the effective implementation of the principle of distribution according to work which " cannot possibly be altered basically before a fundamental change in the social nature of socialism takes place." This concern with piece-rate and other progressive wage instruments attests to the growing importance the régime has placed on material interest as a major motive force in raising the quantity and quality of labour input.[49]

Agriculture.

Although the change in incentive policy in agriculture was foreshadowed in many random dicta on the need to " distribute more and accumulate less " in communes, in the greater use of material rewards, and in inevitable pronouncements declaring (first cautiously and then unabashedly) the primacy of agriculture (and of its problems), the death knell of the old policy was rung abruptly and dramatically. Toward the end of 1960 the small private plots were suddenly returned to commune members. With the development of the communes, these small private plots had been made commune property, taking away a vital income and food source from peasant families and ending rural free markets. The realisation once more that distribution according to labour was " the most vital link for mobilising the masses to carry out production with good results " led logically to the return of private plots. Early in 1961, it was officially admitted that " It is a major economic policy of the Party to allow commune members to possess a small plot of private land

[48] See Ch'en Han-ch'uan, " Strengthening of the Piece-Work System," *Ta Kung Pao*, August 23, 1961, in JPRS, No. 10720.
[49] Lin Fang, " A Discussion on the Forms of Wages," *People's Daily*, October 28, 1961, in JPRS, No. 11969, and " Concerning the Question of Socialist Distribution . . . ," *Ta Kung Pao*, December 15, 1961, in SCMP, No. 2656.

individually and to engage in family side-line occupations on a small scale." [50]

This reversion to an important institution of the pre-commune period represented a significant concession that "the people's enthusiasm in labour is completely low, and the communes have failed to realise fully their superiority." [51] Moreover, the admission that failure to implement the principle of distribution according to labour properly results in "the labour enthusiasm of the commune members [being] unavoidably killed" became the basis for reordering incentives with great emphasis on "rational" rewards linking more output to more income. The greater importance of material incentives was also reflected in reintroduction of piece-rates and a 5 or 7-grade wage scale, stress again on equal pay for equal work, moving labour into desired occupations through flexible use of differential economic rewards, and allowing rural free markets to operate again. Physical exertion superseded ideological purity as the main criterion for model performance. The renewed emphasis on the interests of the individual was paralleled by allowing greater autonomy to the production team. [52]

In the communes the new policy had two main patterns: a sharpening of the effect of money payments for collective work and a return to individual initiative in side-line activities including use of small private plots again. The aims were to boost production and deliveries to the State and to raise peasant income and enthusiasm. Incentive policy was to contribute in a major way to the drive to make the rural communes (in their modified form) a more viable economic unit so that the rapid growth rate of earlier years could be regained.

The approach to heightening material incentives had two aspects. First, there was an attempt to extend the influence of money and rationalise income payment generally. Second, schemes for payment were devised on a progressive basis and implemented as widely as possible. More frequent payment—with monthly payment the ideal—was counted an important means of advancing the personal interests of the commune member and those of the commune and State. The individual would have pocket money and could plan his pattern of consumption more rationally. The closer link between performance and reward would presumably stimulate the peasant's labour input. To the extent that periodic payment at short intervals developed "calculatingness," the

---

[50] "The Nature of Private Plots . . . ." *Ta Kung Pao*, March 15, 1961, in SCMP, No. 2478, April 18, 1961.

[51] *People's Daily*, editorial, November 20, 1960. SCMP, No. 2388, December 1, 1960.

[52] "Relation between Collective Production and Domestic Sideline Occupations Well-handled . . . ," *Nan-fang Daily* (November 14, 1960, in SCMP, No. 2405, December 28, 1960, pp. 11–13.

more rational operation of economic units would be more easily achieved.[53]

The heart of the new incentive policy, of course, was the extension of progressive reward systems heightening income disparities to spur on agricultural production. Wherever possible a system of piece-rate wage payment was to be implemented; where that was not feasible then a time-rate system with rewards based on performance beyond the standard was used. Piece-rate payment is based upon norms for the individual or class of workers; any performance above or below those norms results in payment of a bonus geared to the overfulfilment or a penalty likewise commensurate with the underfulfilment. Though the supply part of commune income distribution still exists, its role has been reduced considerably. Thus, the proportion of income subject to piece-rate determination may sometimes be about 80 per cent. of total income. Piece-rate systems have been modified widely on the basis of the many problems of the 1953–57 period. Differential rewards are geared to skill and allocation needs and the standard work-point payment and over-fulfilment rate have been raised to encourage many important neglected activities.[54]

The return of private plots to individual peasant families is another very important aspect of incentive policy reversal, since it undoubtedly has stimulated peasant production in side-line activities such as vegetable production, raising of live-stock, dairy-farming, etc. Although the size of returned private plots is quite small (in some production brigades the average holding is less than one-thirtieth of an acre), the proportion of pigs and eggs recently sold to the government from peasants' side-line activities reached, in some instances, 40 per cent. of the total purchased. Indicative of the Party's appraisal of side-line activity as an economic spur to peasant output is the improvement of the holiday system in some communes. Instead of the rigid system in which the prescribed number of days was set by custom or a cadre, free selection by commune members, within a unified plan, safeguarding the labour requirements of the commune has been arranged explicitly to allow commune members to develop side-line activity. Moreover, in fixing targets for collective production in the commune, cadres are now required to arrange for time during which the private plots can be properly cared for.[55]

Given the dual aspects of incentive policy in China, and given the Party's desire to maximise labour input with a minimum of

[53] See Wang Shih-hsin, " . . . Pay Wages in Advance Every Month," *People's Daily*, August 8, 1960, in SCMP, No. 2322.

[54] See " Adjust Reward for Supplementary Production Labour," *People's Daily*, May 5, 1961, in JPRS, No. 9669.

[55] See Chu Tai-hsien, " Proper Relationship Between Group Production and Family Side-line Enterprises," *Ta Kung Pao*, June 25, 1961, in JPRS, No. 10563.

consumer goods and services, the meaning of the above pattern of changing incentive emphasis takes shape. The régime is determined to maintain a high level of capital formation and a high rate of economic growth; but it must reckon with the elementary needs of hundreds of millions of peasants. Just as the needs of the peasant masses determine policy on capital formation they shape incentive policy. Ideally, the party leaders would like non-material incentives to become the main motive force impelling the masses on to greater output; this would fulfil significant ideological and economic aims. But these goals must be compromised when the masses' level of living is lowered considerably. Then reliance on material incentives in conventional as well as new ways becomes an imperative if the fundamental stability of the economy and the society are to be maintained. When economic conditions are favourable, non-material incentives are pushed; when unfavourable circumstances arise, pressing on the vulnerably low subsistence level of the masses, too great a dependence on non-material incentives compounds the difficulties. The party will continue to vary incentives in a dualistic way; the limits to which they can push the non-material incentives will depend greatly on the conditions and attitudes of the peasant.

China's Economic Planning and Industry*

By AUDREY DONNITHORNE

ECONOMIC planning in China was pioneered by Kao Kang, Chairman of the North-East Administrative Area in the early days of the Communist régime, who controlled the region formerly known as Manchuria. This was the region which the Japanese had developed into China's foremost centre of heavy industry. It came under Communist rule before most of the country and as early as 1949 the North-East Financial and Economic Commission had made a rough plan for rehabilitating its industry. Two years later a regional planning commission was established.

The beginnings of nation-wide planning also appeared in 1951 when the State Council's Financial and Economic Commission put out control figures for production and capital investment in industry and transport and drew up a plan for state-owned industrial concerns. In November 1952, after it had been announced that the First Five-Year Plan was to begin the following year, a State Planning Committee was set up under Kao Kang. Although we read that in 1953 " a relatively complete set of plans was mapped out and handed down to the lower levels for execution," [1] the First Five-Year Plan as a whole was not published until 1955, half way through the period it was supposed to cover. The State Statistical Bureau was not set up until October 1952. The statistical organs, which the Chinese claimed existed in all provinces and autonomous regions except Tibet by 1953, were usually, no doubt, of a rudimentary type.

With the adoption of the new constitution in 1954 the State Planning Committee was transformed into the State Planning Commission, under the State Council. Meanwhile Kao Kang had been expelled from the Party and had died in mysterious circumstances. Li Fu-ch'un, his former assistant in the North East, was appointed Chairman of the new Planning Commission. The general oversight of capital investment under the Plan was entrusted to another new body, the State Construction Commission.

* Economic Planning is discussed more fully in the author's forthcoming book *China's Economic System*, to be published by Allen & Unwin.

[1] Ku Tso-hsin, " The Development of the Planning of Industrial Construction in the Past Decade," *Chi-hua yü T'ung-chi* (*Planning and Statistics*), No. 13, July 1959. Translated in *Extracts from China Mainland Magazines* (E.C.M.M.) (Hong Kong: U.S. Consulate-General), No. 204.

Two years later, in 1956, long-term and short-term planning were separated. The State Planning Commission was now supposedly free to concentrate on five-year plans and on the longer perspective plans. Since then, however, little has been heard of perspective planning.[2] Formulating and adjusting plans of up to one year's duration was handed over to the newly formed State Economic Commission which, like the State Planning Commission, came directly under the State Council.

The State Economic Commission also had to balance the national supply and demand of raw materials. Chinese planning is in fact primarily "planning by material balances." There is little information about how it is done. Presumably Soviet methods have been used as a rough guide, and future requirements of raw materials and capital equipment have been calculated on the basis of technical coefficients. This demand is then compared with supplies likely to be available in the country as a whole (national balancing) or in the particular area (*e.g.*, province) for which the balancing is being done, and decisions are taken on imports and exports and the transfer of supplies within the country. This is called " balance transfers " (*Ch'a-e tiao-p'o*).[3]

As the First Five-Year period went on, insufficient supplies of raw materials caused serious bottlenecks. This prompted the establishment in 1956 of yet another organ directly subordinate to the State Council, the General Bureau for the Supply of Raw Materials, for controlling supplies and reserves of raw materials. The State Technological Commission, established at the same time, had among its duties that of formulating five-year and perspective plans for technical development.[4]

Summing up the achievements of economic planning during the First Five-Year Plan, an article written on the basis of reports made by Soviet experts in Peking claimed that " a system for the balancing and distribution of products was introduced and the stock reserve system and the comprehensive financial plan of the State were brought close to perfection." The other achievements were said to include the inauguration of a planning and control system for capital construction, the fixing of targets, arrangements for control at different levels and the laying down of procedure for the approval of reports on tasks planned.[5]

2 An Indian Mission which visited the State Planning Commission in 1956 and reported on its organisation just before these changes, stated that no special group was working on perspective plans but that each department concerned itself with them in addition to five-year plans. (Mimeographed report.)

3 *Report of the Indian Delegation to China on Agricultural Planning and Techniques*, pp. 55–56. Also see She Yi-san, " A Discussion of the Change in the Allocation System for Raw Materials, *Chi-hua Ching-chi (Planned Economy)*, No. 10, October 1958, pp. 34–35; Ku Tso-hsin, *op. cit.*; and A. Nove, *The Soviet Economy* (London: Allen & Unwin, 1961), pp. 80–81, 207.

4 *Collected Laws and Regulations of the Chinese People's Republic*, III (Peking: Legal Publishing House), p. 82.

5 Ku Tso-hsin, *op. cit.*

Certainly during this period plans were formulated more quickly. While the First Five-Year Plan was not published until half way through the period for which it ran, the figures for the second (1958–62) were adopted by the Eighth National Congress of the Chinese Communist Party in September 1956.

Towards the end of the First Five-Year Plan, the administrative machinery was clearly overloaded and showed signs of strain. Ever since the abolition of the six great administrative regions in 1954 the government had attempted to maintain centralised control over the whole economy. This was liable to hamstring the pace of development. Indeed it appears that this degree of centralisation was so unworkable that the system had broken down. Some areas were said to " decide on major items of capital construction without the approval of the state or of higher levels. For these purposes they divert raw materials from key construction projects of the state, and in some cases even detain materials in transit. In some places investment in capital construction far exceeds the figure approved by the state and by higher levels." [6] Moreover, some plans were drawn up carelessly and repeatedly revised with the result that " non-productive construction hampers productive construction and unimportant construction hampers essential construction. Capital and materials are both wasted and the fulfilment of production plans is very unbalanced." [7] The " erroneous views " which led to this situation were said (in November 1958) to have been most prevalent in the second half of 1957 and the first half of 1958; they included the opinions that state control of planning should be reduced, that state plans should not be unified and that the maximum flexibility should be allowed to various localities and departments. These are contrasted with " erroneous views " of the opposite type, that is of excessive centralisation, which were said to have been more popular before 1957. [8] The decision to decentralise in 1957–58 was thus partly a belated recognition that highly centralised control was impossible and that in fact the local authorities had already in many cases taken over some of the functions supposedly reserved for the centre. By attempting central control on a smaller front, it may have been hoped to get an effective command of certain key points in the economy. The decentralisation measures were intended to re-shape economic planning, taxation, industrial management and commerce. It must be remembered that this administrative decentralisation was counterbalanced by the control exercised at all levels by branches of the Communist Party which ensured,

[6] Yang Ying-chieh, " On Unified Planning and Decentralised Control," *Planned Economy*, No. 11, November 1958, pp. 3–4.
[7] *Ibid.*
[8] *Ibid.*

as far as possible, that the policies laid down by the centre would be pursued throughout the country. The net result was probably that a good deal of the initiative on how to carry out policies was transferred from the Central Government to the party committees of local authorities and of individual enterprises. The provincial party first secretaries became especially important.

The chief changes in economic planning which the 1958 regulations were designed to effect were given in an article in the State Planning Commission's journal *Planned Economy*[9] as follows: (1) The former system of planning, in which the lead was taken by the specialised ministries of the Central Government was changed into what was called a " double-track " system in which local equilibrium was to play a leading part and the ministries and local authorities were to co-operate. (2) Decentralised control. (3) Strengthened co-operation and co-ordination. (4) The central authorities were to distribute only the " balance transfers " of the major local authorities and not the total production of the country.

Previously the planning activities of provinces, autonomous regions and municipalities under the direct jurisdiction of the Central Government were restricted to drafting plans for local enterprises and businesses. Now they were also to include in their plans the draft plans of concerns under the administration of Central Government economic ministries. It was hoped that the plans of both centrally and locally administered concerns in any one area would be linked together to form a complete economic plan for the area as a whole. In the same way, the formal plans, which at the end of the process of planning are issued by the Central Government as operational orders to the major local authorities, were in future to refer to both types of enterprise. It should here be mentioned that because of another administrative change at this time, control over many economic enterprises was transferred from central ministries to local authorities. The planning regulations to which we now refer were concerned, therefore, only with those enterprises still under central control. Even for these the major local authorities now had power to regulate and balance production, to co-ordinate, and to distribute materials and labour, so long as the fulfilment of state plans was guaranteed. Yet another change was instituted in 1959 whereby enterprises under central control were, with certain exceptions, to apply to the local authorities for raw materials allocated by the state instead of to state organs at higher levels. Changes were also to be made in planning labour resources. In the past there were frequently great discrepancies in wages and amenities within a city between factories which came under the Central Government and those which came under the local

9 Wang Kuei-wu, " An Important Change in the Method of Drawing Up Annual Plans," *Planned Economy*, No. 9, September 1958, p. 13 *et seq*.

authority. From 1959 onwards the labour plans of both types of enterprises were to be incorporated into the local labour plan.[10]

However, while the powers of local authorities were enlarged, the new regulations emphasised the importance of centralised leadership by the ministries " to prevent blind local development and dislocation between localities." The Central Government ministries were to assemble and balance all draft plans according to industries. The draft plans of each ministry were to cover both the draft plans of enterprises under their direct administration and local draft plans for the ministry's particular branch of industry. Besides this, the industrial ministries were to draft plans for local distribution and transfer of those materials coming under their control. The Ministry of Labour, together with other relevant ministries, was to draft labour plans for both regions and ministries.

The formal plans finally issued by the Central Government to the ministries were to include the plans of the enterprise directly under them and the plans for production, business affairs (this phrase is as vague in Chinese as it is in English) and capital construction under their charge— presumably the grand totals for the branch of industry concerned, including the output of locally-owned enterprises. To avoid omissions in local and ministerial plans the State Economic Commission was to unify, balance and formulate draft plans on a national scale.[11]

As from 1959 the number of targets controlled by the Central Government was reduced to the following seven: (1) Output and "balance transfers" of certain major industrial products (*e.g.*, steel, iron, coal, lathes, cotton yarn); (2) Output and "balance transfers" of major agricultural products (*e.g.*, grain, cotton, vegetable oil, pigs); (3) Total exports and imports and the volume of important export and import commodities; (4) Volume of freight of railways and of transport undertakings directly under the Ministry of Communications; (5) Total investment, new productive capacity, major projects, and scale of basic capital construction; (6) Total wages and average number of staff and workers; and (7) Enrolment in higher educational institutions and allocation of graduates.

Other targets which now ceased to be fixed by the central authorities included total value of industrial output, irrigated acreage, arable acreage, total circulation of commodities, total retail sales, local transport, rate and total of cost reduction, and volumes of building and installation work. These targets were in future to be settled by the local authorities and the ministries between themselves. In order to provide flexibility,

[10] Wang Kuei-wu, *op. cit.*, p. 13.
[11] *Ibid.* p. 14.

even the centrally controlled targets might be adjusted by local authorities so long as state plans were fulfilled and more especially those plans concerning construction projects, productive capacity, level of production, " balance transfers " and revenue.[12]

To co-ordinate plans, it was suggested that the local authorities and the ministries might invite each other to planning conferences. The major local authorities, after drawing up their draft plans, should send copies to the central ministries for reference purposes. The ministries were to use these as the basis for their own draft plans. There should also be a general exchange of copies of plans between the ministries and the local authorities. The Ministries of Labour and of Education must maintain close contact with other ministries concerned when formulating their nation-wide plans. In accordance with the principle of " balance transfer," embodied in the new regulations, each local authority had first to make a preliminary balance of industrial and agricultural products within its own area and then forward to the Central Government its schemes for transfers into and out of its area. On the basis of such local schemes, the Central Government's State Economic Commission would then effect balances on a national scale; for raw materials, the task of making these balances was transferred to the State Planning Commission. A final and no doubt very welcome reform embodied in the new regulations was a 70 per cent. reduction in the number of forms used in planning.[13]

The 1959 annual plan was the first to be drawn up under this new system. The drafting of this began in the previous June, discussions with the co-ordinating regions (seven somewhat shadowy units between the central government and the provinces) took place in July, the Central Government set a control figure in August (this may refer to the percentage of national income to be devoted to investment), the formal drafting of local plans was carried out from September to November and (in an article appearing early that November) it was thought that the final plan would be completed during November and December.[14] Target figures for the four most important items—steel, grain, coal and cotton—were set by the sixth plenary session of the Eighth Plenum of the Party's Central Committee which met at Wuchang in November-December 1958.[15] The plan as a whole was approved by the State Council on April 16, 1959, and the report on it delivered by Li Fu-ch'un to the National People's Congress five days later. In August of that year the principal targets for the year's plan were readjusted—in plain words were

12 *Ibid.* p. 14.
13 She Yi-san, *op. cit.*, p. 34, and Wang Kuei-wu, *op. cit.*, pp. 14–15.
14 Chao Pai, " On the Question of Comprehensive Financial Plans," *Planned Economy*, No. 11, November 1958, p. 31.
15 *People's Daily*, editorial, February 2, 1959.

drastically reduced. Originally the targets for 1959 had been calculated on the basis of the supposed output of 1958, the year of the Great Leap. The original 1958 figures were, however, found to be greatly exaggerated with the result that the 1959 targets based on them were clearly unattainable.

In February 1958 the State Construction Commission had been abolished and its duties divided between the State Planning Commission, the State Economic Commission and the Ministry of Construction Engineering. Nine months later the setting up of a State Basic Construction Commission was reported. This body was in turn abolished in January 1961 and its duties transferred to the State Planning Commission.[16] After that date the two main central planning organs were the State Planning Commission for long-term planning and the State Economic Commission which dealt with plans for one year or less. It has already been mentioned that in 1958 the State Planning Commission had been given the responsibility for effecting a nation-wide balance of raw materials. In the same year the General Bureau for the Supply of Raw Materials which, it will be remembered, was supposed to co-ordinate the allocation of raw materials, was put under the State Economic Commission.[17] It is not clear how the division of labour between the two commissions worked out in this sphere. In September 1959 we read of steel for farm tools being allocated by the State Planning Commission.[18] Then six months later in March 1960 the " State Economic Commission and other departments concerned " were allocating rolled steel, tinplate, copper, rubber, quicksilver and other products " to certain industries which were not meeting demand." In yet another instance, in December 1959, the directive in a shock campaign to collect factory rejects and waste materials was signed jointly by the State Planning Commission, the Ministry of Commerce and the Ministry of Public Health.[19]

We have seen that the central authorities retained official control of certain important aspects of capital construction although in this sector, as in others, a measure of decentralisation was decreed. But whatever the formal degree of decentralisation of decisions on capital construction, both the State and the provinces found difficulty in exercising effective control, at least as far as the province of Kwangtung was concerned. In May 1962, the provincial daily carried an editorial demanding that work on all projects not in the plan should stop at once. " The

[16] *People's Daily*, January 31, 1961, p. 1, and *Collected Laws and Regulations, op. cit.*, VII, p. 61, and *ibid*, VIII, p. 95.

[17] *Collected Laws and Regulations, op. cit.*, VII, p. 64.

[18] New China News Agency (NCNA), September 16, 1959. Translated in *Survey of China Mainland Press* (SCMP) (Hong Kong: U.S. Consulate-General), No. 2105.

[19] NCNA (Canton), March 27, 1960. Translated in SCMP No. 2234. And NCNA, February 23, 1960, in SCMP No. 2207.

Party Central Committee and the Provincial Party Committee," we read, " long ago issued a directive strictly prohibiting all capital construction projects not in the state plan and the immediate suspension of those projects already under way. However," it complained, " some areas and units have adopted an indifferent attitude towards the directive, as shown by the fact that many extra-plan projects are still in progress " with funds, raw materials and labour obtained for the most part through illicit channels.[20] So with respect to construction projects, matters had apparently not improved over the situation at the end of the First Five-Year Plan period which decentralisation was designed to remedy.

In November 1962 seven new vice-chairmen—four of them vice-premiers—joined the fifteen vice-chairmen of the State Planning Commission. The new men were: Po I-po, Director of the State Council's Office of Industry and Communications and concurrently Chairman of the State Economic Commission; T'an Chen-lin, Director of the State Council's Office of Agriculture and Forestry; Teng Tzu-hui, the Director of the Rural Work Department of the Central Committee of the Party; Li Hsien-nien, the Director of the State Council's Office of Finance and Trade and concurrently Minister of Finance; Ch'en Po-ta, the Editor-in-Chief of *Red Flag* and Vice-Director of the Party Central Committee's Propaganda Department, and two economists, Sung Shao-wen and Yang Ying-chieh. Yang's case is interesting because in 1959 he was dismissed from the position to which he was now once again appointed, that of Vice-Chairman of the State Planning Commission, for criticising the Great Leap Forward. These appointments are thought to have been made in order to strengthen the Commission when it was engaged on drawing up the Third Five-Year Plan, for 1963–67. Three months later, in February 1963, three of the old vice-chairmen —Chu hi-chih, Han Che-Yi and Sung P'ing—were relieved of their posts.

In addition to the State Planning Commission and the State Economic Commission, Central Government organs concerned with planning include the planning bureaus inside various ministries. Planning organs also exist at all levels of local government in order to carry out the " double track " system of planning, thus making possible the " organic integration of specialised balancing (*i.e.*, by sectors) and local balancing." [21] This policy has not been conspicuously successful. In August 1962, in the course of an academic discussion on the topic, it was said that local authorities and central government ministries were frequently at odds on planning and that local planning bodies found it difficult to

---

20 *Southern Daily*, May 15, 1962, editorial in SCMP No. 2757.
21 " National Economic Planning Group of Hupeh Economic Society Discusses Question of Local Composite Balancing," *Ta Kung Pao*, August 29, 1962.

incorporate the plans of central government enterprises in their area into the plans for achieving local balance of commodities. "The relationship of the two sides in planning," it was stated "is thus limited to reports and the exchange of plans, and the double-track system exists only in form." [22] However, all agreed that when local balancing was properly organised, the Central Government enterprises should not be omitted.

In the process of planning, considerable use is made of conferences at which the various interested bodies are represented. To give one example, in November 1958 a conference held at Peking under the auspices of the State Planning Commission, the State Economic Commission, the First Ministry of Machine Building and the Ministry of Metallurgical Industry, came to a decision to build more medium and heavy steel rolling mills. In addition to representatives of the sponsoring departments, the conference was attended by officials of machine building and metallurgical departments from various provinces and also by staff from machine building factories.[23] Telephone conferences, a favourite device in China, are sometimes held for the purpose of announcing short-term plans to lower levels. We hear, for instance, of a telephone conference held in July 1959 by the Ministry of Communications at which a vice-minister reported on work for the first half of the year and on the programme for fulfilling the plan for the second half.[24]

Weaknesses of the statistical system greatly impede the attempt to plan the economy. Chinese industrial statistics, however, are in general considerably more reliable than those of agriculture, and statistics of modern industry are better than those of small-scale industry and handicrafts.

Connected with the weakness of the statistical system is the fact that targets have not been a wholly unambiguous concept. Targets may, according to an article of January 1959,[25] be divided into "those hoped for" and "those which must be realised" or "those which are guaranteed" and "those striven after." Those which are guaranteed and must be realised are to be decided "after more accurate computation and made to conform with objective realities as much as possible"; the other sort suffer no such restriction. The situation was formalised by the official use of two sets of targets under the "system of planning with dual accounts" which was instituted in 1958. By this system the authorities at each level had two sets of targets, the second and larger being that passed down to the level beneath them, for which it formed the

[22] *Ibid.*   [23] NCNA, November 30, 1958, in SCMP No. 1908.
[24] *Ta Kung Pao*, July 26, 1959, p. 1, in SCMP No. 2075.
[25] Chiang Hsia, "On High Targets," *Chün-tsung (The Masses)*, January 16, 1959, translated in ECMM No. 165.

first set, while a new and yet larger second set would be sent down to the next level. The second set formed "a target for struggle" which, it was held, would give fuller scope to the initiative of the masses which had been restrained by the planners during the First Five-Year Plan period. In one province in 1958 the second set of accounts, as far as industry was concerned, exceeded the first set by 33 per cent. At the beginning of 1960 the practice of dual targets was being condemned. However in 1961 the "production target" of production brigades was said to be generally around 10 per cent. above their "target for guaranteed output" which suggests that the system had not died out although it was being used with greater moderation than previously.[26] As each level felt it obligatory to report fulfilment or over-fulfilment of the targets handed down to it, the result was the gross inflation of output statistics which occurred in 1958 and which was in part corrected by the revised figures issued in the summer of 1959.

One aspect of the reaction to the "Great Leap" mentality was that more emphasis was put on targets other than those of mere volume of output. Thus towards the end of 1959 a *People's Daily* editorial stated that while a great part of the annual plan had been fulfilled, difficulties existed in producing the full variety of goods planned. Some industrial enterprises, it complained "might have emphasised only the attainment of targets of quantity and value of output while paying less attention to targets of quality, variety and cost." [27] Two years later, in October 1961, an article in *Red Flag* felt it necessary to make the same point: that enterprises must fulfil all the targets set whereas they tended to overstress quantity and value of output without regard to quality, variety, cost of production, profit and loss and social need.[28] It is of course advantageous for an enterprise to have its targets set low and Party branches are supposed to counteract the tendency to try to get an "easy plan." [29]

In addition to setting targets for individual items, an economic plan should attempt to co-ordinate the economy by achieving a certain proportionate development between different sectors. The theoretical

26 See Liao Chi-li, "A Discussion on Dual Accounting," *Planned Economy*, No. 5, May 1958, pp. 9–10; Wei Yi, "A Revolution in Methods of Planning," *Hsueh-hsi (Study)*, No. 8, April 18, 1958, p. 10; Liu Tsun-hsiu, "Continue to Oppose Rightist Tendencies, Exert Efforts and Take a Big Leap Forward in Agricultural Production this Year," *Kiangsi Daily*, January 2, 1960, in SCMP No. 2226; Yen Yung-ch'ien, "A Tentative Discussion on Differential Net Income from Land and its Distribution," *Kuang-ming Daily*, September 18, 1961. See also Choh-ming Li, *Statistical System of Communist China* (Berkeley: University of California Press, 1959), pp. 71–72.
27 *People's Daily*, November 26, 1959, editorial.
28 Li Cheng-jui and Tse Ch'un-t'ai, "Several problems concerning Economic Accounting in Socialist Enterprises," *Red Flag*, No. 19, October 1, 1961, p. 20.
29 "Party Branch of Fatshan Municipal Metal Company carries out Ideological Work carefully and penetratingly," *Ta Kung Pao*, April 16, 1962.

problems of planned and proportionate development, of balance and imbalance, have generated much discussion in China. That the national economy can be developed at high speed and at the same time proportionally is held to be an objective law of socialist construction, as well as an expression of the great superiority of the socialist system. Nevertheless balance is relative and temporary while imbalance is absolute and perpetual. So no matter how hard one tries to achieve balance, imbalance will inevitably occur. However signs of imbalance and disharmony should be analysed as soon as they appear.[30] According to an article published by Yang Ying-chieh in November 1962, in which month he was appointed a Vice-Chairman of the State Planning Commission, the six ratios to be kept in balance are those between agriculture and industry; between the output of means of production and that of consumption goods; between accumulation and consumption in the national income; between transport on the one hand and agriculture and industry on the other; between the supply of commodities and total purchasing power; and finally between investment for cultural purposes and economic investment.[31] Three years earlier, the same author writing on the same theme had added that while much could be learned from "a study of the experience of construction in fraternal countries" nevertheless the ratios used by them were not to be introduced, without modification, into the Chinese plans.[32] In 1962, apparently, Yang no longer felt this warning was necessary. In this connection it is interesting to note that at one time there must have been a considerable number of Soviet experts working in the State Planning Commission. They published four volumes of reports, of which the first two were announced in September 1958.[33] Many of the mistakes of the past years had been due to a disregard of the type of ratios which Yang listed, as exemplified by the excessive concentration on industry and neglect of agriculture and of transport, the over-emphasis on producer goods, or, to quote a more specific instance, in the lack of co-ordination in plans for electric power and for industrial development.

Supervising and controlling the execution of plans has been a constant problem. In 1954 a Ministry of Supervision was established with branches at ministry, provincial and enterprise levels. It was abolished in 1959. However, other bodies were already in existence charged with the specific function of supervising the execution of plans.

[30] Yang Chien-pai, "Seeking Balance in High Speed Development," *People's Daily*, November 18, 1959.
[31] Yang Ying-chieh, "On Comprehensive Balance," *Economic Research*, No. 11, November 1962, pp. 4–8.
[32] Yang Ying-chieh, "On the Questions of Ratios, Priorities and Rate of Growth in the National Economy," *ibid*. No. 5, May 1959, p. 13.
[33] *Planned Economy*, September 1958, p. 15.

By 1958 a number of specialised organs had been established "to inspect and ensure the carrying out of state plans of all kinds" and to make quarterly checks on the progress of the plans for agricultural and industrial production, capital construction, the distribution of raw materials and for other major items. Before that time, quarterly plans had been left to ministries and local authorities to draw up on the basis of the state's annual plan. "According to the practical experience of the last few years," stated an article in November 1958, "the arrangements made (for quarterly planning) by the various ministries and local authorities alone were insufficient"[34] hence the establishment of central organs to carry out this task. This, then, is a measure of greater centralisation taken in a year in which the administrative machinery, as distinct from party control, was being decentralised. "Disciplinary punishment," this article insisted, "should be meted out to those who wilfully refuse to fulfil the state plan or intentionally damage it." "Repeated propaganda" was recognised as the chief and first method to ensure plan fulfillment, "but when necessary discipline might and should be employed."[35]

One example of inspection by Central Government organs was in 1959 when the 8th Bureau of the First Ministry of Machine Building sent special technical teams to visit factories to check on the quality of electric motors, steam turbines and certain other types of machinery. This Bureau also convened a meeting for chiefs of technical inspection departments of key factories. By these means it discovered a serious decline in the quality of electrical goods.[36] When state supervisory organs discover that sub-standard goods are being turned out, they are empowered to reduce their prices, suspend delivery or even production.[37]

The banks and financial departments are expected to play a major part in ensuring that production proceeds as planned. They have to see that plans for credit loans to enterprises accord closely with national economic plans (especially those for industrial production and the circulation of commodities) and also with the state budget. Banks must insist that the distinction between working capital and investment funds is maintained. This has been a perennial source of trouble, as on many occasions loans provided as working capital have been diverted by enterprise to purposes of capital construction.

[34] Yang Ying-chieh, "On Unified Planning and Decentralised Control," *Planned Economy*, No. 11, November 9, 1958, p. 5.

[35] *Ibid.*

[36] "Instructions concerning the speedy Adoption of Measures to ensure the Quality of Electrical Products, issued by 8th Bureau of First Ministry of Machine Building," *Tien-chi Kung-yeh (Electric Motor Industry)*, No. 10, May 25, 1959, p. 1.

[37] Han Kuang, "Some problems concerning technical work in industry," *Red Flag*, No. 24, December 16, 1961, p. 4.

Despite all these arrangements for supervision, control over implementation of plans still remained defective. To quote one example, in October 1962 a warning was needed of the harm done when plants supposed to be making spare parts and accessories took up instead the manufacture of complete machines, contrary to state plans.[38]

The chief criticism that must be levelled at the economic planning system set up in the first decade of Communist rule is that of being over-ambitious for China's stage of development. For a large part of the economy the statistical basis was too shaky to support either the sound formulation or the checking of plans. While this was particularly so in agriculture, industrial planning was also hampered by this deficiency. Nor were the administrative services capable of enforcing compliance with planning directives. In view of this, any description of the machinery for planning must include a warning that the system viewed at close quarters in operation is likely to appear very different from what it is supposed to be in theory. Illustrations of this divergence have been given above. However a further cautionary note to this end is not out of place. One element in the gap between theory and fact was mentioned when discussing the decentralisation of 1957–58. It is the controlling power wielded by the Party over all organs of the state, including of course those concerned with planning.

On the development of the planning system from 1960, it is difficult to speak, for no annual plans were published for several years thereafter. In October 1963 the Prime Minister, Chou En-lai said that the Third Five-Year Plan, which was due to begin that year, was under preparation and meanwhile China was operating on the basis of annual plans. Little statistical information about the economy has been made public (by the beginning of 1964) for any year after 1959. Occasional figures for the output of one or two isolated products have been given from Peking, others have seeped out from the Soviet Union or have been estimated by observers, but nothing comprehensive has been published. In July 1963 it was reported that the State Council and the Standing Committee of the National People's Congress had accepted the report on the adjusted plan for the last two years (1961–62) of the Second Five-Year Plan but no further information was given. The communique after the National People's Congress meeting of November-December 1963, stated that Li Fu-ch'un, Chairman of the State Planning Commission had given a report on the implementation of the 1963 plan and the draft plan for 1964. Comment on the evolution since 1960 of the

---

[38] Lin Pin and Chao Hua-ling, " Several Questions Concerning Production Co-operation in Light Industry," *Chung-kuo Ch'ing Kung-yeh (Chinese Light Industry)*, No. 10, October 1962 (SCMM No. 348).

machinery of planning must await publication of some of this material at present withheld.

However one new policy emerged which may have facilitated the planners' task. The decision to give agriculture an over-riding priority should have introduced a unifying influence into the drawing up of plans. It gave a clear criterion by which all proposals could be judged: how far do they assist agricultural production? For example, in heavy industry precedence was given to assisting the technical transformation of agriculture, and the order went forth that the proportional relationship between different departments of heavy industry should be fixed according to this end.[39] It only remains to be seen whether this priority for agriculture has been successfully maintained, in fact as well as in theory, when many other interests would doubtless wish priorities to be arranged in a different manner.

[39] Chieh Yuan, " Practical and Theoretical Economists in Peking Discuss how to Conduct Further Study on the Question of Developing Agricultural Production through Implementing the Principle of Taking Agriculture as the Foundation," *Economic Research*, No. 12, December 1962, p. 64; Yang Chien-pai, " Redirect Industry in Accordance with the Policy of ' Agriculture the Foundation,' " *Ta Kung Pao*, January 30, 1963.

Changes in the Location of China's Steel Industry*

By RONALD HSIA

THE importance of examining the location of China's steel development is not confined solely to the steel industry. It reflects to a large extent, the Communist policy on industrial location in general. The new steel centres have been planned to form the nuclei of industrial complexes. To counteract the pre-Communist concentration of industry in the coastal areas,[1] the Communist régime has emphasised from the beginning that a wide dispersion of industry is desirable from the standpoint of economic development and national defence. In planning new capital construction, therefore, regional development constitutes a key-note while sources of raw materials and fuel supply, consumption centres, future mechanisation of agriculture and national security become the major determinants of industrial locations. As a result of adherence to this policy, a new pattern has emerged for the location of China's steel industry.

Changes in location are traced in this article in terms of the distribution of capacity (in the case of blast furnaces) or the distribution of output (in the case of ingot steel) among seven economic regions. These regions, as defined by the Party's Central Committee in March 1958, are given in Table 1.

WARTIME CHANGES

With the outbreak of the Sino-Japanese hostilities and in anticipation of Japanese occupation smelting equipment was dismantled and removed to the interior. The removal and subsequent wartime construction and expansion of iron and steel plants, particularly in the Japanese occupied areas, resulted in a relative shift of China's steel industry away from Central China to the North-east. Central China's share of the country's aggregate blast furnace capacity declined from the pre-war 8·4 per cent. to 0·3 per cent. at the time of Japanese surrender in August 1945.

* This article is based on a chapter of the author's forthcoming book, *Steel in Communist China*, a study prepared under the auspices of the Committee on the Economy of China, Social Science Research Council.
[1] In pre-Communist China, over three-quarters of the value of industrial output came from the coastal areas, which constituted less than 10 per cent. of the country.

The share of the North-east region, on the other hand, rose from 60·6 to 67·8 per cent. during the same period. For the remaining regions in which iron-smelting capacity existed,[2] changes in their shares in the overall capacity distribution were negligible during the war.

Table 1

ECONOMIC REGIONS AS DEFINED BY THE CCP CENTRAL COMMITTEE March 1958

Economic Region	Components (Province or Autonomous Region)
North-east	Heilungkiang, Kirin, Liaoning
North	Inner Mongolia, Hopei, Shansi
East	Shantung, Kiangsu, Anhwei, Chekiang, Kiangsi, Fukien
Central	Honan, Hupei, Hunan
South	Kwangtung, Kwangsi
North-west	Sinkiang, Kansu, Shensi, Chinghai
South-west	Szechwan, Kweichow, Yunnan

LOCATIONAL CHANGES UNDER PLANNING

The Communists aimed at widening the dispersion of industrial centres by planned capital construction.[3] In the restoration period this policy appears to have exerted itself (see Columns 1 and 2 of Table 2). In actual fact, however, the change was brought about through a substantial decrease in the nation's overall blast furnace capacity. This can be attributed primarily to the Soviet Union removing metallurgical equipment and other installations from iron and steel centres in the North-east. The doubling of the share of the South-west in the nation's aggregate blast furnace capacity primarily represented no increase in its absolute capacity. Without Soviet removals the share of the North-east would not have dwindled so much and the dispersion of blast furnace capacity could not have widened so much, in spite of the Communist policy regarding industrial locations.

In contrast to the illusory widening of dispersion in the reconstruction phase, the implementation of the First Five-Year Plan brought about a greater concentration, as can be seen from Column 3 of Table 2. This is more or less expected inasmuch as the reconstruction and expansion of Anshan Steel[4] was envisaged in the First Five-Year Plan as the

---

2 These include the North, the East and the South-west, as no smelting facilities were installed in the South or the North-west.

3 For planning rehabilitation, the policy of industrial dispersion was subservient to the objective of maximising the capital-output ratio.

4 Anshan Steel is the abbreviated form for the Anshan Iron and Steel Corporation. Wuhan Steel, etc., are similar abbreviations.

most urgent task, and the building of the two new key steel bases did not get started till the latter part of the Plan. While this priority scheme accentuated the concentration of the steel industry in the North-east, it did not conflict with the long-run policy of widening locational dispersion. On the contrary, the extension of the existing steel bases was a *sine qua non* for the establishment of new bases in terms of technical support and material supply. Anshan Steel was the largest single supplier of iron and steel for the construction of steel bases in the First Five-Year Plan. Thus the share of the North-east in the country's overall blast furnace capacity rose from 59·0 per cent. in 1953 to 79·6 per cent. in 1957. This enhanced the share of the all-important North-east at the expense of the other regions. The exceptionally large percentage decrease in the share of the South-west reflected a negligible change in its blast furnace capacity.

Table 2

REGIONAL DISTRIBUTION OF BLAST FURNACE CAPACITY
1945,[a] 1953 and 1957

Economic Region	1945 [a]	1953	1957
	Figures in percentages		
	(1)	(2)	(3)
North-east	67·8	59·1	79·6
North	19·7	25·1	14·4
East	7·6	5·7	4·0
Central	0·3	0·8	0·5
South-west	4·6	9·3	1·5
Total	100·0	100·0	100·0

[a] Before Soviet dismantling and removal of equipment and installations.

Changes in regional distribution of the steel industry in terms of ingot steel output are shown in Table 3, which presents a somewhat different picture from that of blast furnace capacity distribution. The nature of the available data does not permit an examination of regional distribution in terms of ingot steel capacity, but it should be noted that changes in *output* distribution among regions can be attributed to variations in furnace productivity in addition to capital construction. Bearing in mind the discrepancy between capacity and output, the data given in Table 3 can be examined.

Regional distribution in terms of ingot steel output show a slightly wider dispersion in 1953 than in 1945.[5] Here again, the percentage redistribution during the rehabilitation phase has little to do with the

[5] Before Soviet dismantling and removal of equipment and installations.

Communist policy on industrial location. Speedy restoration of output in Shanghai and Tayeh accounted especially for the increased shares of East and Central China. The virtually unchanged share of the North-east can be attributed chiefly to difficulties encountered in restoring Anshan's No. 2 steel plant which was completely stripped by the Russians.[6]

Table 3 reveals that the spread of ingot steel output increased during the First Five-Year Plan. The shares of the East and the Central regions continued to increase mainly because capacity expanded and the per-formance of the steel mills in Shanghai and Tayeh improved. Ingot steel output in Shanghai increased from 75,000 tons in 1952 to 480,000 tons in 1957, as a result of additional new facilities the reconstruction and renovation of the existing facilities (notably in No. 3 Iron and Steel Plant) and improvements in furnace productivity. The construction of

Table 3

REGIONAL DISTRIBUTION OF INGOT STEEL OUTPUT
1945,[a] 1953 and 1957

Economic Region	1945 [a]	1953	1957
	Figures in percentages		
	(1)	(2)	(3)
North-east	65·3	65·9	67·8
North	30·5	25·4	10·7
East	1·7	5·5	14·7
Central	0·6	2·1	4·1
South-west	1·9	1·1	2·7
Total	100·0	100·0	100·0

[a] Before Soviet dismantling and removal of equipment and installations.

two new converter shops in Shanghai's No. 1 Iron and Steel Plant in 1956, for instance, gave East China an additional rated capacity of 250,000 tons per annum; the installation of six more converters in Shanghai's No. 6 Iron and Steel Plant in 1957 added another 50,000 tons of annual rated capacity. Improvements in furnace productivity can be illustrated by Shanghai's No. 3 Iron and Steel Plant. The utilisation coefficients of its open hearths showed an annual average increase of 34 per cent. during the First Five-Year Plan.[7] Tayeh's ingot steel output was boosted chiefly by the four large open hearths and four electric

[6] No. 2 steel plant was rehabilitated between November 1954 and December 1956.
[7] Computed on the basis of data given in *Kang-tieh (Metallurgy)*, Semi-monthly, Peking, No. 18, 1959, p. 806.

furnaces moved there from Dairen in 1955, in addition to the new open hearth built in 1954.

The share of the North-east in the country's overall ingot steel output in 1957 also showed a slight increase. Chiefly responsible for this increase were the rehabilitation of open hearths Nos. 10–15 in Anshan's No. 2 steel plant and the construction of open hearths Nos. 16–19, both completed by the end of 1956. In addition, the average open-hearth coefficient of Anshan Steel rose from 5·17 in 1953 to 6·76 in 1957.[8] The more than doubling of the relative importance of the South-west in ingot steel production can be credited mainly to the rapid reconstruction of plants Nos. 101, 102 and 105 in the region. The fact that these were included among the Soviet-aid projects of the First Five-Year Plan indicates their importance. Consequently, the 1957 share of the South-west in the nation's total was more than restored to its 1945 level, in spite of its decrease in 1953. The 1957 shares of the four regions were enhanced apparently at the expense of North China, where the development of steel refining facilities during the Plan was practically confined to the relatively small steel plants at Tangshan and Tientsin.

THE EMERGING PATTERN

The location of China's steel industry in 1961 can be seen from the map, and from Table 4. Whereas the former shows the geographical distribution of the larger iron and steel producers, the table gives the percentage distribution of blast furnace capacity and ingot steel output by economic regions. Despite the different bases used, a decidedly wider dispersion was attained in 1961 through the rise of iron and steel bases in regions in which they were hitherto absent, and through a higher rate of growth in regions other than the all-important North-east. Undoubtedly all this would not have been feasible in a matter of years without the 1958 all-out steel campaign and the subsequent rise of a small-scale production front.

South China and the North-west, neither of which produced any noticeable amount of either steel or iron in 1957, have since become iron and steel producing regions. Whereas the contribution of South China to the country's overall iron-smelting capacity or steel output amounts to not much more than 2 per cent., the relative importance of the North-west has surpassed that of the South-west by a sizeable margin particularly in iron-smelting, as can be seen from Column 1 of Table 4. Behind the rising importance of the North-west was the construction, beginning in 1958, of two sizeable new iron and steel works in Sinkiang,

[8] *Chi-hua ching-chi (Planned Economy)*, No. 4, 1958, p. 22.

the Payi and the Hami. In view of the discovery in 1958 of extensive iron ore deposits in Chingtiehshan, Kansu and the subsequent
organisation of the Chiuchuan Iron and Steel Corporation comparable in
scale to Paotow Steel, the importance of the North-West is likely to
increase.

Central China's share of the overall blast furnace capacity increased
30-fold between 1957 and 1961. For this spectacular gain, while the
contribution particularly of two new iron and steel combines (the
Lienyuan in Hunan and the Anyang in Honan) should not be overlooked,
major credit was due to Wuhan Steel whose iron-smelting capacity rose
from nil in 1957 to more than 8 per cent. of the national total in 1961.

Table 4

REGIONAL DISTRIBUTION OF IRON AND STEEL
1961

Economic Region	Blast Furnace Capacity	Ingot Steel Output
	Figures in percentages	
	(1)	(2)
North-east	31·8	20·7
North	17·5	17·9
East	15·8	29·5
Central	15·6	13·3
South	2·2	2·1
North-west	13·5	9·5
South-west	3·6	7·0
Total	100·0	100·0

Prior to 1958, pig iron production in East China was more or less
confined to Maanshan, Anhwei. The blast furnace capacity of the region
was under 600 cubic metres in 1957. By 1961, it grew to above 8,000
cubic metres. Consequently, the region's share in the national total
nearly quadrupled (see Column 3 of Table 2 and Column 1 of Table 4).
Although in 1961, Anhwei remained the province with the largest blast
furnace capacity in the region, its prominence was reduced by the rise in
importance of Kiangsu and Shantung as iron-producing provinces. In
Kiangsu, for instance, Shanghai's No. 1 Iron and Steel Plant built two 255
cubic metre furnaces in 1959. In the same year, two blast furnaces of
equal size were erected in the Nanking Iron and Steel Works. Similarly
in Shantung, four blast furnaces with an aggregate capacity of 710 cubic
metres were installed in the Tsinan Iron and Steel Works in 1959. In
addition, other provinces in the region such as Kiangsi and Fukien which

had no iron-smelting facilities to speak of during the First Five-Year Plan subsequently became iron producers. For example, the Sanming Iron and Steel Works in Fukien built in 1959 two blast furnaces with an aggregate capacity of 510 cubic metres, and the Pinghsiang Iron and Steel Works in Kiangsi built in 1960 seven furnaces with a total capacity of 982 cubic metres.

The doubling of South-west China's share in the overall blast furnace capacity between 1957 and 1961 was not sufficient to elevate the region to prominence. Although it surpassed the South in terms of iron-smelting capacity available, it still lagged far behind the other regions. Within the South-west region, the rising importance of Yunnan is worth noting. Between 1958 and 1961, the Kunming Iron and Steel Corporation built four sizeable blast furnaces (Nos. 1–4). By 1961, Yunnan threatened Szechwan as the leading iron-producing province of the region, despite the expansion of capacity at the Chungking Iron and Steel Corporation.

The share of North China in the overall blast furnace capacity of the country rose from 14·4 per cent. in 1957 to 17·9 per cent. in 1961 (see Column 3 of Table 2 and Column 1 of Table 4). This comparatively small increase was attributable notably to the relatively late start of Paotow Steel [9] coupled with the cut-back in industrial capital construction in 1961. On the other hand, the rising importance of other producers in the region should not be overlooked, particularly the Lungyen Iron and Steel Corporation in Hopei and the Taiyuan Iron and Steel Corporation in Shansi, where seventeen blast furnaces with a combined capacity of 2,550 cubic metres were built between 1958 and 1961.

The substantial decline in the relative importance of the North-east as revealed in Table 4 should not conceal the absolute increase in its blast furnace capacity between 1957 and 1961. In Anshan, the 1513 cubic metre No. 10 blast furnace was completed late in 1958 in addition to 140 small furnaces with an aggregate capacity of 4,440 cubic metres. Also, two medium-sized blast furnaces were built in Tunghua, Kirin, in 1959.

The geographical centres of steel output in 1961 is shown in Column 2 of Table 4. Whereas the North-east remains the leading iron-smelting region, its lead in ingot steel production has passed on to East China. The explanation lies chiefly in the speedy rise in the share of converter steel in the overall ingot steel output, together with the concentration of open hearth steel in the North-east. The share of converter steel rose from 14·7 per cent. in 1957 to 51·9 per cent. in 1960, while as late as

---

[9] The blast furnace capacity of Paotow Steel constituted less than 4 per cent. of the 1961 national total.

1961 Anshan alone accounted for more than half of the nation's open-hearth steel output. The speedy rise in the importance of converter steel originates from the campaign for small-scale production, which more than the introduction of overall planning has hastened the locational dispersion of China's steel industry.

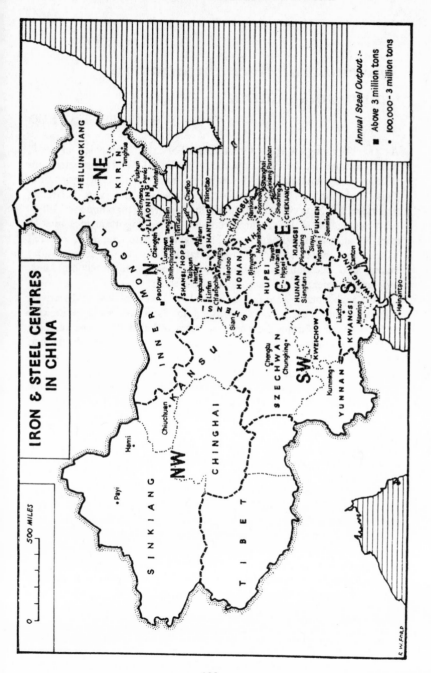

Agricultural Mechanisation in Communist China*

By LESLIE T. C. KUO

AT the beginning of the "Great Leap Forward" campaign of 1958, Mao Tse-tung declared the now much publicised "eight-character constitution of agriculture" for the technical transformation of agriculture. This "constitution" was essentially a condensed and more appealing version of the National Agricultural Development Programme for 1956–67, promulgated in 1956, which contains twelve important measures to improve agricultural production. The eight Chinese characters referred to are: *shui*, water conservation; *fei*, fertilisation; *t'u*, soil conservation; *chung*, seed selection; *mi*, dense planting; *pao*, plant protection; *kung*, tool improvement; and *kuan*, field management.

Although many accomplishments have been claimed, directives, criticisms and self-criticisms published in the Communist periodicals and newspapers during the past few years revealed that none of these eight major measures had actually progressed as successfully as had been expected. The Chinese authorities have blamed the natural calamities, particularly floods, drought and pests, as the sole factor for the three consecutive years of crop failure. But it is apparent that the failure should also be attributed to the mis-management of practically all aspects in Mao's "agricultural constitution," as well as the indifference, discontented mood and lack of incentive to work on the part of the peasants under the commune system. This perhaps can best be illustrated by the situation of agricultural machinery and implements, or *kung* in Mao's "constitution."

For centuries before the Communist régime, Chinese peasants had used ploughs, spades, hoes, picks, sickles, rakes and other small and medium-sized implements for their farming. These tools were designed according to climate, soil, topography and other local conditions and were the products of the long evolution of primitive farming. The general policy at the outset of the Communist régime was to develop and improve these farm implements and to move gradually toward mechanisation. During the "economic recovery period" (1949–52), efforts were

* This article is based on a study of the technical transformation of agriculture in Communist China, which I have conducted under the sponsorship of the Joint Committee on Contemporary China, the Social Science Research Council and the American Council of Learned Societies, New York.

made to increase the supplies of old-fashioned implements and to popularise some new implements through demonstrations. According to the Communist account, more than 59 million units of old-fashioned implements were added, and more than two million small farm tools were issued free of charge in minority regions in an attempt to ease the general shortage. In the dry plains of Northeast and North China, some new types of animal-drawn implements, including ploughs, sowers, harvesters and threshers, were demonstrated and popularised with the farmers through the combined methods of lease, lending, and sale by the local agrotechnical stations and by the experimental farm implement stations in North China.

During the First Five-Year Plan period (1953–57), many innovations of farm implements were developed as a first step toward semi-mechanisation. Some 5,110,000 improved and modern farm implements for ploughing, tilling, raking, pressing, sowing, harvesting and threshing purposes were made available to farmers. The principal items were ploughs, including 3,200,000 old-fashioned ploughs, improved ploughs, double-wheel-double-share ploughs and double-wheel-single-share ploughs. Also, during this period, 390 tractor stations were set up on an experimental basis, with a total of more than 12,000 standard tractors (15 h.p. per unit), which were said to be able to serve approximately 27 million *mou* (4,500,000 acres) of land, or one tractor for an average of 375 acres.[1]

As in other aspects of the " Great Leap Forward," the policy of " walking on two legs " was adopted in the Chinese Communists' efforts to improve agricultural tools. This means modern mechanisation of farming simultaneous with the improvement and innovation of native tools and implements. The Chinese Communists believe that by using the combined methods of old and new, native and foreign, scientific and primitive, mechanical and manual, the motive power for agricultural production can be increased at a higher speed.

MECHANISATION OF FARMING

Although the Chinese Communists realise that agriculture in China can only be mechanised gradually in view of limited industrial capacity and raw materials, nation-wide farm mechanisation has been one of the great benefits which the new régime has promised to bring to the peasants from the outset. It was first emphasised during the land reform in 1951–52 and again during the co-operativisation of agriculture in 1955–56. The number of tractors is said to have increased from 401 in

---

[1] " Gradual Realisation of Agricultural Mechanisation Through Tool Innovation," by Li Ching-yü, Director of the Agricultural Machinery Administration, the Ministry of Agriculture, *Nung-yeh Chi-hsieh (Agricultural Machinery)*, No. 18, 1959, pp. 1–5.

1949 to 24,629 in 1957.[2] But it was not until the launching of the " Great Leap Forward " campaign and the establishment of the communes in 1958 that an ambitious programme of agricultural mechanisation was mapped out. In order to expedite farm mechanisation, the State Council set up the Ministry of Agricultural Machine-building Industry in August 1959. The first big tractor plant went into full production in November 1959 at Loyang, Honan Province. It was built with technical aid from the Soviet Union and is estimated to have an annual capacity of 15,000 54-h.p. tractors. Several other tractor plants have since been added in Tientsin, Nanchang, Changchun, Anshan and Shenyang. Also a number of other agricultural machinery factories have been established or expanded.

According to Ch'en Cheng-jen, Minister of Agricultural Machine-building Industry, the general aim was to enable agriculture, forestry, animal husbandry, fishery and side occupations to advance gradually toward over-all mechanisation and electrification within about ten years. Owing to insufficient production of machinery, however, primary attention would be given to agriculture and animal husbandry during the first four years, striving first to mechanise a small part of agricultural and pastoral production and the fundamental portion of farmland irrigation. During this period emphasis would be placed on the suburbs of the big cities, the centres of grain production, of other economic crops and of pastoral farming. Ch'en estimated that the supply of farm machinery would be adequate for over half the task to be completed in seven years and finished in ten years.[3]

The actual progress of agricultural mechanisation since the beginning of the " Great Leap Forward " campaign, as disclosed by the Chinese Communist authorities, may be summarised as follows:

TRACTORS

Of the 45,330 tractors in operation in 1958, 957 were produced in China for the first time. Production figures for more recent years are not available, but it is claimed that the country now is manufacturing many types of tractors, including heavy and medium caterpillar tractors for large-scale land reclamation and contouring, medium-sized wheeled tractors for ordinary field work, light tractors for garden-type cultivation, and tractors specially designed for rice paddies. Emphasis has been given to the production of multi-purpose models and to that of large models, in view of the deep ploughing programme.

2 *Wei-ta ti Shih-nien* (*The Great Ten Years*) (Peking: State Statistical Bureau, 1959), p. 120.
3 " Speed Up Technical Transformation of Agriculture," by Ch'en Cheng-jen, *Red Flag* (*Hung Ch'i*), No. 4, 1960, pp. 4–10.

AGRICULTURAL MECHANISATION IN COMMUNIST CHINA

	1958[a]	1959[b]	1961[c]	1962[d]
Agricultural machinery in operation				
Tractors	45,330 units	59,000 units	99,000 units	100,000 units
Harvester-combines	3,452 units	4,900 units	—	—
Motor threshers	5,516 units	7,500 units	—	—
Irrigation & drainage equipment	1,600,000 h.p.	3,380,000 h.p.	6,680,000 h.p.	—
Other major mechanised agricultural implements	80,000 units	100,000 units	174,000 units	—
Total mechanical power in rural areas	—	5,200,000 h.p.	—	—
Percentage of cultivated land on which mechanised farming was practised	—	4–5%	—	"less than 10%"
Percentage of irrigated area that was irrigated mechanically	—	10%	—	—
Percentage of land under mechanised irrigation and drainage as of the total land that needs mechanised irrigation and drainage	—	20%	—	—

137

[a] The 1958 figure for tractors is from p. 120, *Wei-ta ti Shih-nien (The Great Ten Years)*; all other 1958 figures from " Gradual Realization of Agricultural Mechanisation Through Tool Innovation," by Li Ching-yü, *op. cit.*

[b] From " Speed Up the Technical Transformation of Agriculture," by Ch'en Cheng-jen, Minister of Agricultural Machine-building Industry, *op. cit.*

[c] Figures based on " Produce Suitable Agricultural Machinery to Support Agriculture," by Chang Feng-shih, Vice-Minister of Agricultural Machine-building Industry, *Kung-jen Jih-pao (Daily Worker)*, January 18, 1962, p. 1.

[d] *People's Daily*, editorial, November 9, 1962, pp. 1–2.

The most popular domestic-made models are "Tungfanghung" (East Is Red), "Hungch'i" (Red Flag), "T'iehniu" (Iron Ox) and "Fengshou" (Bumper Harvest). The "Tungfanghung-54" caterpillar-track tractor, produced by the Loyang No. 1 Tractor Plant, can be operated to carry out singly or simultaneously such farm jobs as ploughing and harrowing of land, sowing of seeds, harvesting of crops, and compacting of the soil. Under general soil conditions, the tractor is said to be able to plough the land to a depth of up to 18 centimetres (7 inches) and to plough 80 *mou* (13 acres) of land in ten hours. With attachments it can be used for moving earth, towing native-made machines, building reservoirs or other construction work. Equipped with transmission belts the tractor can be used for such fixed jobs as grinding flour, threshing, watering, and generating power.

The "T'iehniu-40" wheeled tractor is produced by the Tientsin Tractor Plant. Equipped with such farm tools as three-blade ploughs, dragging ploughs and rakes, it can be used for ploughing and harrowing land. The tractor can also be used for sowing seeds and pulling combine-harvesters for reaping paddy crops. It can be operated to plough 50 to 60 *mou* (8 to 10 acres) of land in a shift of ten work-hours. It can plough to a maximum depth of 27 centimetres (10·6 inches). The tractor can also be used for transport and for operating various kinds of agricultural machines for fixed jobs.

The "Hungch'i-80" caterpillar tractor, manufactured by the Anshan Tractor Plant, weighs eleven tons with a tow capacity of nine tons. Using two five-claw cultivators, the tractor can clear 12 *mou* (2·0 acres) of uncultivated land in one hour. The "Fengshou-6" all-purpose small model tractor, produced by the Hangchow Tractor Plant, has a capacity of tilling 1·5 *mou* (0·25 acres) of land per hour. It is designed for the use on both paddies and fields. With appropriate attachments, it can also be used for processing grains.

Among the many models of imported tractors used in various provinces are the "Stalin-80" and "DT-54" heavy-duty caterpillar-track tractors from the Soviet Union, the "Zetor-25" wheeled tractors from Czechoslovakia, the "DK-35" medium caterpillar-track tractors from Rumania, and the "DT-413" heavy-duty caterpillar-track tractors from Hungary.[4]

The number of tractors is said to have increased rapidly from 24,629 in 1957 to 45,330 in 1958, or an increase of 84 per cent. and from less than 1,000 in 1949 to 100,000 in 1962, or about 100 times, as a result of the "Great Leap Forward" campaign. This increase was, however, far from being sufficient to meet the current needs. As the *People's Daily*

---

[4] "A Brief Explanation of Tractors Generally Used in Kwangtung Province," *Nan-fang Daily*, Canton, April 29, 1962, p. 1.

pointed out, on the basis of one tractor for 1,500 *mou* (250 acres), more than one million tractors, as against the present 100,000, would be required for the mechanisation of the estimated 1·6 billion *mou* (267,000,000 acres) of farmland in China.[5]

The low degree of mechanisation was further indicated by the fact that by the end of 1960, only 5 per cent. of the cultivated land of the country was cultivated with machines (the target for that year was 6·9 per cent.), 15 per cent. with semi-mechanisation, and 80 per cent. with improved small implements.[6]

Toward the end of 1962, the area farmed by tractors still accounted for less than 10 per cent. of the cultivated land.[7] Mechanisation materialised primarily on the state farms, which produce mainly for exports; and some large communes used a few tractors and other agricultural machines. In Heilungkiang Province, where many state farms are located, 20 per cent. of the cultivated land was cultivated in 1960 by machines and more than 30 per cent. by modern animal-drawn implements.[8] Among other areas where the acreage of mechanised farming makes up an important portion of the total area of cultivated land are Hopei and Shantung provinces, Sinkiang Autonomous Region and the suburbs of Peking and Shanghai.

How many of the reported 100,000 tractors in operation in 1962 were domestically manufactured has not been revealed. Domestic production of tractors and other agricultural machines since 1958 has apparently been handicapped by the shortage of raw materials, particularly steel. The few centres of the steel industry have been experimenting with new products suitable for agricultural machinery, but the amount is not commensurate with the needs of the country. Certain types of steel products and essential parts of agricultural machinery cannot be produced in China and have therefore to be imported. The " East Is Red " tractor, for example, consists of some 10,000 parts requiring more than 450 kinds of metal. When the tractor was first manufactured in 1959, most of these metals were imported. The variety of metals produced domestically has increased during the past two or three years. But even in 1962, there were still more than thirty kinds of metal needed for making farm machinery, which China could not produce or could produce only in small quantities. Furthermore, the quality of some of the metals and parts produced in China was below the required standard.[9]

[5] *People's Daily*, editorial, November 9, 1962, pp. 1–2.
[6] *People's Daily*, April 11, 1960, p. 3; October 28, 1960, p. 4.
[7] *People's Daily*, editorial, November 9, 1962, pp. 1–2.
[8] *People's Daily*, October 27, 1960, p. 1.
[9] *People's Daily*, January 7, 1962, p. 1.

Aside from the lagging production, there are other serious problems that have handicapped the mechanisation of agriculture. Tractors were first managed by the State-operated tractor stations, but many of them have been turned over to the communes since 1958. Despite the claimed advantages, management under the communes has been far from satisfactory. The depreciation rate and maintenance costs have been high, partly because of "the lack of the sense of political responsibility to take good care of tractors on the part of drivers." In 1961, about 20 per cent. of tractors and 20–30 per cent. of irrigation machines needed repair. And yet, there were no repair networks, nor sufficient spare parts. Also, many tractors were without machine-drawn farm tools; and irrigation and drainage machines without pipes and pumps. Moreover, operators and maintenance personnel of tractors and other farm machines generally had undergone only a very short period of technical training.[10]

The use of a great variety of agricultural machines has created additional technical problems. A visitor to the six production brigades in Shulu *hsien*, Hopei Province, found that as many as eight models of motors of different horsepower and consuming different fuels (natural gas, gasoline and so on) were used for various agricultural machines. And in the Ningpo District, Chekiang Province, more than forty types of internal combustion machines were used for drainage and irrigation. This situation made it difficult for the technicians to handle the machines, because most of them had had only limited technical training. It also created the problem of getting an adequate supply of all kinds of fuel and accessories.[11]

Another technical problem is that farm land in many areas still does not meet the conditions required for mechanised farming. In Pingku *hsien* of the Municipality of Peking, for example, the local authorities instructed in 1962 that land of less than ten *mou* (1·7 acres) or of less than 165 yards in length should not be cultivated with caterpillar tractors; and that land of less than five *mou* (0·85 acre) or less than 110 yards in length should not be cultivated with wheeled tractors. Under these instructions, there is very little land suitable for mechanical cultivation. Moreover, even after the agricultural collectivisation, many pieces of land still have not been properly adjusted to make them suitable for mechanisation. Within each piece of land, there are abandoned wells and ditches not yet flattened or boundary stones not yet removed. Also, on some pieces of land, irrigation canals are not well located, sometimes dividing the land into a number of small fragments so that mechanisation of farming can hardly be carried out. Finally, some roads, bridges and

---

[10] "Current Problems in Agricultural Mechanisation," by Chao Hsüeh, *Ta Kung Pao*, May 15, 1961, p. 3.   [11] *People's Daily*, December 18, 1962, p. 2.

tunnels between the farms are not wide or strong enough for the passage of large farm machines, and sometimes detours have to be made to get to one place from another.[12]

Despite the slow progress, even toward the end of 1960, the *People's Daily* still maintained that modernisation of small agricultural implements would be solved in four years beginning 1959, that of medium-sized implements in seven years, and complete agricultural mechanisation in ten years.[18] It was not until the beginning of 1962, after three consecutive years of bad harvest, that the failure of agricultural mechanisation was admitted. As revealed by Chang Feng-shih, Vice-Minister of Agricultural Machinery, " In the two years of 1960 and 1961, the agricultural machinery industry has supplied agriculture with 40,000 standard tractors, 37,000 motor-powered ploughs, 37,000 motor-powered harrows, 3,300,000 horsepower of agricultural irrigation equipment, 150,000 rubber-wheel animal-drawn carts, 11,500,000 rubber-wheel hand carts, 800,000,000 small agricultural tools and many other semi-mechanised agricultural tools. But these are far from satisfying the agricultural needs. Furthermore, the quality of certain products is not high, they are not properly co-ordinated, and their supply is not in time." [14]

ELECTRIFICATION

A special mention should be made of one aspect of agricultural mechanisation, namely, electrification, because it has frequently been publicised by the Chinese Communists as an important measure to transform the country's agriculture. The " walking on two legs " policy calls for the establishment of large modern electric power plants under the auspices of the central and provincial governments simultaneous with the construction of small plants by the communes.

A national conference held in 1958 recommended, however, that emphasis be given to the construction of small hydro-electric plants, each with a generating capacity of not more than 50 kilowatts. It was suggested that such power plants would require no specialised technique, equipment and scarce material. At the end of 1958, there were 4,878 rural hydro-electric power plants in the country with a total capacity of 151,826 kilowatts, or an average capacity of 31 kilowatts. Of these plants, 4,334 with a total capacity of 131,502 kilowatts, were built in 1958, the first " leap forward " year. Like the numerous primitive blast furnaces constructed during that year for steel production, many of these

---

[12] *People's Daily*, December 8, 1962, p. 2.
[18] *People's Daily*, November 5, 1960, p. 7.
[14] " Produce Suitable Agricultural Machinery to Support Agriculture," by Chang Feng-shih, *Daily Worker*, January 18, 1962, p. 1; translated in JPRS 12909, March 9, 1962, pp. 1–13.

LESLIE T. C. KUO

small plants were ineffective. Some of them were constructed with only one water turbine, mostly made of wood, and had a generating capacity of as small as three or four kilowatts each. The larger hydro-electric power plants, though in general more effective, had to cease operation during the low water seasons.

The development of rural hydro-electric plants after 1958 has been even less successful. In the first half of 1959, the total capacity of such plants was increased by only something over 30,000 kilowatts. The shortage of technical personnel and equipment was reported to be the major cause of the slow progress.[15] It probably also was due to the ineffectiveness of the small plants constructed in 1958. The development has also been handicapped by the high cost of construction. Moreover, there is a lack of over-all planning and of accurate data needed for planning. Only in some isolated regions have surveys of hydraulic resources been conducted.

A number of larger hydro-electric plants have been constructed in connection with the projects for multiple purposes—flood control, electric and water supply for industrial, domestic as well as agricultural uses. These plants are in general considerably more efficient and economical than the small hydro-electric plants.[16]

Only a small number of thermal electric power plants have been constructed. Their total number at the end of 1958 was 2,112. One of the major problems here is that most of the equipment and tools used are more complicated and have to be imported, while those for hydro-electric plants can be partly manufactured in China. Another difficulty is the shortage of coal, caused by the great demand in other industries and by inadequate transportation.

Besides the hydro-electric plants and the thermal electric plants, another major source of electric supply in rural China is the transformer substations of big electric power stations in urban and suburban areas. Power transmission lines, however, are still poorly developed, partly because of the shortage of metals and cement. Electric power networks of 35-, 10-, 6·6-, and 3·3-kilovolt transmission lines are the most common ones, but even these networks are rather scarce. The slow development of power transmission lines is a handicap to the development of reasonably large rural power plants.

Electric power is used in rural China primarily for the processing of agricultural products, especially rice husking and flour grinding, for the preparation of fertilisers and animal feed, and for illumination. The use of electricity for irrigation and drainage is increasing, but still not widespread. The total area of land irrigated by electricity now amounts

15 *People's Daily*, January 26, 1960, p. 7.
16 *Shui-li Fa-tien (Hydroelectrics)*, No. 12, 1958, p. 54.

to approximately 10,000,000 *mou* (1,700,000 acres), or about 1 per cent. of the total area irrigated by all means. Most of the electrically irrigated farms are located in the areas producing rice, wheat, cotton and vegetables.

Electric power has also been used on an experimental basis in the cultivation of land with a new type of plough operated by rope traction. It is claimed that compared with tractors, the " electric ploughs " have the advantages of lower cost of manufacturing, less steel required, higher efficiency of operation, especially on paddy fields, and being able to be operated with human and animal power, wind as well as electricity.[17] But so far no definite success has been revealed.

The use of tide, wind, marsh gas and other sources of natural energy began to be gradually popularised in July 1958. Special attention has been given to the transformation of tidal energy into electricity for agricultural uses. It is maintained that with a total coastal line of more than 11,000 kilometres (6,830 miles), China has the possibility of developing a tremendous amount of tidal energy. As an experiment, several small tidal electric power stations have been built along the seacoast with capacities ranging from 15 to 250 kilowatts. Preliminary results indicate that although the construction of tidal electric stations is less expensive than that of the ordinary hydro-electric plants, tidal energy is not dependable because of the wide fluctuations of the tide.[18]

IMPROVEMENT OF OLD-TYPE IMPLEMENTS

Meanwhile, the programme for the improvement and innovation of medium-sized and small old-fashioned agricultural implements has proceeded just as unsatisfactorily as that for the mechanisation of farms. The chaotic state in handling these tools existed even before the " leap forward " campaign. In 1956, for example, it was planned to popularise and use some 6 million double-wheel-double-share ploughs and double-wheel-single-share ploughs throughout the country within three to five years. Both types were animal-drawn and regarded as suitable for cultivating sandy or light clay soils, and the single-share type was also regarded as being suitable for reclaiming wasteland.[19]

17 " Energetically Popularise Rope Traction Machines," *Nung-yeh Chi-hsieh* (*Agricultural Machinery*) editorial, No. 7, 1958, p. 1; " A Rapid Way Towards the Mechanisation and Electrification of Cultivation," *People's Daily*, editorial, September 12, 1958, p. 1; *Nung-yeh K'o-hsueh T'ung-hsun* (*Agriculture Science Bulletin*), No. 10, 1958, pp. 518-520.

18 Report by Chang Han-ying, Vice-Minister of Water Conservation and Electricity, to the National Conference on the Transformation of Tidal Energy into Electricity held in Shanghai in October 1958, *Shui-li Shui-tien Chien-she* (*Water Conservation and Hydroelectric Construction*), No. 2, 1958, pp. 3-5.

19 " How to Use Double-wheel-double-share Ploughs and Double-wheel-single-share Ploughs," by Ni Ts'ai-wang, *Sheng-wu hsueh T'ung-pao* (*Biological Bulletin*), September 1956, pp. 65-68.

This plan was, however, almost a complete failure. The ploughs were mainly copies of ploughs used in the broad, flat wheat lands of the Soviet Union and were unsuited to China's terraced and small farm plots. Many farmers complained that the ploughs were too heavy, their farm animals were too few and too weak to pull the ploughs, and that they had no means of repairing them even if they had been able to use them successfully. In South China, farmers complained that the rice paddies were too small and too muddy for the ploughs. Consequently, the plan was revised to include only 3,500,000 ploughs, and finally only 100,000 to 150,000 were distributed to farmers.[20] Another report reveals that in 1957 only 72,000 double-wheel-double-share ploughs were distributed to farmers and 800,000 were left idle, and that many of those distributed were later returned or destroyed by farmers.[21]

A further effort was made at the beginning of the " leap forward " campaign in 1958 to popularise the double-wheel-double-share ploughs in areas other than the rice fields of South China.[22] It was also reported that a modified type, which eliminated the drawbacks of the original type, had been designed by the Chekiang Agricultural Research Institute in Hangchow, and was personally tried by Mao Tse-tung during his visit to the institute in January 1958.[23]

Besides ploughs, many other farm tools and implements were reported to have been developed or innovated by the masses during the three years of " leap forward " for use in water conservation, manure accumulation, transport, irrigation, drainage, tilling, processing of farm products and other purposes.[24] But many of these tools and implements were lost, wasted or destroyed, partly because of the over-emphasis on the mechanisation. " They were left scattered in the open air in the field where rains and winds ruined them." [25]

It was not until the latter part of 1960 that the responsibilities toward farm tools and implements were clearly defined for the commune and its components (the large production brigade, the small production brigade, and the individual commune member). After the country had suffered two consecutive years of bad harvest, the policy of " taking agriculture as the foundation of the national economy " was

20 " Why the Demand and Production of Double-wheel-double-share Ploughs Have Stopped?", by the Editor, *Chi-hua Ching-chi (Planned Economy)*, No. 9, 1956, pp. 1–4.
21 " Raise the Effectiveness of the Double-wheel-double-share Ploughs," *People's Daily*, editorial, April 16, 1958, p. 1; *Hsin-Hua Pan-yueh K'an (New China Semi-monthly)*, No. 9, 1958, pp. 86–88.
22 " Ten Years of Great Accomplishment and Experience in Farm Machinery Work in China," *Nung-yeh Chi-hsieh (Agricultural Machinery)*, No. 18, 1959, pp. 10–14.
23 *K'o-hsueh T'ung-hsun (Science Bulletin)*, No. 2, 1958, pp. 62–63.
24 " Gradual Realisation of Agricultural Mechanisation Through Tool Innovation," by Li Ching-yü, *Nung-yeh Chi-hsieh (Agricultural Machinery)*, No. 18, 1959, pp. 1–5.
25 *People's Daily*, editorial, November 15, 1960, p. 1.

adopted. A movement was started in August 1960 to send all available hands to the fields and all available land was to be devoted to grain production. These people should not of course go to the fields empty-handed, and the importance of medium-sized and small tools and implements was again emphasised.[26]

Under the new directives, medium-sized implements, such as ploughs, harrows, weeding discs, water wheels, carts, fertiliser dispensers, threshers, and so on, should be under the care of the commune or of the large or small production brigade using them. A shed should be built to store them. A commune member " known for his high consciousness and his zeal for common property " should be appointed guard, and he should also inspect these implements and see that they are repaired in good time. Individual commune members are responsible for the care and use of small implements (spades, hoes, picks, sickles and so on).[27] In all cases, a pressing duty should be " the education of the masses toward love of the common property." [28]

It was further admitted that the mere care of the existing implements would not be enough for the millions who had been urged to take part in agricultural production. There was an urgent need for the manufacture of new implements as well as the repair of old ones. Survey reports from a number of communes revealed almost uniformly that the shortage of farm implements was felt very seriously.[29]

But the manufacturing and repair were impeded by an acute shortage of steel and other necessary materials. Although it was reported that in 1962 the state allocated and made arrangements for the delivery of some 2 million cubic metres of lumber and " corresponding quantities " of rolled steel, copper and hemp to various localities for the repair, maintenance and manufacturing of farm implements, many *hsien* (counties) had to obtain much of the materials locally, had to use various kinds of substitutes, and had to collect scrap iron, pieces of wood, split bamboo, nails and screws. The process of casting, instead of forging, had to be adopted for making implements and spare parts, because the " native " iron cannot be forged. The use of cheap native iron and steel has resulted in the breakdown and deterioration of millions of implements produced or repaired in innumerable improvised small factories.[30]

DRAFT ANIMALS

Many medium-sized farm implements depend on draft animals as a principal source of power for operation. Even in some areas with a

[26] *People's Daily*, December 26, 1960, p. 3.
[27] *People's Daily*, November 18, 1960, p. 3.
[28] *People's Daily*, December 2, 1960, p. 2.
[29] *People's Daily*, November 16, 1960, p. 1; November 18, 1960,
[30] *People's Daily*, December 29, 1960, p. 2

higher degree of mechanisation, draft animals are needed because of the particular types of farming and because of the limitations of climatic and soil conditions. The cultivated land of Heilungkiang, for example, is composed of black, yellowish black and light salty soil, which is sticky

DRAFT ANIMALS IN COMMUNIST CHINA
1949 and 1952–59

Unit: 1,000 head

Year	Cattle	Horses	Donkeys	Mules	Total
1949	43,936	4,874	9,494	1,471	59,775
1952	56,600	6,130	11,806	1,637	76,173
1953	60,083	6,512	12,215	1,645	80,455
1954	63,623	6,939	12,700	1,717	84,979
1955	65,951	7,312	12,402	1,723	87,388
1956	66,601	7,372	11,686	1,711	87,370
1957	65,860	7,510	10,900	1,840	86,110
1958	64,952	7,512	10,601	1,624	84,689
1959	—	—	—	—	85,400

Sources:

Figures for 1949 and 1958 are from "Accomplishments in Animal Husbandry in the Past Decade," by Ts'ai Tzu-wei, Vice-minister of Agriculture, *Chung-kuo Hsu-mu-hsueh Tsa-chih (Chinese Animal Husbandry Magazine)*. Peking, No. 10, 1959, pp. 289–293.

Figures for 1952–1957 are from *Development of the Economy and Foreign Economic Contacts of the People's Republic of China*, by Yu N. Kapelinskiy and others, 1959, p. 311, translated from Russian by the United States Joint Publications Research Service, Washington, D.C.

Total figure for 1959 is from the *People's Daily*, January 26, 1960, p. 3. Breakdown figures for various animals for that year are not available.

and with a comparatively low speed of evaporation. After a downpour, tractors are of no use, and certain kinds of farming would be impossible without draft animals. A combined use of machines, horses, and oxen will remain therefore essential to agricultural production.[31]

As shown in the accompanying table, the increase in the number of draft animals in Communist China since 1949 has not been impressive. In fact, from 1955 to 1958 the number decreased steadily while agricultural work in the fields was intensified. There were several causes for the slow increase or even decrease of the animals. First, many animals weakened or died because of overwork, sometimes under excessive heat or cold. Draft animals were used in China traditionally for irrigation, for turning the primitive village mills and for local transport. Their functions increased tremendously during the " leap forward " years

[31] " Positively Develop Draft Animals and Accelerate Agricultural Production," by Yang I-ch'eng, *People's Daily*, May 9, 1961, p. 7.

when the deep-ploughing practice was introduced. It was not until the summer of 1960, however, that orders were issued by several provincial authorities for the strengthening of draft animals. In Heilungkiang, a directive was issued that animals should be granted some rest and that females during gestation should be exempted from work for one month.[32]

Another factor was the absence of incentive among the herdsmen and those in charge of animals in the co-operatives or communes because of low wages. Cases of purposed neglect and secret slaughters have been reported in some areas. Under the communes there were practically no systems of care, which did exist at the time of agricultural producers' co-operatives, and the men in charge of animals were paid uniformly whether the work was well or badly done. The need to reintroduce a regular system of management was emphasised at the end of 1960, and it was urged that the small brigades and the persons in charge of animals must get a premium if they do their work well.[33] Beginning the spring of 1961, the care of animals and their mating was given over to the large production brigades or the small production brigades, and the payment to the persons in charge of animals was readjusted.[34]

The shortage of fodder has been another cause for the failure in improving the situation of draft animals. An improvement in the feeding of livestock and in the related problems of management is a prerequisite to any substantial livestock improvement programme through breeding. And yet, draft animals in China have been fed primarily on roughage and received only limited amounts of concentrates, although the Chinese Communists have made efforts to improve the feeding of farm animals. It is reported that, up to the end of 1958, the chemical composition of 1,032 kinds of feed from different parts of the country had been analysed. Of these, 581 are green feeds, many of which grow wild and have a fairly high nutritive value. Studies have also been made of methods of expanding the cultivation in various parts of the country of certain high quality feeds.[35]

Studies have reportedly been made on the use of certain industrial and agricultural by-products for feeding of animals. An extensive study of the grazing lands in Sinkiang and Inner Mongolia, and experimental studies of the seeding of grasslands in the cold areas above 3,000 metres elevation are also said to have been undertaken. It was reported that toward the end of 1962, more than twenty improved varieties of fodder

[32] *People's Daily*, July 28, 1960, p. 2; March 27, 1961, p. 2.

[33] *People's Daily*, editorial, December 23, 1960, p. 1.

[34] *People's Daily*, April 12, 1961, p. 3.

[35] " Accomplishments of Animal Husbandry in the Past Decade," by Ts'ai Tzu-wei, Vice-minister of Agriculture; and " A Brief Account of the Accomplishments of Scientific Research in Animal Husbandry in the Past Decade," by Hsu Chi, Deputy Director of the Animal Husbandry Research Institute, *Chung-kuo Hsu-mu-hsueh Tsa-chih* (*China Animal Husbandry Magazine*), No. 10, 1959, pp. 289–294.

and some measures for preventing the deterioration of grazing land had been developed by technical workers in Inner Mongolia.[36]

Despite all these efforts, the supply of fodder has remained insufficient. The situation has been worsened by the three consecutive years of natural calamities, which caused draft animals to be badly underfed.

Finally, the breeding of draft animals was adversely affected by the shortage of technical personnel and necessary instruments. A directive on the promotion of mating of big animals issued in February 1959 by the central government indicated that there were 27 million head of female animals at the right age of propagation, of which 15 million were in pregnancy. In order to increase the number of big animals by 10 per cent. by the end of 1959, artificial insemination was encouraged, but there were not enough trained technicians and necessary instruments for this task.[37] The shortage of veterinarians remained very acute in 1962 and 1963, and the strengthening of the veterinary centres throughout the country was urged.[38]

THE PROSPECTS

Thus, after more than a decade of strenuous efforts, the general situation of farm implements, or *kung* in Mao Tse-tung's " Eight-character constitution of agriculture," has deteriorated rather than improved. Neither of the " two legs "—mechanisation of farming and the innovation of old-fashioned implements—has walked satisfactorily. The problem had become so serious that a series of emergency measures were taken in 1962. The first national conference for the scientific discussion on agricultural machinery was held in Peking for three weeks in June and July, attended by Vice-premier Teng Tzu-hui; Han Kuang, Vice-chairman of the State Science and Technology Commission; Ch'en Cheng-jen and Chang Feng-shih, Minister and Vice-minister of Agricultural Machinery, respectively; and others. This was followed by the establishment of the Chinese Academy of Agricultural Mechanisation in Peking on July 16, 1962.[39]

The most important step taken was a thorough discussion on the problem of agricultural mechanisation at the Tenth Plenary Session of the Eighth Central Committee of the Chinese Communist Party held in November 1962. It was realised at the meeting that the " arduous and complicated " task of mechanisation of agriculture would require a period of twenty to twenty-five years, rather than ten years as originally planned, and that semi-mechanised and improved farm tools would

---

[36] *Kuang-ming Daily*, December 2, 1962, p. 1.
[37] *People's Daily*, February 23, 1959, p. 1.
[38] *People's Daily*, November 17, 1962, p. 2; and editorial, February 17, 1963, p. 2.
[39] *Nung-yeh Chi-hsieh Chi-shu (Agricultural Machinery Technology)*, No. 5, 1962, pp. 2–3.

remain in a very important position for a long time to come.[40] In a full-page article in the *People's Daily* by a veteran Party member, it was suggested that agricultural mechanisation in different regions of the country should not be carried out at a uniform speed, but should be based on the prevailing crops and other local conditions.[41]

Although this revised plan is much less ambitious than the original one, whether or not it could be carried out according to schedule remains to be seen. The shortage of technical personnel, steel and other raw materials and the somewhat improved but still inefficient management under the communes will undoubtedly continue to give the Chinese Communists difficulties in their production and maintenance of agricultural machinery and tools.

In connection with the supply of production materials, the government has repeatedly ordered that industry above all must satisfy the needs of technical innovation of agriculture. In 1962, according to an article in the *Ta Kung Pao*, industry's aid to agriculture improved not only in quantity but also in variety and quality. For example, from January to August of that year, steel industry experimented successfully with 119 new types of steel, half of which were destined for agriculture and light industry, and 40 types for agricultural machinery alone. Also, 330,000 tons more of chemical fertiliser, 2,900 tons more of 666 DDT and other principal types of insecticides were produced in the first eight months of 1962 than in the corresponding period of 1961.

Despite the increased industrial aid to agriculture, however, says the author, the supply of production materials is far below the need of the " big collective rural market." The country needs 1,000,000 tractors for the land suitable for mechanical cultivation instead of 100,000 tractors as available at present; tens of million horsepower of machines for irrigation and drainage, as compared to several million horsepower; and more than one hundred *chin* (catties) of chemical fertiliser for each *mou* of cultivated land each year rather than the present three or four *chin*.[42]

The programme of intensive industrial aid to agriculture, however, involves many serious economic problems. First, it is an extra burden added to the already heavy tasks of industry. Steel, for example, is badly needed in many fields, including agricultural machinery. Then, there is the question of to what extent industry can change its objectives and its structure without suffering financial loss and reducing

40 *People's Daily*, editorial, " Actively and Systematically Bring About the Technical Transformation of Our Country's Agriculture," November 9, 1962, p. 1.
41 " Certain Problems of Agricultural Mechanisation," by Hsiang Nan, *People's Daily*, December 22, 1962, p. 5.
42 " Heavy Industry Should Make Agriculture Its Important Market," by Liu Jih-hsin, *Ta Kung Pao*, January 7, 1963, p. 3.

production efficiency. This leads to another question: even with the readjustment, how much agricultural machinery can actually be produced?

In the meanwhile, how much mechanisation will agriculture be able to absorb profitably? Is there really a " big collective rural market " for an expanded production of agricultural machinery? It is generally believed that economic and social conditions in Communist China will probably remain immature for a nationwide agricultural mechanisation for some time to come.

Handicrafts in Communist China

By PETER SCHRAN

EVEN though it is a truism, it is worth pointing out that with relatively little foreign trade and even less foreign aid, Communist China's economic growth must in the main result *directly* from the development of her indigenous resources. In her comparatively backward economy, most of those resources were to be found initially in two traditional sectors of production: in agriculture, and in various crafts and trades. Due to limited division of labour, these two traditional sectors were not separated sharply from each other, but overlapped in the person of the peasant-craftsman who was relatively common in the countryside.

To permit the growth of a modern sector of production through the initial development of a modern producer goods industry,[1] these two traditional sectors have to generate " surpluses " which will make the following three changes possible: (a) exports of consumer goods to pay for imports of producer goods for producer goods production; (b) re-allocation of labour from the traditional sectors to the expanding producer goods industry upon the absorption of unemployed labour; and (c) sustenance of the growing labour force in producer goods production with consumer goods and services. Similar statements can be made with respect to the development of any modern sector, since all of them initially require portions of the surpluses of the traditional sectors without being able at first to compensate those sectors with modern goods and services.

To generate such surpluses, various measures can be taken. Attempts can be made to increase production by increasing work efforts with given means and according to given methods of production, by improving both traditional means and traditional methods of production, and by increasing these means of production. In addition, attempts can be made to decrease consumption, at least relative to production.

All of these measures have been taken and have been studied intensively in the case of Chinese agriculture. Similar occurrences in the handicraft sector have not yet received as much attention. In my attempt to outline these developments the limitations of the data have forced me to concentrate on the years 1949–57.

---

[1] For a discussion of the rationality of such a choice see Hugh T. Patrick and Peter Schran, " Economic Contrasts: China, India, and Japan," *Journal of International Affairs*, Vol. 17, No. 2, 1963, pp. 168–184.

The Concept of Handicrafts and the Chinese Communist Theory of Developing Handicrafts [2]

In conformity with Marxist usage, the term *handicraft* (*shou-kung-yeh*) signifies to the Chinese Communists a traditional and technically out-moded method of production which combines labour with a few simple tools and implements without the aid of mechanical power. The hand-ling of the tools demands certain skills from the craftsman, but such skill requirements are not very complex in most instances. Because of their technical characteristics, handicrafts can be practised usually with small amounts of capital in small production units, but they also yield usually small amounts of output and in particular very little *surplus value*, *i.e.*, value in excess of the sustenance and replacement costs.

Traditional techniques of production are not altogether homogeneous. Although there appears to be a continuum of increasingly complex handi-craft techniques, three ranges of complexity should be distinguished for the reason that they are significant for the initial Communist system of handicraft classification.[3]

At their lowest, skill and tool requirements are so limited that there is no need even for occupational specialisation and commodity produc-tion. Instead, handicrafts can be practised as domestic subsistence activities in addition to other subsistence or commodity production. At least until 1957, peasant households in particular engaged in many so-called *subsistence activities* of this kind.

Intermediately, skill and tool requirements are sufficiently complex to warrant occupational specialisation and commodity production at least in the rudimentary form of a part-time activity (peasant-craftsman). Yet, they are still so limited that they do not lead to individual specialisa-tion within and to corresponding social division of the process of handi-craft production. A craftsman in this range usually owns his means of production and practises his craft or trade individually or familially, possibly with the help of a journeyman or apprentice. The Chinese Communists spoke of *individual handicrafts* for this reason and classified as such all handicraft establishments with less than four gainfully occupied persons, including family members.

In the higher reaches, skill and tool requirements are so complex that usually there is at least some individual specialisation within and

---

[2] For a comprehensive study of the problems of definition see C. T. Lu, *An Interim Understanding of the Concept of Handicraft as the Term is Used in Communist China*, Prepared for the First Research Conference of the Social Science Research Council Committee on the Economy of China, Berkeley, California, 1963 (mimeo-graphed manuscript).

[3] *Cf.* Chao I-wen, *Hsin Chung-kuo ti Kung-yeh* (*New China's Industry*) (Peking: T'ung-chi Publishing Co., 1957), pp. 87–99, for a discussion of these types.

some social division of the process of handicraft production. Production is organised in so-called *handicraft workshops* which require amounts of capital that are beyond the individual means of most craftsmen. Traditionally, the majority of establishments in this range were *small capitalist handicraft workshops* with at least four and less than ten gainfully occupied persons, including proprietors and their helping family members as well as craftsmen who were employed as wage labourers.

As a rule, the greater the skill and tool requirements and the correspondingly greater the degrees of individual specialisation and of social division of labour in handicraft production, the greater the value as well as the surplus value of handicraft production per craftsman. Changes from subsistence handicraft activities to individual handicrafts and to handicraft workshops result therefore in increases in the productivity of handicraft labour which in historical perspective reflect technical progress. The trend of increasing labour productivity continues with the change from handicraft workshops to industries which are distinguished by the addition of mechanical power to the process of production.

The existence of all three types of handicrafts and of industries at the same time is indicative of a state of economic backwardness which is to be overcome in an historical process of economic development on Socialist premises.[4] Different states of technical development and correspondingly different forms of social organisation of handicraft production require different patterns of technical change and correspondingly different patterns of socialist transformation. If total socialist industrialisation is the goal, the three types of handicrafts have to be transformed and developed as follows:

Capitalist handicraft workshops are already capitalist establishments and are similar in this respect to capitalist industries. They still have to be turned into industries, however. In the interest of this goal as well as of increases in the value and surplus value of production generally, all of which are served best according to doctrine by " distribution according to labour," handicraft capitalists have to be expropriated and made to depend on wage income. The Chinese Communists assert that this objective can be realised best through a gradual process of " utilising, restricting, and reconstructing " which applies to all members of the *national bourgeoisie*.

Individual craftsmen have not yet become capitalists, but technically they also have not yet reached the handicraft workshop stage. Under conditions of Communist political domination, the latter task has to be

---

4 For a summary presentation of Mao Tse-tung's rationalisation of the " new democratic revolution " or " people's democratic revolution " *cf.* Ch'en Po-ta, *Mao Tse-tung on the Chinese Revolution* (Peking: Foreign Languages Press, 1953), esp. pp. 14–30.

accomplished in non-capitalist forms. The Chinese Communists assert that it can be done best through a gradual process of collectivisation, beginning with joint tool groups, advancing to handicraft marketing co-operatives and to small handicraft groups, and ending with handicraft production co-operatives. These are then to be transformed into co-operative factories or handicraft workshops. The change turns the craftsman-co-operator into a wage labourer and thus consummates the process of transition toward the Socialist system of distribution. Co-operative handicraft workshops finally have to be developed into modern industries.

Subsistence handicraft activities of peasant households have to be eliminated in favour of individual occupational specialisation either in agriculture or in handicrafts. The Chinese Communists assert that this immediate goal can be reached best through a gradual process of agricultural collectivisation which involves peasants increasingly in agricultural work and requires increasingly comprehensive and complex handicraft activities in relation to agriculture. The rural communes, finally, bring about not only individual occupational specialisation, but also the formation of communal handicraft workshops and the introduction of Socialist wage systems. Communal handicraft workshops, too, have to be developed into modern industries eventually.

Besides serving to explain the handicraft policies of the Chinese Communists, the above statements and deductions also contribute to an understanding of their practices in classifying handicraft statistics. From the beginning, the Chinese Communists added subsistence handicrafts to agriculture and handicraft workshops to industry, thus limiting the statistical category handicrafts to individual handicrafts. During the course of Socialist transformation, the category handicrafts covered both individual and collective forms of organisation. Furthermore, only handicraft production co-operatives were listed separately in aggregate statistics as fully collectivised forms, while joint tool groups, handicraft marketing co-operatives, and small handicraft groups were still included among individual handicrafts. Finally, with the transition to co-operative handicraft workshops or "factories," the category handicrafts disappeared altogether statistically, and handicraft production cannot be separated any more from industrial production since 1958.

THE STATE OF HANDICRAFTS IN 1954

If we are to relate theory to practice first with respect to a given state of affairs, we unfortunately cannot discuss with any confidence the state of Chinese handicrafts at the time when the Chinese Communists came to power. The only comprehensive description which has become available resulted from the 1954 investigation of individual handicrafts. It also covers to some extent handicraft collectives and small capitalist handicraft workshops as well as small industrial enterprises generally. But it does not contain information on subsistence handicrafts.[5] A bare minimum of such facts can be derived from other sources, however, and we may begin our review by assembling some data on the contributions of the three forms of handicraft production to agricultural plus industrial production in 1954 (see the following tabulation). It appears that handicraft production accounted for about one quarter of the gross value and probably for about 17 per cent. of the net value of agricultural plus industrial production. On the whole, subsistence handicrafts, handicrafts, and handicraft workshops contributed similar shares to the total handicraft product.

Sector	Gross value of production Billion* yuan[b]	Per cent.	Net value of production[a] Billion yuan[b]	Per cent.
Agriculture plus hunting, fishing, and gathering	43·2[c]	41·7	33·9	61·7
Subsistence handicrafts plus preliminary processing...	8·4[e]	8·1	4·2[d]	7·7
Handicrafts	10·5[e]	10·1	3·2	5·8
Handicraft workshops	7·5[e]	7·2 ⎫	13·6	24·8
Modern industry	34·0[e]	32·9 ⎭		

* Billion = a thousand million
[a] Choh-ming Li, *Economic Development of Communist China*, (Berkeley: University of California Press, 1959), pp. 88-96.
[b] At 1952 prices.
[c] *Ching-chi Yen-chiu*, (*Economic Research*) No. 5 (1956), p. 26.
[d] Estimate based on William W. Hollister, *China's Gross National Product and Social Accounts* 1950-1957, (Glencoe: The Free Press, 1958), p. 31.
[e] Chinese Academy of Sciences, Economic Research Section, Handicrafts Group, Editor (1954-*nien Ch'üan Kuo Ko-t'i Shou-kung-yeh Tiao-ch'a Tzu-liao*) (Peking: San Lien Bookstore, 1957), p. 252.

In combination with the information that more than half of the gross value of individual handicraft production originated in the countryside (III.2), the above data demonstrate also the largely rural nature of handicraft production.

Subsistence handicrafts. In the absence of precise information on the composition of the product, its distribution by households, and its relation to rural means of handicraft production, we must limit ourselves to relating the gross value of production to the number of peasant households and to the peasant labour force. The latter can be estimated as twice the number of households. Since there were said to be 117·3

---

[5] A summary of the more relevant findings is presented in the statistical appendix. Subsequent references to tables in the appendix will be given in Roman numerals in the text.

million peasant households in 1954,[6] the average annual gross value of subsistence handicraft production plus preliminary processing was 72 yuan per household and 36 yuan per labouring peasant. The corresponding average annual net value estimates are 36 yuan and 18 yuan, at 1952 prices. Since there are various difficulties involved in estimating the value of subsistence handicraft production, these figures are not particularly reliable as estimates, but they seem to indicate the range of magnitudes which must be considered.

Handicrafts. Aggregate information on the structure of production of handicrafts is somewhat more detailed. In 1954, 91·8 per cent. of the gross value of handicraft production originated still in individual establishments and merely 3 per cent. were partly collectivised (II). Of the individual portion 57·1 per cent. was produced in the countryside, and 26·9 per cent. by peasants who engaged in handicraft *commodity* production on a part-time basis (III.2). Production was heavily concentrated in 13 out of a " thousand " trades which accounted for 48·75 per cent. of the gross value of handicraft production. Among them, the needle trades, cotton spinning, metal manufacturing, and processing of wood, bamboo, etc., were most important (III.3). Producer goods trades accounted for about 23 per cent. and consumer goods trades for about 77 per cent. of the gross value of production of individual handicrafts (III.4). Industrial producer goods dominated among the producer goods.

Aggregate information on handicraft capital and handicraft investment could not be found, and data on the number of part time craftsmen are also missing.[7] The available information permits us to infer, however, that the average annual gross value of production at 1952 prices per *full-time* craftsman amounted to 884 yuan in 1954 (II). The corresponding average annual net value can be estimated as approximately 30 per cent. of the gross value[8] or 265 yuan. Allowing for taxes, fees etc., in a roundabout fashion leaves at best 240 yuan average net earnings per annum or 20 yuan average net earnings per month. Yet, handicrafts were not at all homogeneous, and in addition to the average value, some measures of the degree of heterogeneity have to be taken into consideration. For lack of space, this review must be all too brief.

Provincial data generally reveal a fairly clear pattern of regional differentiation. The average gross value of production per gainfully occupied craftsman (VIII) appears to be related positively to the relative

---

6 Derived from State Statistical Bureau, *Ten Great Years* (Peking: Foreign Languages Press, 1960), pp. 34–35.

7 There are indications that the gross value of production of part-time craftsmen was estimated on the basis of rural trade statistics and that the number of part-time craftsmen was not ascertained in most provinces. *Cf.* Chinese Academy of Sciences, *op. cit.*, *e.g.*, p. 205.

8 *Cf.* Choh-ming Li, *op. cit.*, p. 94.

contribution of industry (including handicrafts) to the gross value of production of industry plus agriculture (IV) as well as to the degree of urban concentration of handicraft production (IX) and also to the degree of its concentration on producer goods production (X).[9] Urban-rural and inter-provincial price and cost of living differentials [10] suggest that inter-provincial differences in the average gross value of production per crafts-man were in part apparent rather than real. The pattern of deflated values (in declining order big cities, North-East, North-West, South, and Central Plains) seems to correspond to the patterns of peasant earnings [11] as well as of handicraft earnings.[12]

The magnitudes of some specific differences are fairly striking. Typically, urban craftsmen produced at least twice as much gross value as rural craftsmen (IX) who in turn produced at least twice as much as rural part-time craftsmen (VIII).[13] Differences of similar magnitude appear between the average gross values of production of (VIII) stationary and ambulatory craftsmen as well as (X) craftsmen engaged in producer goods production and consumer goods production. They can also be assumed to have existed among the various crafts and trades. So far as earnings are concerned, urban-rural and inter-craft differentials seem to be evident, and the latter seem to correspond to the pattern of inter-industry differentials.[14]

All these patterns of differentiation tend to obscure the significance of one distinction which is particularly important from the point of view of Chinese Communist theory of handicraft development: the distinction between individual and collective forms of handicraft organis-ation. The 1954 nation-wide data shows that the average annual gross value of production per member of handicraft production co-operatives was 185·7 per cent. of the average per craftsman generally and almost twice as much as the average per individual craftsman. But individual handicrafts included partly collectivised organisations (handicraft market-ing co-operatives plus small handicraft groups), and the average annual gross value of production per craftsman in these organisations was merely

[9] Correspondingly, it is related negatively to the relative contribution of handicrafts to the gross value of production of industry plus handicrafts (IV).

[10] For a crude inter-regional cost of living index cf. Peter Schran, *The Structure of Income in Communist China* (unpublished Ph.D. dissertation; Berkeley: University of California, 1961), p. 61.

[11] *Ibid.*, pp. 142 *et seq.*

[12] *Cf.* Chinese Academy of Sciences, *op. cit.*, pp. 62, 111, 195, and Cheng Chu-yuan, *Income and Standard of Living in Mainland China* (Hong Kong: Union Research Institute, 2nd ed., 1958), I, pp. 151-152.

[13] Urban-rural productivity differences are in part attributable to urban-rural price and cost of living differences. *Cf.* Peter Schran, *op. cit.*, pp. 54 *et seq.*

[14] *Cf. Peter Schran, op. cit.*, pp. 272 *et seq.*, Chinese Academy of Sciences, *op. cit.*, pp. 62, 86, 213, 214, and Cheng Chu-yuan, *op. cit.*, I, pp. 161, 162.

57·4 per cent. of the average per craftsman. If partly and fully collectivised organisations are aggregated, their average annual gross value of production per craftsman-co-operator exceeded that in the residual category (which still includes members of joint tool groups) only by a relatively small 20 per cent. (II).

While provincial data tend to confirm these relations (VIII), they also suggest that individual and co operative establishments may not have differed much from each other in their capital—labour ratios (V, VI) and show that on an average per capita basis, members of production co-operatives did not always outproduce individual stationary craftsmen, urban craftsmen generally, and craftsmen engaged in producer goods production. In the absence of more specific information, then, productivity differences between collective and individual handicrafts can be attributed to a fair degree of concentration of production co-operatives on urban stationary producer goods production as well as to improvements resulting from collectivisation. Correspondingly, the relatively small average annual gross value of production per craftsman in partly collectivised organisations can be related to concentration on rural areas, on ambulatory crafts and trades, and on consumer goods production as well as to possible negative consequences of collectivisation.

Lack of information and especially of aggregate information makes it difficult to say much about the effects of collectivisation on handicraft capital formation and on handicraft earnings.[15] There are indications that the former increased due to share capital requirements and to various forms of collective accumulation. And there is also evidence that the earnings differentials between craftsmen-proprietors and employed craftsmen disappeared to the disadvantage of the former during the course of transition to various forms of " distribution according to labour." But it is practically impossible to ascertain the impact of these changes on the earnings level.[16]

Handicraft workshops. Because employment data have not become available, little can be said in comparison about the state of handicraft workshops in general. In 1954, they produced 14·5 per cent. of the gross value of production of industry (including handicrafts), and 39·3 per cent. of this contribution originated in private establishments (including state agents and capitalists proper) (I), most of it apparently in small-scale workshops. Some additional information on the latter can be derived from provincial data. The pattern of regional differentiation of the average gross value of production per gainfully occupied person

---

15 For an extensive discussion of many unrelated bits of evidence on capital formation and earnings, *cf.* Cheng Chu-yuan, *op. cit.*, I, pp. 148 *et seq.*
16 Cheng asserts a decrease in the level of earnings as a result of collectivisation. *Cf. ibid.*, pp. 158–162.

seems to correspond to that for craftsmen generally (VIII). In all provinces covered, the average gross value of production per gainfully occupied person in handicraft workshops exceeded the average values for practically all types of craftsmen, and frequently to a considerable extent. Only in Shensi Province were members of handicraft production co-operatives more productive on the average (VIII). The greater labour productivity in small capitalist handicraft workshops and in small-scale industrial establishments generally appears to be related to higher capital-labour ratios (V, VI). The provincial data seem to indicate that the nation-wide average gross value of production per gainfully occupied person in small capitalist handicraft workshops ranged between 2,000 and 3,000 yuan.[17] Since the relation between gross value and net value was probably similar to that for handicrafts, the corresponding net value can be expected to have ranged in between 700 and 1,000 yuan. Practically nothing can be said about its distribution and about earnings levels in particular.[18]

THE DEVELOPMENT OF HANDICRAFTS, 1952–59

Corresponding to our discussion of the state of handicrafts in 1954, we may begin our review of developments with a look at changes in the contributions of the three forms of handicraft production to industrial plus agricultural production. Disregarding the years 1949–51 for the reason that gains are attributable both to recuperation from war-time conditions and to improving statistical coverage, the following picture emerges:

Sector	Gross value of production[a] (Billion yuan at 1952 prices)					
	1952	1953	1954	1955	1956	1957
Agriculture plus hunting, fishing, and gathering	40·8	41·6	43·2	46·7	49·4	50·0
Subsistence handicrafts plus preliminary processing	7·6	8·3	8·4	8·8	8·9[b]	10·4[b]
Handicrafts	7·3	9·1	10·5	10·1	11·7	13·4
Handicraft workshops	5·0	6·8	7·5	7·7 ⎱	58·7	65·0
Modern industry	22·0	28·8	34·0	37·1 ⎰		

[a] For 1952-55 cf. references to preceding tabulation. For 1956-57 cf. State Statistical Bureau, *Ten Great Years*, p. 16.

[b] Personal estimate.

[17] For comparison, note that private industry as a whole produced on the average 5,757 yuan gross value per person in 1954. The value of net assets per person was 1,094 yuan in 1954. Cf. Ch'ien Hua et al., *Ch'i Nien lai Wo Kuo Ssu-ying Kung-shang-yeh ti Pien-hua (1949-1956 nien)* (Peking: Ts'ai-cheng Publishing Co., 1957), p. 8.

[18] Practically all available data concern private industry as a whole which may not be representative of handicraft workshops that accounted for the majority of establishments but only for a small share of output. Cf. *ibid.*, p. 88.

The three forms of handicraft production seem to have increased their contribution almost continuously in absolute terms, and at least handicrafts and handicraft workshops accelerated their production also relative to agriculture. Since the statistical coverage was far from perfect at most times and especially during the early fifties, all of these changes have to be viewed with some reservations.

Subsistence handicrafts. Contrary to what might be expected on the basis of doctrinal pronouncements, the gross value of subsistence handicraft production does not seem to have declined as a result of rural collectivisation. It should also be noted, however, that the most significant increase depends on a personal estimate. The gross value of production appears to have increased even on the average per household as follows: 1952—67 yuan; 1953—71 yuan; 1954—72 yuan; 1955—74 yuan; 1956—73 yuan; 1957—84 yuan.[19] The minor decline in 1956, also estimated, coincides with the high tide of rural collectivisation and with the mass winter campaign for soil improvement, irrigation, etc. While it may be reasonable to infer from the above data that collectivisation did not affect subsistence handicrafts significantly, the same cannot be assumed for rural communisation. Yet, the effect of the latter event cannot be ascertained statistically, due to changes in the coverage of the agricultural production account.

Handicrafts. The gross value of production of handicrafts increased considerably until 1954, decreased slightly in 1955, and grew again importantly until 1957 when the handicraft series terminated. The major wave of collectivisation which occurred in 1956 and brought immediate transition to handicraft production co-operatives in most instances does not seem to have had an adverse affect on handicraft production (II). Because the gross value of production of part-time craftsmen can only be identified for 1954 and because the numbers of part-time craftsmen are not known for any year, no general statements can be made on the development of the average gross value of production per craftsman. In consequence of the rapidly extending coverage of the handicrafts sector by co-operatives, little analytical significance can be attached to the ups and downs in the average gross value of production per co-operator. Most important appears to have been the decline in the number of craftsmen from 1954 to 1955 and especially from 1955 to 1956, during the main period of collectivisation. The State Statistical Bureau attributes this decrease to the absorption of urban craftsmen by industry and of rural craftsmen by agricultural production co-operatives. Practically nothing is known about the impact of the latter transfer on rural division of

---

[19] Derived from data in the above tabulation and from household data implicit in State Statistical Bureau, *Ten Great Years*, pp. 42–43. 1957 value equal to average of 1956 and 1958 values.

labour. So far as earnings are concerned, transfer to agricultural production co-operatives seems to have implied at least minor decreases,[20] while transfer to industry may have led to no change at all.

Handicraft workshops. Both the development and the pattern of socialist transformation of handicraft workshops are largely unknown. During the years 1952–55, handicraft workshops contributed almost constantly 14–15 per cent. of the gross value of production of industry and handicrafts. Private handicraft workshops accounted for 52·3 per cent. of this portion in 1953, for 39·3 per cent. of it in 1954, and for 30·0 per cent. of it in 1955. At the same time, so-called co-operative factories which apparently consisted primarily of consolidated workshops, increased their share of the gross value of production of industry and handicrafts from 2·5 per cent. in 1952 to 3·9 per cent in 1955 and to 7·5 per cent. in 1956. Later data could not be found, and the distribution of handicraft workshops on state-operated and joint-public-private enterprises has not become available either.

New handicraft workshops. In 1958, efforts were made to transform all handicraft production co-operatives into handicraft workshops on the pattern of co-operative factories as well as to organise rural handicraft production in so-called communal industries. For lack of adequate information, hardly anything can be said about the results of the campaign in the urban sector.[21] The gross value of production of communal industries was given as six billion yuan in 1958 and as 10 billion yuan in 1959.[22] The 1958 figure corresponds roughly to the 1954 figure for the rural share in the gross value of production of handicrafts. In 1958 and in 1959, however, the gross value of production of communal industries is significantly smaller than the combined gross value of production of subsistence handicrafts and of rural handicrafts in 1954.

Data on the composition of output of communal industries which were gathered in 60 rural communes during April 1959, indicate that traditional products of rural handicrafts were still very important, even though the great leap manifested itself in large output shares of native fertilisers and insecticides as most important chemical products:

Item					Output share
Foods ...	...	...	...	...	27 per cent.
Chemicals	...	...	...	...	21 per cent.
Textiles ...	...	...	...	...	11 per cent.

[20] *Cf.* Cheng Chu-yuan, *op. cit.,* p. 162. Note that according to most indications, the earnings of rural craftsmen did not exceed those of peasants by much on the average.

[21] *Cf. Far Eastern Economic Review,* No. 23 (December 4, 1958), p. 715, for a note on a report of a national handicraft conference in Peking in September 1958 which dealt with the subject of co-operative factories.

[22] *Cf. Chi-hua yü T'ung-chi,* No. 4 (April 1960), p. 11.

Item (cont.)				Output share (cont.)
Metal processing	...	...	...	10 per cent.
Needle trades ...	...	...	...	7 per cent.
Construction materials ...	...	...	7 per cent.
Wooden materials	...	...	...	5 per cent.
Other ...	...	...	...	12 per cent.

Since the residual 12 per cent. include mining and smelting in addition to many other activities, the relative importance of backyard furnaces and of rural mining does not seem to have been great in 1959.

In the latter part of 1959, 700,000 rural industrial establishments were said to have been in operation.[24] The average gross value per establishment seems to have been near 15,000 yuan. The number of craftsmen is not known but it may be noted that it would take merely 30 persons on the average per establishment to reduce the gross value per person to traditional rural levels.

Finally, mention should be made of the urban communes as a new form of handicraft organisation, even though lack of space prevents us from discussing the limited amount of evidence which has been made available on them.

RELATIONS BETWEEN SECTORS

In conclusion, we may review our limited findings on the state and development of Chinese handicrafts in the light of our initial discussion of the requirements of Chinese development policy. The goal of increasing surplus from the handicraft sector necessitated that the following changes be induced;

First, increases in the supplies of handicraft products to other sectors and notably to the modern producer goods sector. Separate marketing data for handicraft products have not become available,[25] but it appears that the collectivisation and socialisation of commerce achieved this result. It seems also, however, that handicraft marketing co-operatives were a relatively unimportant instrument in pursuit of that goal.

Second, increases in handicraft production. To the extent that handicraft production statistics can be accepted, increases in the gross value of production are evident.

Third, changes in the composition of output from consumer to producer goods. Such changes are apparent in particular for rural communal industries. Lack of aggregate information prevents statements concerning the urban sector.

24 Ibid.
25 Chinese Academy of Sciences, op. cit., contains various references to the state of controlled marketing of handicraft products in 1954.

Fourth, increases in handicraft investment. Increases in collective capital formation have been asserted, but it is practically impossible to verify these claims in the aggregate.

Fifth, improvements in handicraft production technology. Major improvements are said to have occurred and to have resulted in particular from collectivisation and communisation, but cannot be ascertained in a satisfactory manner.

Sixth, increases in handicraft labour productivity as a result of increases in investment and/or improvements in technology. Incomplete labour force data make it impossible to demonstrate the claimed achievement of this goal.

Seventh, transfer of handicraftsmen to other sectors of the economy. Such changes have been asserted as a result of collectivisation, but their magnitude cannot be established for lack of data on the sectoral distribution of transfers and on their subsequent occupations.

Eighth, decreases in handicraft earnings at least relative to production and to earnings in the modern sector.[26] While absolute decreases are indicated for certain groups of craftsmen, little can be said about changes in the earnings level.[27]

Ninth, decreases and changes in the composition of consumption. Such changes cannot be identified for handicraftsmen, but can be presumed to have occurred as a result of rationing and other measures aimed at consumption control.

In addition to the above developments, increases in raw material supplies to the handicrafts sector became necessary. Since handicrafts depend primarily on agricultural and subsidiary products for this purpose,[28] the growth of handicraft production was in large measure determined by the growth of agricultural production. We have shown above that according to official statistics handicraft output grew relatively to the output of agriculture. As a result, raw material supplies became a bottleneck as early as in 1954 [29] and probably increasingly so in subsequent years as frequent references indicate.

---

[26] *Cf.* Chinese Academy of Sciences, *op. cit.*, p. 73 (Heilungkiang), for the assertion that handicraft earnings were too high relative to earnings in state and co-operative enterprises.

[27] Note that the adjustment of earnings levels may have occurred on the pattern typical for private industry which concentrated on consumer goods production, too. Earnings stagnated during the course of socialist transformation in 1955 and 1956, relatively speaking, while earnings in state industries increased as a result of the 1956 wage reform. *Cf.* Peter Schran, *op. cit.*, pp. 272 *et seq.*

[28] The general rule seems to be that 80 per cent. of the raw material inputs of consumer goods industries originate in agriculture. See also Chao I-wen, *op. cit.*, p. 27.

[29] *Cf.* Chinese Academy of Sciences, *op. cit.*, especially p. 21, for the assertion that handicraft development in other areas diminishes both commodity markets and raw material markets for Shanghai handicrafts.

Given the Chinese strategy of development, then, virtually everything seems to depend in the end on the development of agriculture. We may well end our discussion of the state and development of handicrafts in China on this sombre note.

Statistical Appendix

Selected Data on the State of Chinese Handicrafts

BECAUSE data on Chinese handicrafts—scarce as they are—have been published primarily in Chinese and in a relatively unsystematic fashion, a summary presentation of the available evidence seems to be desirable. Lack of space, however, requires concentration on the major statements in the paper. The following statistical tables have been compiled from three sources:

State Statistical Bureau, *Ten Great Years* (Peking: Foreign Languages Press, 1960);

Chao I-wen, *Hsin Chung-kuo ti Kung-yeh* (*New China's Industry*) (Peking: T'ung-chi Publishing Co., 1957);

Chinese Academy of Sciences, Economic Research Section, Handicrafts Group, Editor, *1954-nien Ch-üan-kuo Ko-t'i Shou-kung-yeh Tiao-ch'a Tzu-liao* (*Materials on the Nation-wide Investigation of Individual Handicrafts in 1954*) (Peking: San Lien Bookstore, 1957).

Incompleteness, inconsistency, incomparability and other shortcomings of the data manifest themselves in tabular gaps as well as in qualifying remarks and references. At least for the early years, the accuracy of the data is subject to doubt, and on the whole it seems to be safe to assume that rates of growth reflect also increasing and improving statistical coverage of the handicraft sector. Heterogeneity of the statistical apparatus becomes apparent in the absence of various provinces from our compilations of provincial data as well as in the relative frequency of gaps in provincial data.

The following tables do not cover fully the substance of the third source. In particular, relatively superior data for a large number of major provincial cities have not been used in the interest of presenting a picture which is somewhat more indicative of the national structure. And the structure of trades in various provinces has been excluded for the sake of brevity.

Table I

RELATIVE IMPORTANCE OF INDUSTRY AND OF HANDICRAFTS IN INDUSTRY:

Industry's relative share of the annual gross value of production (GVP) of industry plus agriculture; relative shares of handicrafts and of handicraft workshops in gainfully occupied persons (GOP) and annual gross value of production (GVP) of industry; nationwide 1949 to 1957. Figures in percentages.

	Industrial GVP[a]	Handicrafts[d]: Total GOP[b]	Handicrafts[d]: Total GVP[c]	Individual[e] GOP[b]	Individual[e] GVP[c]	Farm[f] GVP[c]	Collective[g] GOP[b]	Collective[g] GVP[b]	Handicraft-workshops Total[h] GVP[c]	Private[i] GVP[c]	Co-operative factories[j] GVP[c]
1949 ...	30·1		23·1						20·5		0·3
1950 ...	33·3		26·5								
1951 ...	38·6		23·3								
1952 ...	41·5		21·3		12·9	5·0			14·5	7·9	2·5
1953 ...	47·2	59·1	20·4	57·2		20·6	1·8	0·7	15·1	5·7	2·7
1954 ...	50·2	54·9	20·1	52·8		19·3	2·1	1·1	14·5	4·2	3·1
1955 ...	49·7	57·2	18·4	49·9			7·3	2·2	14·0		3·9
1956 ...	54·7	54·6	16·6	42·1		14·8	12·5	3·7			7·5
1957 ...	56·5	42·0	17·1	9·5		2·7	32·5	14·0			

a Per cent. of GVP of industry plus agriculture. State Statistical Bureau, *op. cit.*, p. 17.

b Per cent. of GOP in industry. In the absence of adequate data on total industrial employment, the total has been approximated by adding the total number of craftsmen, the number of industrial workers, and the number of engineers and technicians. *Ibid.*, pp. 36, 183, 184. Since the estimated total does not include administrative personnel, all estimated GOP shares overstate the actual shares to some extent.

c Per cent. of industry's GVP.

d *Ibid.*, p. 16.

e *Ibid.*, and Table II. Including stationary and ambulatory craftsmen plus joint tool groups.

f *Ibid.*, gross value of the market production of subsidiary farm crafts. The number of craftsmen is not known.

g *Ibid.*, including handicraft production co-operatives, handicraft marketing co-operatives, and small handicraft production groups, plus " other " collective activities in 1956.

h Chinese Academy of Sciences, *op. cit.*, p. 252.

i Ch'ien Hua et al., *Ch'i Nien lai Wo Kuo Ssu-ying Kung-shang-yeh ti Pien-hua (1949–1956 Nien)* (Peking: Ts'ai-cheng Publishing Co., 1957, p. 88.)

j Chinese Academy of Sciences, *op. cit.*, p. 252, 1956: Choh-ming Li. *Economic Development of Communist China* (Berkeley: University of California Press, 1959), p. 111.

Table II

Distribution of gainfully occupied persons (GOP) and annual gross value of production (GVP) of handicrafts on individual, partly collective, and fully collective forms of handicraft organisation in China, 1952 to 1956.

Item Year	Handicrafts total		Individual handicrafts		incl. partly collective		Production cooperatives		Total: collective		Residual: Individual	
GVP*	Million yuan^a	Per cent.	Million yuan^b	Per cent.	Million yuan^c	Per cent.	Million yuan^d	Per cent.	Million yuan^e	Per cent.	Million yuan^f	Per cent.
1952	7,312	100	7,006	96·6	9	0·1	246	3·4	255	3·5	7,057	96·5
1953	9,119	100	8,633	94·7	20	0·2	486	5·3	506	5·5	8,613	94·5
1954	10,462	100	9,606	91·8	313	3·0	856	8·2	1,169	11·2	9,293	88·8
1955	10,123	100	8,822	87·1	715	7·1	1,301	12·9	2,016	19·9	8,107	80·1
1956	11,700	100	4,959	42·4	3,083	26·4	6,741	57·6	9,824	84·0	1,876	16·0
GOP	1,000 persons^g	Per cent.	1,000 persons^h	Per cent.	1,000 persons^c	Per cent.	1,000 persons^d	Per cent.	1,000 persons^e	Per cent.	1,000 persons^f	Per cent.
1952	7,364	100	7,146	97·0	10	0·1	218	3·0	228	3·1	7,136*	96·9
1953	7,789	100	7,518	96·5	30	0·4	271	3·5	301	3·9	7,488	96·1
1954	8,910	100	8,389	94·2	618	6·9	521	5·8	1,139	12·8	7,771^i	87·2
1955	8,202	100	7,353	89·6	1,026	12·5	849	10·4	1,875	22·9	6,327^i	77·1
1956	6,583	100	2,885	43·8	1,397	21·2	3,698	56·2	5,095	77·4	1,488^i	22·6
GVP per GOP*	Yuan	Index	Yuan	Index	Yuan	Index	Yuan	Index	Yuan	Index	Yuan	Index
1952					894		1,130		1,120			
1953					672		1,792		1,680			
1954	884^j	100	837^i	94·7	507	57·4	1,642	185·7	1,027	116·2	863	97·6
1955					697		1,532		1,075			
1956					2,206		1,823		1,961			

* at 1952 prices.

166

a Chinese Academy of Sciences, *op. cit.*, p. 252, and State Statistical **Bureau**, *op. cit.*, p. 16. Including gross value of the market production of subsidiary farm crafts.

b Chinese Academy of Sciences, *op. cit.*, p. 252, 1956: total minus production co-operatives.

c Chao I-wen, *op. cit.*, pp. 109, 111:

Year	Gross value of production (1,000 yuan)				Gainfully occupied persons (persons)			
	Collect. total	Product. co-ops	Markets. co-ops	Small. groups	Collect. Total	Product. co-ops	Market co-ops	Small groups
1952	255,140	246,405	7,406	1,329	227,786	218,018	4,288	5,480
1953	506,364	486,405	12,280	8,014	301,487	271,297	15,851	14,339
1954	1,169,389	855,703	91,209	222,477	1,139,009	521,209	227,216	390,584
1955	2,015,737	1,301,651	187,528	526,558	1,874,590	849,485	507,343	517,762
1956	9,824,363	6,741,293	367,853	508,217	5,095,186	3,697,834	674,578	332,774

In 1956, there appear residuals of 2,207 million yuan gross value of production and 390 thousand gainfully occupied persons, both of which remain unexplained.

d *Ibid.*, p. 111, and Chinese Academy of Sciences, *op. cit*, p. 252.

e Partly collective plus production co-operatives.

f Total minus the total: collective.

g State Statistical Bureau, *op. cit.*, p. 36. Not including persons engaged in subsidiary farm crafts.

"Notes: 1. In 1955 and 1956 the number of handicraftsmen decreased because in the course of forming co-operatives some of the handicraftsmen in the cities were absorbed by the industrial enterprises, while in the countryside some of the handicraftsmen joined the agricultural producers' co-operatives.

2. The figure for co-op handicraftsmen in 1956 covers more than 1,000,000 handicraftsmen belonging to fishing and salt co-ops."

h Total minus production co-operatives.

i The residual includes an unexplained share of collectivised craftsmen (possibly members of joint tool groups). The numbers are for 1954: 74,000 persons; 1955: 331,000 persons; 1956: 944,000 persons. *Cf.* State Statistical Bureau, *op. cit.*, p. 36, and Chao I-wen, *op. cit.*, p. 109.

j Gross value of (total, individual, residual: individual) production minus gross value of market production of subsidiary farm crafts (1954: 26.9 per cent of individual handicraft production or 2,584 million yuan), divided by corresponding number of gainfully occupied persons. *Cf.* Chao I-wen, *op. cit.*, pp. 102–104.

Table III

GROSS VALUE AND STRUCTURE OF HANDICRAFT PRODUCTION, 1954
Results of the 1954 Nation-wide Handicraft Investigation [a]

1. *Gross Value of Handicraft Production by Organisation.*[b]

Total gross value of handicraft production	10,462 million yuan
Individual handicraft production	9,606
Handicraft marketing co-operatives	91
Small handicraft groups	222
Co-operative handicraft production	856

2. *Gross Value of Handicraft Production by Location.*[c]

Gross value of individual handicraft production	100·0 per cent.
Rural handicraft production	57·1
Peasant part-time production	26·9
Full-time handicraft production	30·2
Urban handicraft production	42·9

3. *Gross Value of Handicraft Production by Trades.*[d]

Gross value of total handicraft production	100·00 per cent.
Gross product of 13 important trades	48·75
Needle trades	13·62
Cotton spinning	8·19
Bamboo, rattan, coir, straw	6·17
Metal manufacturing	6·03
Wood processing	5·97
Edible oils and fats	3·09
Sugar refining	1·66
Leather manufacturing	1·23
Specialty handicrafts	0·93
Weaving	0·87
Pottery	0·57
Coal and charcoal mining	0·30
Silk reeling	0·12

4. *Gross Value of Handicraft Production by Final Use.*[e]

Gross value of individual handicraft production	100·00 per cent.
Gross product of producer goods trades	22·96
Agricultural producer goods	5·88
Industrial producer goods	12·45
Other (construction)	4·63
Gross product of consumer goods trades	77·04
Daily necessities	69·52
Other (cultural and educational)	7·52

a Chao I-wen, *op. cit.*, pp. 101–104, 109, 111.
b *Ibid.*, pp. 104, 109, 111, and Chinese Academy of Sciences, *op. cit.*, p. 252.
c Chao I-wen, *op. cit.*, pp. 102 and 103. Note that Chao uses the terms " small commodity producing individual handicrafts " and " small commodity producing handicrafts " and " individual handicrafts " interchangeably.
d *Ibid.*, p. 103. Chao does not make explicit that these are the thirteen *most* important trades.
e *Ibid.*, pp. 101, and 102. Chao lists the gross product of other producer goods trades (mainly construction trades) as 0.63 per cent, and at the same time fails to account at all for four per cent. of the total. In view of the relative importance of construction, this correction seems to be appropriate.

Table IV

RELATIVE IMPORTANCE OF INDUSTRY AND OF HANDICRAFTS IN INDUSTRY:

Industry's relative share of the annual gross value of production (GVP) of industry plus agriculture; relative shares of handicrafts and of capitalist small scale handicraft workshops in gainfully occupied persons (GOP) and annual gross value of production (GVP) of industry; in selected cities, provinces and regions, in 1954. Figures in percentages.

City / Province / Region	Industrial GVP[a]	Handicrafts: Total GOP[b]	Handicrafts: Total GVP[c]	Individual[d] GOP[b]	Individual[d] GVP[c]	Farm[e] GVP[c]	Collective[f] GOP[b]	Collective[f] GVP[c]	Small scale capitalists GOP[b]	Small scale capitalists GVP[c]
Peking				21·26	12·85	0·15			8·87[h]	6·15[h]
Tientsin					5·91					
Liaoning	52·35				5·0	0·4				
Kirin	57·90				8·22[i]					
Heilungkiang		23·12	9·94	20·17	7·46	0·63	2·95	1·85	5·19[j]	6·52[j]
Inner Mongolia					19·64			4·04		7·30[k]
Shansi	39·9		20·81		10·83	2·62		7·36		2·26[l]
Chekiang	42·6		29·62		22·43	5·05		2·14		
Anhwei	33·1	82·23	38·85	76·80	28·23	7·86	5·43	2·76	0·61?	2·23?
Fukien	43		56		37	17		2		
Honan	28·0		46·87		26·17	15·92		4·78		8·20[m]
Szechwan	35·8	53·93	26·47	49·64	20·09	5·61	4·29	1·22	3·44[l]	3·02[o]
Yünnan	32·0				36·14			2·22		
Kweichow	29·9				46·08[n]					
Shensi		61·67	29·72	53·36	27·31[n]		8·31	2·41	8·50[h]	4·55[h]
Kansu[p]	26·1		49·73		36·73	10·41[n]		2·59		6·22[o]
Sinkiang					54·79[n]					

* Derived from Chinese Academy of Sciences, op. cit.
a Per cent. of GVP of agriculture plus industry.
b Per cent. of GOP of industry.
c Per cent. of GVP of industry.
d Including stationary and ambulatory craftsmen, plus joint tool groups. The coverage of servicing trades, fishing, etc., is irregular.
e Gross value of the market production of subsidiary farm crafts. The numbers of craftsmen are usually not known.
f Including handicraft production co-operatives, handicraft marketing co-operatives, and small handicraft production groups.
g Handicraft workshops with four to nine gainfully occupied persons, unless otherwise stated.
h Including modern small scale enterprises.
i Not including scattered rural craftsmen and fisheries.
j Private industry, including handicraft workshops.
k Including capitalist handicraft workshops with more than ten gainfully occupied persons.
l Possibly including modern small scale enterprises.
m Including state operated, local state operated, joint public-private and private handicraft workshops.
n The gross value of the market production of subsidiary farm crafts cannot be identified.
o Capitalist handicraft workshops.
p At 1952 prices.

Table V

Average numbers of gainfully occupied persons in individual and co-operative handicraft establishments and in capitalist handicraft workshops, in selected cities, provinces and regions, 1954.

City Province Region	Total	Individual handicrafts – Total	Individual Craftsmen – Stationary	Individual Craftsmen – Ambulatory	Joint tool groups	Subsidiary farm crafts	Handicraft co-operatives – Total	Production	Marketing	Small production groups	Capitalist handicraft workshops (4-9 pers.)
Peking ...	2·76	2·46	2·78	1·29	5·35		74·5	79·0	32·6	21·2	5·16
Shanghai ...			2·21				58·8				5·65
Tientsin ...	2·52	1·41	1·71	1·03			92·7				
Liaoning ...	1·63	1·78									
Kirin ...	2·27	1·57			3·20		22·7	28·6	110·8	10·3	8·52
Heilungkiang ...	1·78	1·62			4·68		31·8	35·8	191·6	14·0	9·38
Inner Mongolia ...	1·87				3·77		26·0				8·52
Hopei ...	2·81				4·99			38·5			
Chekiang ...	2·07					1·58					
Anhwei ...	2·11	1·90	2·01	1·45	10·06		20·0				1·58(?)
Fukien ...	2·43		2·37	1·42	3·53		19·5	36·0	63·4	14·1	
Honan ...	3·07	2·68	2·68	2·66	3·78						
Kiangsi ...	1·89	1·78	1·82	1·72	5·10						
Szechwan ...	2·00	1·52	1·84	1·00	10·05		16·4				5·86
Kweichow ...	1·67		1·62				15·6	27·6	12·4	26·6	
Shensi ...	1·92						14·6	28·8	39·5	11·0	
Kansu ...	1·75	1·65			5·82		15·6				7·20
Sinkiang ...	1·51	1·47	1·50	1·15	3·24		15·1				6·62

170

* Derived from: Chinese Academy of Sciences, *op. cit.* Cf. references to Table IV.

Table VI

Average amounts of funds (*tzu-chin*) per establishment in individual handicrafts, handicraft production co-operatives, and capitalist handicraft workshops, in selected cities, provinces, regions and Hsiens, 1954.

Figures in Yuan at current prices.*

City, Province Region, Hsien	Individual handicraftsmen	Handicraft production co-ops	Capitalist handicraft workshops	All handicraft establishments
Tientsin	563			
Kirin	583			
Inner Mongolia	233			
Shansi, T'ai-yuan City	314		2,957	665 a
Kiangsi, Nan-ch'ang Region ...	78			
Hupeh, Wu-han City	293			
Hunan, Ch'ang-sha City ...		2,767 b		972
Szechwan			2,513	
Shensi		6,464		
Tsinghai, Ch'i-t'ai Hsien ...	138·5			
P'i-shan Hsien ...	92·2			

* Derived from: Chinese Academy of Sciences, *op. cit.* *Cf.* references to Table IV.
a Individual handicrafts plus capitalist handicraft workshops.
b Share capital. Co-operative funds should have been much higher.

Table VII

Distribution of all handicraft establishments in T'ai-yuan and of all individual handicraft establishments sampled in Yunnan according to amounts of funds.

Unit: Yuan at current prices, per cent.*

Amount of funds	T'ai-yuan:-all handicraft establishments	Yunnan: individual handicraft establishments
– 100	33·33	81·07
100– 500	41·94	16·91
500– 5,000	22·69	2·02
5,000–10,000	1·48	
10,000–	0·56	
Total	100·00	100·00 a

* Chinese Academy of Sciences, *op. cit.*, pp. 100, 218.
a 2,193 establishments.

Table VIII

Average annual gross value of output per gainfully occupied person in individual and co-operative handicraft establishments and in capitalist handicraft workshops, in selected cities, provinces and regions, 1954. Figures in Yuan at current prices.

City Province Region	Total	Individual handicrafts			Joint tool groups	Subsidiary farm crafts	Handicraft co-operatives			Small production groups	Capitalist handicraft workshops (4-9 pers.)
		Total	Individual Craftsmen				Total	Production	Marketing		
			Stationary	Ambulatory							
Peking ...	1,851	1,937	1,993	1,497	1,444		2,682				4,252
Shanghai ...		1,677	2,061	378			2,250				5,930
Tientsin ...	2,482		2,442	303							
Liaoning ...	1,784	1,642									
Kirin ...	1,664	1,664			2,281	25	2,381	2,783	310	940	5,936
Heilungkiang ...	1,708	1,684			1,663	232	2,862	3,764	886	1,087	2,648
Inner Mongolia	1,310	1,309			1,804		1,665				1,640
Hopei ...	982				1,314	238	1,305				2,297
Shansi ...	900					291	773				
Chekiang ...	565	560	618	247		59	233				5,721 (?)
Anhwei ...	576	1,108	1,176	418	689		797				
Fukien ...	1,038	861	956	258	781		800	1,170	293	664	
Honan ...	860	568	752	268	860						
Kiangsi ...	602		897		965						
Szechwan ...	888						623				1,927
Yünnan ...	763						640	680			
Shensi ...	1,197						871	2,371			1,612
Kansu ...	1,477	1,531			878		608				1,687

172

* Derived from: Chinese Academy of Sciences, *op. cit. Cf.* references to Table IV.

Table IX

Relative distribution of establishments, gainfully occupied persons, and annual gross value of production of individual handicrafts on urban and rural areas (unit: per cent.); and average annual gross value of production per gainfully occupied person in urban and rural areas (unit: yuan at current prices); in selected cities, provinces, and regions, 1954*.

City Province Region	Establishments		Persons		Gross value of Production (A)		Gross value of Production (B)		Average value (B)	
	Urban	Rural	Urban	Rural	Urban	Rural	Urban	Rural	Urban	Rural
Peking ...	95·17	4·83	92·13	7·87	93·45	6·55	94·6	5·4	1,900	1,277
Liaoning ...	47·3	52·7	49·4	50·6	71	29	77	23	2,778	814
Heilungkiang ...	67·09	32·91	68·83	31·17	77·12	22·88	83·6	16·4	2,075	897
Inner Mongolia ...	48·78	51·22	52·38	47·62			78·01	21·99	1,951	605
Anhwei ...	29·8	70·2	31·5	68·5			49·8	50·2	910	422
Fukien ...	33·2	66·8	31·1	68·9	31·1	68·9	45·3	54·7	1,513	824
Honan ...	41·35	58·65	27·98	70·02	25·28	74·72	63·99	36·01	1,268	702
Kansu ...	43·4	56·6	45·3	54·7	34·27	65·73	44·0	56·0	1,434	1,513
Tsinghai ...	43·9	56·1	35·6	64·4			43·2	56·8	2,181	1,585

* Derived from: Chinese Academy of Sciences, *op. cit.* *Cf.* references to Table IV.
(A) Including the gross value of production of subsidiary farm crafts.
(B) Excluding the gross value of production of subsidiary farm crafts.

173

Table X

Relative distribution of establishments, gainfully occupied persons, and annual gross value of production of individual handicrafts on producer goods and consumer goods (unit: per cent.); and average annual gross value of production per occupied person in producer goods production and in consumer goods production (unit: yuan at current prices); in selected cities, provinces, and regions, 1954*.

City Province Region	Producer goods production			Consumer goods production			Average gross value	
	Establishments	Occupied persons	Gross value	Establishments	Occupied persons	Gross value	Producer goods	Consumer goods
Shanghai ...	13·86	13·28	23·85a	86·14	86·72	76·15a	3,027	1,480
Tientsin ...	15·18	17·76	24·42a	84·82	82·24	75·58a	3,417	2,281
Liaoning ...	20·5	23·1	21·0	79·5	76·9	79·0		
Heilungkiang ...	13·2	18·2	15·1a	86·8	81·8	84·9a	1,264	1,581
Anhwei ...	26·1	27·7	16·5	73·9	72·3	83·5		
Fukien ...	13·2	15·1	18·9a	86·8	84·9	81·1a	1,300	962
Kiangsi ...	30·22	32·85	18·98	69·65	67·16	81·01		
Szechwan ...		29	16		71	84		
Kansu ...	27·8	28·5	11·6	72·2	71·5	88·6		

* Derived from: Chinese Academy of Sciences, *op. cit.* *Cf.* references to Table IV.
a Not including the gross value of market production of subsidiary farm crafts.

The Terms of
Sino-Soviet Trade*

By FENG-HWA MAH

THE development of the ideological controversy between Communist China and the Soviet Union in recent years has aroused increased interest in a more careful evaluation of Sino-Soviet economic relations.[1] In this paper, I attempt to deal with one specific aspect of this broad area, that is the price problem in Sino-Soviet trade.

During the last few years, intensive analyses of the terms of trade between the Soviet Union and other Communist countries have been made by Horst Mendershausen and Franklyn D. Holzman.[2] By comparing the average unit values of Soviet trade with the European satellites, and those of Soviet trade with Western Europe, Mendershausen reached the conclusion that the Soviet Union discriminated against the European satellites, charging them higher prices for Soviet exports and paying them lower prices for Soviet imports, compared with Soviet trade in similar commodities with Western European countries. Working on Bulgarian foreign trade statistics, Holzman found that there were even greater apparent discriminations against the bloc (including Russia) by Bulgaria than by the Soviet Union. He suggested that these apparent discriminations ought not to be interpreted as losses due to relative bargaining power but rather the cost of bloc autarky to each of the Communist

---

* Based on a paper presented at the First Research Conference of the Social Science Research Council Committee on the Economy of China, Berkeley, California, January 31 to February 2, 1963. This paper is a summary of the preliminary findings of a forthcoming RAND study. The author is grateful to Dr. Oleg Hoeffding for his advice and suggestions on that study. The views expressed here are those of the author.

1 See, for example, Oleg Hoeffding, " Sino-Soviet Economic Relations in Recent Years," in *Unity and Contradiction: Major Aspects of Sino-Soviet Relations*, Kurt London (ed.) (New York: Frederick A. Praeger, 1962), pp. 295–312; Walter Galenson, " Economic Relations between the Soviet Union and Communist China," in *Study of the Soviet Economy*, Nicolas Spulber (ed.) (Bloomington: Indiana University, 1961); and Alexander Eckstein, " Sino-Soviet Economic Relations: A Reappraisal " (unpublished), 1961.

2 Horst Mendershausen, " Terms of Trade between the Soviet Union and Smaller Communist Countries, 1955–57," *Review of Economics and Statistics (RE and S)*, May 1959, pp. 106–118; " The Terms of Soviet-Satellite Trade: A Broadened Analysis," *RE and S*, May 1960, pp. 152–163; and *The Terms of the Soviet-Satellite Trade: 1955–1959*, RAND RM 2507–1–PR (Santa Monica: The RAND Corporation, March 1962). Franklyn D. Holzman, " Soviet Foreign Trade Pricing and the Question of Discrimination," *RE and S*, May 1962, pp. 134–147; and the discussions between Mendershausen and Holzman in *RE and S*, November 1962, pp. 493–499.

countries under study. Their analyses, however, do not include trade between the Soviet Union and Communist China. Therefore, it is not certain whether or not their findings and conclusions are applicable to Sino-Soviet trade.

There is virtually no published statistical data on prices in Communist China's foreign trade. The only information from Communist China in this connection is in a speech by its Minister of Foreign Trade, Yeh Chi-chuang, in which he stated that prices in Communist China's trade with the Soviet Union and other Communist countries were fixed through negotiations based on the principle of "equality and mutual benefit." He added that while prices of individual commodities in Sino-Soviet trade might differ from world market prices, yet for all import and export commodities and over a number of years, the prices under the Sino-Soviet trade agreement were "reasonable and fair." [3]

Since 1958, the Soviet Ministry of Foreign Trade has published detailed statistics of the Soviet Union's foreign trade from 1955 onwards.[4] From this data it is possible to calculate the unit rouble values of many commodities traded between Russia and China. In addition, the United States Department of Commerce publishes, from time to time, statistics of trade between non-Communist and Communist countries.[5] For many items both the quantity and value (in U.S. dollars) are reported. Therefore, unit values of a number of commodities traded between Communist China and non-Communist countries can also be computed.[6]

PURPOSE AND METHOD

Working primarily from the official Soviet and American sources just mentioned, I have attempted:

(1) To compare, where data is available, the unit values of a sample of commodities traded between Communist China and the Soviet Union between 1955 and 1959 with the average unit values of similar commodities traded between (a) Russia and non-Communist countries, (b) Russia and Communist countries other than China, and (c) Communist China

---

[3] Yeh Chi-chuang, "The Foreign Trade of China," speech delivered to National People's Congress on July 11, 1957, *Hsin-hua Pan-yueh-k'an* (*New China Semimonthly*), No. 16, 1957, p. 90.

[4] *Vneshniaia Torgovlia SSSR za 1956 god—Statisticheskii Obzor* (*Foreign Trade of the USSR in 1956—Stastical Summary*) (Moscow: 1958); and same for later years.

[5] U.S. Department of Commerce, International Trade Analysis Division, *Country by-Commodity Series*.

[6] The unit values of selected commodities are derived by dividing the annual trade values of these commodities by their respective quantities as reported in the Soviet and American sources. The unit values thus computed are different from the prices of these commodities as the former may include such non-price elements as transport and insurance costs, etc., depending on the methods of valuation used in the statistical reports.

and non-Communist countries.[7] This comparison sample (sample B) includes 25 Chinese import items (about 17 per cent. to 33 per cent. of China's annual import from Russia between 1955 and 1959) and 24 Chinese export items (roughly 33 per cent. to 44 per cent. of China's annual export to the Soviet Union during the same period). This comparison is to discover whether there are significant price or unit value differences in Sino-Soviet trade as compared with each country's trade with other partners.

(2) For the purpose of testing the quantitative significance of the unit value differences which may be found in the above comparison, I have tried to estimate Communist China's " over-receipts " (or " over-payments "), and to compute indexes of Communist China's comparative price advantage (or disadvantage) in trading with the Soviet Union during this period.[8] This is done by calculating and comparing the actual payments and receipts of Communist China's imports from and exports to the Soviet Union in the selected commodities with the hypothetical payments and receipts if the trade had been carried on at the unit values in Soviet trade with Western Europe, or at world market prices [9] when the Soviet figures are not available. In symbols, Communist China's import price advantage (or disadvantage) is

$$\frac{\sum P_{mf} Q_{mc}}{\sum P_{mc} Q_{mc}}$$

where P_{mf} is the unit value of Western Europe's import from the Soviet Union, P_{mc} is that of China's import from the Soviet Union, and Q_{mc} is

---

[7] The countries included in my calculations and the abbreviations used for these countries and country groups in this paper are as follows:

CC: Communist China; SU: Soviet Union.

WE: Western Europe (13 countries: Austria, England, Finland, France, West Germany, Greece, Holland, Iceland, Italy, Norway, Sweden, Switzerland and Yugoslavia).

NCA: Non-Communist Asia (7 countries: Burma, India, Indonesia, Japan, Malaya, Pakistan and Hong Kong).

EE: Eastern Europe (7 countries: Albania, Bulgaria, Czechoslovakia, East Germany, Hungary, Poland and Rumania).

ACC: Asian Communist Countries (3 countries: North Korea, Outer Mongolia and North Vietnam).

The following notation is also used in this paper:

SU-WE: (average unit value of) Soviet Union's exports to Western Europe, or WE imports from SU.

WE-CC: (average unit value of) Communist China's imports from Western Europe, or WE exports to CC, etc.

[8] The term " advantage " and " disadvantage " used here are in the " comparative " sense. They do not necessarily imply " discrimination in favour of " or " discrimination against," although such possibilities are not ruled out.

[9] Whenever data permits, Hong Kong prices are used to represent " world market prices." In the absence of Hong Kong prices, the import and export prices of the United Kingdom are used as a second choice and those of Japan as a third choice. Only one " world market price " is used (for 1959) in the import comparison. The number of " world market prices " used in the export comparison are 10 for 1955 and 8 for each of the four subsequent years.

the quantity of the Chinese import from the Soviet Union. Any computed percentage below 100 is a disadvantage to China. Similarly, Communist China's export price advantage (or disadvantage) is

$$\frac{\sum P_{xo} Q_{xo}}{\sum P_{xt} Q_{xo}}$$

where P_{xt} is the unit value of Western Europe's export to the Soviet Union, P_{xo} is that of Communist China's export to the Soviet Union, and Q_{xo} is the quantity of the Chinese export to the Soviet Union. Here again any percentage under 100 is a disadvantage to Communist China.

(3) To construct overall import and export unit value indexes, and unit value indexes for some important groups of commodities in Sino-Soviet trade. The sample for the overall indexes (sample A) includes 43 Chinese import items (21·7 per cent. of the total value of Chinese imports from Russia in 1955) and 51 Chinese export items (78·5 per cent. of the total value of Chinese exports to Russia in 1955). The indexes are weighted arithmetic mean of price (unit value) relatives using base year (1955) value weights. The choice of 1955 as the base year is arbitrary, but it is felt that any one of the first three years (1955, 1956 and 1957) is better than 1958 or 1959 as a base year, because of the apparently drastic price adjustments in Sino-Soviet trade in 1958 and/or 1959. These unit value indexes in Sino-Soviet trade are then compared with the import and export unit value indexes of non-Communist Asian countries.

The limitations of such an analysis must be emphasised. The selection of commodities in this study depends primarily on the availability of information and the comparability of the commodities reported in the Soviet source. With regard to the availability of information, the limitations are: (a) only those commodities for which both physical quantities and values are given in the Soviet source can be considered for inclusion, (b) only those commodities which appear both in bloc trade and in Soviet trade with at least some of the selected non-Communist countries can be included, and (c) the quantities of some commodities are reported in very vague units of measure which make comparison almost meaningless. For example, it is clearly not very meaningful to compare machinery and equipment by " numbers " or " complete sets," and unfortunately during the period under study between 30 and 60 per cent. of Communist China's imports from the Soviet Union were machinery and equipment. These limitations are more serious than they appear to be. Basically the difficulties in selecting commodities for international comparison lie in the countries involved having different patterns of foreign trade. For example, China is primarily an exporter of agricultural and mineral products and an importer of capital goods. Many of the Western European countries, on the other hand, are exporters of manufactured goods and importers of basic materials. Thus the number of commodities that the Soviet Union imports from both China and Western Europe, or exports to both China and Western Europe, is inherently limited to a very narrow range. It is within this narrow range that the above-mentioned limitations on the availability and usefulness of information available are encountered.

Then there is the problem of comparability. This is perhaps the most serious difficulty in selecting commodities. The aim is to select items which can "reasonably" be compared. The two main problems in doing this are (a) whether an item exported from, say, China, to different countries, even though it bears the same name, is likely to be of the same quality and design, and (b) whether a commodity imported by, say, China, from different countries is more or less standardised internationally. In many cases, it is not possible to match Soviet commodity descriptions with those of non-Communist countries. This is especially true when commodities are reported in groups or sub-groups. Even where the commodity group seems from the name to be identical, we cannot be sure of comparability. For example, "metal-cutting lathes" exported from the Soviet Union to China may or may not be comparable with items classified under the same name exported from West Germany to China. For even if we knew that the two classifications included identical items, which is not necessarily so, it would be entirely possible that China imported metal-cutting lathes of very different types, prices and quality from the Soviet Union and West Germany. The same is true for Chinese or Soviet exports of some commodities or commodity groups, such as silk textiles. In these cases the differences in unit values would probably be not very meaningful.

On the other hand, however, there is reason to believe that international comparison is not entirely impossible. The repeated claims of Communist countries that prices in their trade with each other, are based on "world market prices" imply that their internationally traded commodities are to some extent comparable with similar commodities of Western origin.

Because of these limitations our sample for calculating unit value indexes (sample A) includes only forty-three commodities which the Chinese import from the Soviet Union, out of a total of 153 import items reported in the Soviet source both in quantity and value, and fifty-one commodities which the Chinese export to the Soviet Union, out of a total of 123 items which are reported in both quantity and value. As mentioned earlier, for our detailed comparison, only twenty-four Chinese export commodities to the Soviet Union, and twenty-five Chinese import commodities from the Soviet Union are used (sample B). This further narrowing of the scope of this study is necessary because:

(a) a commodity cannot be included for comparison if data for only one year of Sino-Soviet trade is available, for in such a situation the unit value difference or identity may be entirely coincidental.

(b) a commodity is excluded if its unit value during the period shows extreme irregularities, either from year to year over the period, or from country to country. There are cases in which unit values become three or four times as high from one year to another. In such situations we cannot be certain whether the irregularities are the result of price changes or commodity differences.

The names of the commodities in our comparison sample (sample B) and their values in Sino-Soviet trade from 1955 to 1959 are shown in Tables 1 and 2.

Structure and Behaviour of Unit Values

The major findings of this analysis can be summarised as follows:

(a) *China's imports from the Soviet Union.* For most of the commodities which I compared, the unit values of China's imports from Russia are higher than the unit values of Western Europe's imports from Russia. It is also quite obvious that the unit values of Soviet exports to China are higher than those of non-Communist Asia's imports from Russia, for similar commodities.

A comparison of the unit values of Soviet exports to China with other sets of average unit values of similar commodities (Soviet exports to Eastern Europe, Soviet exports to Asian Communist countries, Western European exports to China and China's imports from the non-Communist Asian countries) reveals no clear-cut relationship. The only generalisation that can be made is that the unit values of Soviet exports to China are closer to the average unit values of Soviet exports to Communist countries other than China than are the unit values of Soviet exports to Western Europe or non-Communist Asia. This was the case for seventeen commodities of the twenty-five in the sample.

(b) *China's exports to the Soviet Union.* In this case the picture is less clear. But for about half of the twenty-four selected commodities the unit values of China's exports to Russia were lower than those of Western Europe's exports to Russia or "world market prices." For one-third of the selected commodities, the unit values of Chinese exports to Russia were predominantly higher than those of Western Europe's exports to Russia or world import prices during this period. For the rest of the commodities covered, no clear statement can be made about the difference in unit values.

179

TABLE 1

VOLUME OF IMPORTS

Communist China's Import of 25 Selected Commodities from U.S.S.R.
(million roubles[a])

COMMODITY	1955	1956	1957	1958	1959
Food and Beverages					
Sugar, refined	—	2·6	3·7	4·3	2·1
Crude materials					
Chromium ore	0·6	0·6	0·9	4·8	5·1
Mineral fuels and related materials					
Crude petroleum	56·5	59·3	56·8	59·9	55·0
Gasoline	—	140·5	125·7	104·2	207·3
Kerosene	46·8	43·2	66·6	47·5	52·6
Diesel fuel	39·3	64·3	64·8	89·6	74·9
Paraffin	1·3	1·4	—	0·4	2·1
Chemicals					
Ammonium nitrate	2·4	0·2	0·7	3·9	2·4
Manufactured goods					
Rolled iron and steel	214·9	174·7	85·6	147·1	117·6
Pipes, assorted, petroleum	19·6	29·0	7·2	45·0	42·3
Pipes, gas	3·8	0·9	2·0	2·9	—
Strips, cold drawn	2·5	2·7	2·9	2·7	3·6
Aluminium	0·2	0·2	0·1	36·7	0·8
Rubber, synthetic	0·4	0·6	0·4	1·7	—
Cement	1·5	2·2	1·4	1·3	2·1
Newsprint	0·5	3·5	1·5	0·1	—
Machinery and transport equipment					
Excavators	10·3	7·0	13·1	6·0	8·2
Bulldozers	1·9	7·5	0·5	4·1	3·6
Ball and roller bearings	9·3	5·2	7·5	6·7	20·3
Agricultural tractors	28·9	23·7	1·8	43·1	10·6
Grain drills	0·6	0·4	0·8	5·5	2·0
Motor trucks	62·7	37·8	5·6	207·0	101·5
Automobiles	5·2	4·2	1·7	8·5	10·8
Motorcycles	0·1	0·1	—	2·2	0·2
Bicycles	—	—	6·1	3·1	0·1
Total import of 25 selected commodities[b]	509·4	611·7	457·6	838·0	725·2
Total Communist Chinese imports from U.S.S.R.	2,993·4	2,932·1	2,176·4	2,536·0	3,818·3
Import of selected commodities as % of total	17·0%	20·9%	21·0%	33·0%	19·0%

Notes: a Values are shown in foreign trade roubles effective prior to January 1, 1961
(1 rouble= $0.25).

b The details may not add to the total because of rounding.
—Indicates no trade, or negligibly small trade.

TABLE 2

Communist China's Export of 24 Selected Commodities to U.S.S.R.
(million roubles[a])

COMMODITY	1955	1956	1957	1958	1959
Food and beverages					
Tobacco, raw	87·6	119·8	164·0	125·7	118·7
Oil cakes, whole and broken-up	4·1	4·1	4·2	—	—
Tea	42·3	50·2	48·8	62·4	77·8
Meat, fresh frozen ...	245·3	205·7	77·9	150·5	99·8
Rice	164·7	257·1	101·7	243·2	330·3
Pineapples, fresh ...	0·3	0·5	—	0·5	—
Bananas, fresh	1·2	1·6	0·7	1·3	1·2
Vegetable oils, edible ...	118·4	103·0	52·7	84·5	84·1
Crude materials, except fuels					
Sulphur	3·0	12·0	17·5	11·1	10·7
Rosin	—	15·2	15·2	17·8	6·2
Rubber, natural ...	2·9	51·7	148·8	88·2	72·3
Hemp	13·2	12·9	—	—	—
Wool, coarse	77·8	62·0	66·8	55·4	54·9
Mineral fuels and related materials					
Coal, hard	20·0	8·2	7·8	11·2	10·6
Animal and vegetable oils, inedible					
Tung oil	17·2	27·9	27·5	31·6	35·4
Chemicals					
Sodium hydroxide ...	6·9	13·2	4·0	2·9	1·8
Sodium carbonate ...	10·4	15·9	3·0	6·7	1·7
Ethyl alcohol	—	5·3	5·9	6·4	0·5
Manufactured goods					
Rolled iron and steel ...	—	18·7	8·4	33·0	1·4
Tin	191·7	129·7	182·1	157·4	166·8
Aluminium	12·8	8·7	—	—	—
Cement	22·8	35·4	53·7	59·2	34·1
Wool textile	80·8	141·9	198·6	171·3	199·4
Footwear, leather ...	3·8	14·9	28·5	136·8	146·8
Total export of 24 selected commodities[b]	1,126·9	1,315·6	1,217·6	1,457·2	1,454·5
Total Communist Chinese export to U.S.S.R. ...	2,574·0	3,056·9	2,952·5	3,525·0	4,401·1
Export of selected commodity as % of total ...	43·8%	43·0%	41·2%	41·3%	33·0%

Notes: a Values are shown in foreign trade roubles effective prior to January 1, 1961
(1 rouble=$0.25).

   b The details may not add to the total because of rounding.

   —Indicates no trade, or negligibly small trade.

A comparison of the unit values of China's exports to non-Communist countries (computed from the U.S. Department of Commerce data) with the unit values of China's exports to Russia was made for ten commodities. The results showed that for five of these ten commodities (coal, rosin, rolled iron and steel, sodium hydroxide and sodium carbonate), China received lower average unit values from the Soviet Union than from non-Communist countries. In three cases (rice, tobacco and wool), on the other hand, China received higher unit values from Russia. The unit values for the other two cases (edible vegetable oils and tea) were too irregular to permit generalisation.

(c) *Direction of unit value differentials.* To understand more concretely the extent to which the unit values in China's trade with the Soviet Union exceed or fall below the unit values in Soviet and Chinese trade with Western Europe, I computed the ratios of the unit values in Sino-Soviet trade to the unit values in the trade of these two Communist countries with Western Europe. These ratios show both the level and the structure of the unit value differentials of the commodities covered.[10] The direction of the differentials is given in Table 3.[11]

In Table 3, for Chinese imports, a higher SU-CC unit value is unfavourable to Communist China, and a lower one is favourable. For Chinese exports, a higher CC-SU unit value is favourable to Communist China and a lower one is unfavourable. It can be observed that for the major comparisons in the table (that is, comparing the unit value of Soviet exports to China with Soviet exports to Western Europe and comparing the unit values of China's exports to the Soviet Union with the unit values of Russia's imports from Western Europe), in the case of Chinese imports, for roughly four out of every five commodities sold to both China and Western Europe, Russia charged China higher unit values between 1955 and 1957. In 1958 and 1959 China paid higher unit values for roughly nine out of every ten commodities. Based on a smaller and more homogeneous sample (sample C) which excludes all machinery and transport equipment (figures in parantheses), the situation is slightly more favourable for China between 1955 and 1957 (the unfavourable unit values against China are two out of every three commodities in 1955, and roughly six out of every ten in 1956 and 1957), but rose back to nine out of every ten commodities in 1958 and 1959.

In the case of Chinese exports, the comparison is unfavourable to China in four of the five years (the CC-SU/WE-SU unit value ratio is

---

10 The ratios are not presented in this article.
11 For all the following tables, figures in parentheses are alternative estimates based on a smaller and more homogeneous sample, sample C. The difference in the number of comparisons each year is due to the fact that the unit values for some of the commodities in Sino-Soviet trade or Soviet trade with Western Europe are not available for a number of the years under study.

unity in 1957). The Soviet Union paid to China less than it did to Western Europe for roughly six out of every ten commodities in 1956 and 1959, and seven out of every ten in 1955 and 1958. The picture is not much changed when the comparison is based on the smaller sample.

TABLE 3

Comparison of SU-CC (CC-SU) unit values with SU-WE (WE-SU) WE-CC (CC-WE) unit values 1955-1959

	CC Imports		CC Exports	
	SU-CC/ SU-WE	SU-CC/ WE-CC	CC-SU/ WE-SU	CC-SU/ CC-WE
Number of Commodities for which SU-CC (CC-SU) unit value is:	1955		1955	
Higher	13 (6)	2 (0)	3 (3)	2 (2)
Lower	3 (3)	1 (1)	8 (7)	3 (3)
Equal	1 (1)	0 (0)	0 (0)	0 (0)
Number of Comparisons	17 (10)	3 (1)	11 (10)	5 (5)
Number of Commodities for which SU-CC (CC-SU) unit value is:	1956		1956	
Higher	19 (7)	5 (1)	6 (6)	4 (4)
Lower	5 (5)	2 (0)	9 (8)	4 (4)
Equal	1 (1)	1 (1)	0 (0)	1 (1)
Number of Comparisons	25 (13)	8 (2)	15 (14)	9 (9)
Number of Commodities for which SU-CC (CC-SU) unit value is:	1957		1957	
Higher	15 (5)	3 (1)	6 (6)	3 (3)
Lower	4 (4)	3 (1)	6 (5)	3 (3)
Equal	2 (1)	0 (0)	1 (1)	1 (1)
Number of Comparisons	21 (10)	6 (12)	13 (12)	7 (7)
Number of Commodities for which SU-CC (CC-SU) unit value is:	1958		1958	
Higher	20 (10)	6 (2)	2 (2)	6 (6)
Lower	2 (1)	3 (2)	7 (6)	2 (2)
Equal	2 (1)	0 (0)	1 (1)	1 (1)
Number of Comparisons	24 (12)	9 (4)	10 (9)	9 (9)
Number of Commodities for which SU-CC (CC-SU) unit value is:	1959		1959	
Higher	18 (10)	5 (1)	2 (2)	5 (5)
Lower	2 (0)	1 (0)	5 (4)	3 (3)
Equal	1 (0)	0 (0)	2 (2)	0 (0)
Number of Comparisons	21 (10)	6 (1)	9 (8)	8 (8)

(d) *Extent of apparent advantage or disadvantage.* Tables 4, 5 and 6 show my estimates of China's over-receipts (or overpayments), its import and export price advantage (or disadvantage), and its combined (import and export) price advantage.[12] The latter is estimated by

(Import price advantage) ÷ (1/export price advantage).

Again, any percentage under 100 indicates a price disadvantage to China.

Tables 4, 5 and 6 are self-explanatory, but a few comments are in order. (1) It is interesting to note that according to the estimates based on sample B, China's import (and combined) price disadvantage in trading with Russia decreased until 1958, but increased in 1959. Based on sample C, the disadvantage decreased from 1955 to 1959, but the gap was not entirely closed. (2) The estimate of combined price advantage suggests that, on balance, China had a relative disadvantage in trading with Russia rather than with Western countries. On the basis of these figures, between 1955 and 1959, for roughly 22 per cent. (or 12 per cent. based on sample C) of China's imports from the Soviet Union and about 40 per cent. or 39·8 per cent. of her exports to the Soviet Union, China paid U.S. $187 (U.S. $118) million more to the Soviet Union and received U.S. $31 (U.S. $25) million less from the Soviet Union, giving a net " overpayment " of about U.S. $218 (U.S. $144) million. If we assume that the same degree of unit value differentials are applicable to Sino-Soviet trade as a whole, then China's total overpayment in its trade with the Soviet Union during this period would have reached approximately U.S. $928 (U.S. $1,046) million, which is roughly equal to or slightly greater than China's total imports from the Soviet Union in 1959 (U.S. $955 million at the then official rouble-dollar rate). It is possible, of course, that the unit value differential (to be referred to as the " China differential " hereafter) observed in the sample does not apply to the commodities which are not included in the comparison. One may even argue that the commodities not covered might show a net over-receipt sufficient to more than offset the net overpayment. But without additional information, there is little one can do about these cases beyond recognising such possibilities. I believe the possibility of " more than offset " to be rather small. (3) In the case of China's imports from the Soviet Union when sample C, which excludes machinery and transport equipment, is used in the comparison, China's comparative price disadvantage becomes greater.

12 This is called " percentage advantage of balanced trade," or ' combined import and export relations," in Frederic L. Pryor, *The Communist Foreign Trade System* (Cambridge: M.I.T. Press, 1963), p. 145. The term " comparative price advantage " was suggested by Joseph Berliner and coined by Franklyn D. Holzman in his article, " Soviet Foreign Trade Pricing and the Question of Discrimination," *Review of Economics and Statistics*, May 1962, p. 137, to contrast with the comparative cost concept.

TABLE 4

Total Payment of Chinese Imports of Selected Commodities from Russia, 1955–59

Year	(1) Number of Commodities Included	(2) Value of included Commodities as % of Total Import Value (%)	(3) Actual Payment (million U.S. $)	(4) Hypothetical Payment	(5) Import Price Advantage or Disadvantage (%)
1955	17 (10)	16·19 (5·65)	121·17 (42·25)	78·44 (25·43)	64·74 (60·19)
1956	25 (13)	20·86 (11·82)	152·92 (86·63)	105·21 (56·98)	68·80 (65·77)
1957	21 (10)	21·03 (15·16)	114·31 (82·50)	83·60 (56·76)	73·13 (68·80)
1958	24 (12)	32·98 (15·81)	209·09 (100·23)	197·20 (78·04)	94·31 (77·86)
1959	22 (10)	18·99 (11·63)	181·27 (111·05)	126·97 (87·12)	70·04 (78·45)

Notes: Columns (3) and (4): See text. Figures originally given in roubles are converted to dollars at the then official exchange rate of four roubles to the dollar.

Column (5): Hypothetical payment as a percentage of actual payment.

TABLE 5

Total Receipts from Chinese Exports of Selected Commodities to Russia, 1955–59

Year	(1) Number of Commodities Included	(2) Value of included Commodities as % of Total Export Value (%)	(3) Actual Receipt (million U.S. $)	(4) Hypothetical Receipt	(5) Export Price Advantage or Disadvantage (%)
1955	20 (19)	43·66 (43·65)	280·98 (280·90)	271·09 (270·84)	103·65 (103·71)
1956	23 (21)	42·54 (41·91)	325·11 (320·30)	311·32 (304·11)	104·43 (105·32)
1957	21 (20)	41·24 (40·95)	304·41 (302·30)	312·06 (308·85)	97·55 (97·88)
1958	18 (17)	40·51 (39·57)	356·96 (348·70)	382·29 (372·46)	93·37 (93·62)
1959	17 (16)	32·65 (32·62)	359·27 (358·92)	380·56 (380·14)	94·41 (94·42)

Note: Column (5): Actual receipt as a percentage of hypothetical receipt.

This seems to be consistent with an earlier Soviet statement which claimed that prices paid by China to the Soviet Union for equipment and machinery were on the average 20 per cent. below U.S. and U.K. prices.[13] (4) I wish to emphasise that the above estimates are rough approximations, and the calculations are extremely sensitive to the peculiar behaviour of individual commodities in the sample. Inferences based on these estimates are necessarily tentative.

TABLE 6

China's Over-payment and Over-receipt in Trade of Selected
Commodities with the Soviet Union and Combined Price Advantage,
1955–59 (million U.S. $)

Year	(1) Over-payment for Imports	(2) Over-receipt from Exports	(3) Net Balance (+ or −)	(4) Combined Price Advantage (%)
1955	42·73 (16·82)	9·89 (10·06)	−32·84 (− 6·76)	67·10 (62·42)
1956	47·71 (29·65)	13·79 (16·19)	−33·92 (− 10·76)	71·85 (69·27)
1957	30·71 (25·74)	− 7·65 (− 6·55)	−38·36 (− 32·29)	71·34 (67·34)
1958	11·89 (22·19)	−25·33 (−23·76)	−37·22 (− 45·95)	88·06 (72·90)
1959	54·30 (23·93)	−21·29 (−21·22)	−75·59 (− 45·15)	66·12 (74·07)
Total	187·34 (118·33)	−30·59 (−25·28)	−217·93 (−143·61)	

Sources and notes: Column (1), from Columns (3) and (4) of Table 4.
Column (2), from Columns (3) and (4) of Table 5.
Column (3), Column (2) minus Column (1).
Column (4), computed from Columns (5), Tables 4 and 5.

(e) *Unit value indexes and terms of trade.* Finally the Sino-Soviet unit value indexes were compared with the import and export indexes of non-Communist Asian (NCA) trade with the rest of the world on the grounds that China and most of the non-Communist Asian countries are all labour-abundant, capital-scarce, basically agricultural and developing economies, their foreign trade structure ought not to be too different. As is shown in Table 7 below, the overall import and export unit value indexes in Sino-Soviet trade move closely with those of non-Communist Asia, except for exports in 1958 and imports in 1959. The net barter terms of Sino-Soviet trade also follow a similar pattern to those of non-Communist Asian countries.

[13] S. I. Tiul'panov, *Vozniknovenie i razvitie mirovogo demokraticheskogo rynka* (*Emergence and Expansion of the Democratic World Market*) (Leningrad: 1955), p. 51.

TABLE 7

Comparison of Overall Unit Value Indexes and Terms of Trade
(1955=100)

Year	Import Unit value Index		Export Unit value Index		Terms of Trade[b]	
	SU-CC	NCA[a]	CC-SU	NCA[a]	Sino-Soviet	NCA[a]
1955	100·0	100	100·0	100	100·0	100
1956	96·5	100	97·2	97	100·8	97
1957	101·8	105	98·0	98	96·3	93
1958	94·7	98	98·6	95	104·1	97
1959	105·1	96	97·9	97	93·1	101

Source and note: a United Nations, *Yearbook of International Trade Statistics 1960* (New York: 1962), pp. 28–29. The U.N. indexes are originally given with 1953=100.
 b Unit value indexes of exports divided by unit value indexes of imports.

NATURE OF THE " CHINA DIFFERENTIAL "

The above analysis has found that unit value differentials exist in China's trade with the Soviet Union compared with Chinese or Soviet trade with other countries, especially Soviet trade with Western Europe. The differential is more pronounced in China's imports than in its exports. The question may be asked whether meaningful interpretations can be given to the " China differential," as Communist countries do not use the price system of the textbook type to allocate resources either domestically or internationally. Analysis seems to suggest that " the outlaws have their own laws," even though their rules of the game are not all clear to us. It is with this understanding that I try to look into the nature of the " China differential." Since many of the details of the needed information are missing, interpretations cannot be other than very tentative.

I submit that part of the China differential may be only illusory, that is, the observed unit value differences may actually reflect unit values of commodities (or commodity groups) with different qualities (or different compositions within the groups). I shall refer to this influence on my estimates as the quality difference effect. The rest of the China differential is considered to be " real " or " actual " and I suggest that it ought to be explained by two other factors: the transport cost effect and China's policy of "lean-to-one-side."[14] I would like to comment briefly on these three factors.

1. *Quality difference effect.* The problem of quality differences between commodities or commodity groups bearing the same name is a serious one. To deal with it, I repeated my calculations with a smaller and more homogeneous sample (sample C). As pointed out earlier, with the more homogeneous sample, China's import and combined price disadvantage became greater (except for 1959). This seems to suggest that the commodity quality differences can at most be only partly responsible for the observed differentials.

2. *The "lean-to-one-side" effect.*[15] China's over-dependence on Russia in its trade is shown by the fact that roughly one half of China's foreign trade being with Russia during the period under consideration, compared with 3 per cent. in 1930.[16] Because of the complete divorce of domestic and international prices,[17] the ambiguity of cost relationships and the possibility of non-profit trade in the Communist countries, I believe this shift of trade towards Russia is due not so much to the changed "comparative advantage" and the comparative cost structures in these two Communist countries (even though these may have changed in the meantime), as to the formation of a Communist economic bloc. China's "lean-to-one-side" policy in foreign trade during this period can be explained by its political sympathy for the one side and hostility to the other, by the convenience of conducting planned foreign trade (as an integrated part of the national economic plan) between planned economies, by the availability of the "market" and credit arrangements,[18] and last but not least, also by the non-Communist world's trade controls.

Given this "lean-to-one-side" orientation, what position is Communist China likely to find itself in in dealing with Russia? In a nutshell, it may be said that China would find its demand for Soviet industrial

[14] Since in our comparison, the rouble figures from the Soviet source are converted into dollars consistently at the then official rate of four roubles to the dollar (however arbitrary the rate may be), any possible exchange rate effect is practically ruled out.

[15] Amid the noises of the Moscow-Peking rift, it may be worth mentioning that Mao's "lean-to-one-side" orientation governed China's international economic relations until at least 1957, when Peking's Finance Minister first declared that "we are now in a better position to rely on our own accumulation to carry on material construction." See Mao Tse-tung, *On the People's Democratic Dictatorship* (Shanghai: Hsin Hua Book Store, 1950 edition), p. 8 and pp. 10–11; Li Hsien-nien, "1957 Budget Report," *New China Semi-monthly*, No. 14, 1957, p. 21.

[16] For 1930 trade volume, see article by Robert F. Dernberger in C. F. Remer (ed.), *Three Essays on the International Economics of Communist China* (Ann Arbor: University of Michigan Press, 1959), p. 135, Table 2.

[17] This point is clearly made by Yeh Chi-chuang in his 1957 speech. See Yeh Chi-chuang, *loc. cit.*, p. 93.

[18] *Cf.* A. Boone, "The Foreign Trade of China," *The China Quarterly*, No. 11, July–September 1962, pp. 169–170.

imports rather inelastic, that Soviet demand for Chinese consumer goods was rather low on Moscow's list of preferences, that China's ability to meet its export obligations was limited by low agricultural productivity and uncertain harvests, and that the Soivet commitment to export capital goods to China is directly competitive with Russia's domestic demand and Soviet commitment to other less developed countries. None of these factors is likely to have favourably influenced China's bargaining position with Russia.

In such a situation one can imagine that China, in importing from Russia, finds itself in a " seller's market " and, therefore, has not much choice but to be a price-taker. This is where Russia's superior bargaining power could come into the picture. Although we have no detailed information referring directly to Sino-Soviet price negotiations, it is nevertheless known that price negotiations between Communist countries are not always conducted under " the noblest and loftiest spirit of internationalism." [19] It is thus conceivable that superior bargaining power might have been employed by the Russians in price negotiations with Chinese trade delegations.[20] To the extent that this is the case, the measured price disadvantage perhaps can be partly explained by what we called the " lean-to-one-side " effect.

However, as Table 7 shows, the Sino-Soviet unit value indexes and the United Nations unit value indexes for non-Communist Asia moved in parallel. China's terms of trade with the Soviet Union, compared with those of the non-Communist Asian countries, showed no relative deterioration during this period. This would support the view that even though the possible use of Russia's superior bargaining power cannot be ruled out, perhaps the Russians have not employed " raw exploitation " in trading with China. Thus the " lean-to-one-side " effect, while it may explain some of the " China differentials " on the import side, is not the main explanation for the China differential.

3. *Transport cost effect.* In the Soviet foreign trade statistics the reported values are based on prices f.o.b. seller's port or franco [21] seller's land border. In other words, the exporting country's domestic transport

---

[19] Quotation taken from Li Che-jen " Fraternal Economic Co-operation," *China Reconstructs*, August 1955, p. 7. For some vivid examples of heated price bargaining between the Soviet Union and other Communist countries, see Frederic L. Pryor, *op. cit.*, pp. 136–139.

[20] The worsening of the Sino-Soviet relationship since 1958 and the increase of China's import (and overall) price disadvantage in her trade with Russia in 1959, as demonstrated above, may not be just coincidental. Note that the Chinese expressed their anger at Russia's " unfair economic treatment " in a letter from their central committee to the Soviet Party's central committee, dated June 14, 1963. See *New York Times*, Western edition, June 17, 1963.

[21] Delivered prices at the border.

cost is included in the Soviet valuation. What effect will this Soviet valuation practice have on the unit value?

My major findings are based on two comparisons: Soviet exports to China with Soviet exports to Western Europe for Chinese imports, and Chinese exports to the Soviet Union with Western Europe's exports to the Soviet Union for Chinese exports. In the case of Soviet exports to China and Western Europe, Soviet exports to Western Europe are valued, typically, f.o.b. Soviet European ports, whereas Soviet exports to China go mainly by railway over very long distances. According to a Soviet source, 95 to 98 per cent. of Sino-Soviet trade is transported by rail.[22] The western-most railway border-crossing is just east of Lake Baikal. In 1956–58, only 40 per cent. of Sino-Soviet freight traffic went this way, the rest crossed into Manchuria.[23] It is known that the Soviet freight rates discriminate against very long hauls of this order.[24] All these points suggest that the unit values of Soviet exports to China, including transport charges up to the Chinese border, must be very high. One of the above mentioned Soviet sources suggests that railway freights from Siberia to China are roughly comparable to ocean freights from England or America to China.[25] This implies that the transport cost from European Russia to China must be very much higher than that inside any other European country. Thus, other things (i.e., prices and qualities) being equal, one would expect the above tests to show a " China differential " in the direction obtained in comparing Soviet exports to China with those to Western Europe i.e., a " Chinese disadvantage." In comparing Chinese exports to the Soviet Union with those of Western Europe to the Soviet Union, the observed " China differential " is inconclusive, as noted already. This may be explained, partly at least, by the fact that Soviet import unit values from China valued " franco Sino-Soviet border," contain a much smaller portion of the total transportation cost than Soviet exports to China " franco Sino-Soviet border." For example, in the case of goods moving between Peking and Moscow, the ratio is about one to four or five. Thus, the average " China differential " should be smaller for Chinese exports to the Soviet Union compared to Western European exports to the Soviet Union than for Soviet exports to China compared with Soviet exports to Western Europe.

[22] M. I. Sladovskii, *Ocherki ekonomicheskikh otnoshenii SSSR s Kitaem* (*A Sketch of Economic Relations Between the USSR and China*) (Moscow: Vneshtorgizdat [Foreign Trade Publishing House], 1957), p. 350.
[23] M. I. Sladovskii, " Soviet-Chinese Economic Collaboration," in Soong Ching-lin *et al*, *Ten Years of the People's Republic of China* (a collection of articles), Moscow, 1959 (U.S. Joint Publications Research Service, Translation No. 2825, August 1960, p. 263).
[24] I am indebted to Dr. Oleg Hoeffding for this information.
[25] M. I. Sladkovskii, 1957, p. 348.

Of course we do not know whether all of the differential or only a part of it can be explained by the effect of transport costs. Inspection of the unit value differentials of individual commodities show some inconsistency among the covered items. This indicates that the transport cost effect, though important, cannot be solely responsible for the "China differential."

Concluding Remarks

On the basis of this analysis of the relevant factors which might contribute to the "China differential," I tentatively reach the conclusion that transport cost effect is the major reason for this differential. The quality difference effect and the "lean-to-one-side" effect are both also partly responsible for the "China differential," but in a less significant way. These observations refer to the measured differentials in the level of unit values. The changes over time of Sino-Soviet unit values follow closely those of the non-Communist Asian countries. Communist China's terms of trade with the Soviet Union, compared with those of the non-Communist Asian countries' trade with the rest of the world, do not show relative deterioration during this period, except for 1959.

In concluding this article I would like to make two remarks:

(1) The "China differential," though it clearly indicates a relative disadvantage in China's trade with Russia rather than with non-Communist countries, does not necessarily mean a "loss," since Communist China may not have had realistic alternatives to this high-cost trade during the period under study.

(2) In the present state of our knowledge it is impossible to separate the various factors mentioned above and measure them quantitatively. I submit that all these factors (except the possible effect of quality differences) can be considered as "price modifiers," for they eventually are all included in the total payments from Peking to Moscow. They indicate that Communist China might realise some economic gains by shifting from the Soviet Union to non-Communist markets.

A Study of the Rouble-Yuan Exchange Rate

By KANG CHAO and FENG-HWA MAH

IT is generally known that the exchange rates in Soviet-type economies are disequilibrium exchange rates in the sense that without controls they do not tend to lead to a balance on the international current accounts. Of the two economies involved, it is also known that these exchange rates are unrealistic, in the sense that they have no relation to the gold content of currencies involved, if the currencies have a gold content, and that these rates do not reflect the relative domestic purchasing power of the two currencies on internationally traded commodities.[1] In the case of the exchange rate between the Soviet rouble and the Communist Chinese yuan, even this disequilibrium and unrealistic exchange rate has in the main been veiled in secrecy since 1950. This secrecy has caused considerable difficulties in working with the Communist foreign trade statistics.

There had been no public announcement on the part of Communist China of the rouble-yuan rate until a few years ago. Western studies of the rouble-yuan rate for the early 1950s have produced different results. For example, in connection with the valuation of Soviet loan supplies to Communist China, Professor Choh-Ming Li has estimated that the rate was roughly 1 rouble to 2 yuan.[2] A U.N. source claimed that the rate was " officially fixed " in 1951 at 2 roubles to 1 yuan, but it also pointed out that, since 1952, the exchange rate implied by the volume of Sino-Soviet trade expressed in yuan, as computed from Communist Chinese data, and the same trade volume expressed in roubles, as reported in Soviet official publications, was approximately 1 rouble to 1 yuan.[3] This 1 to 1 rate has also been used in other

---

[1] For more detailed discussion of the nature of the exchange rates in Soviet-type economics, see Franklyn D. Holzman, " Some Financial Aspects of Soviet Foreign Trade," in U.S. Congress Joint Economic Committee, *Comparisons of the United States and Soviet Economies*, Part II, 1962, pp. 427–428; Frederic L. Pryor, *The Communist Foreign Trade System* (Cambridge: The M.I.T. Press, 1963), pp. 237–240.

[2] The precise rate estimated by Li is 1 rouble = 2·177 yuan. See Choh-Ming Li, *Economic Development of Communist China* (Berkeley: University of California Press, 1959), pp. 171–173.

[3] The source of the alleged 1951 official exchange rate was not given in the U.N. publication; see United Nations, *Economic Survey of Asia and the Far East 1958*, p. 35.

United Nations publications.[4] Finally, it was reported that on July 1, 1959, the quotation of the Communist Bank of China gave the rate for "foreign trade rouble" as 1 rouble to 0·50 yuan (2 roubles=1 yuan), and that for "non-commercial rouble" as 1 rouble to 0·1667 yuan (6 roubles=1 yuan).[5] The purpose of this paper is to determine and to analyse the effective rouble-yuan exchange rate since 1950, and to present the results of our estimate of the rouble-yuan purchasing power parity.

THE ROUBLE-YUAN EXCHANGE RATE, 1950–1960

On the basis of available information, we may reconstruct the story of the rouble-yuan exchange rate since 1950. It is quite certain that from the signing of the Sino-Soviet trade agreement on April 19, 1950, to the end of 1957, the effective rouble-yuan exchange rate was approximately 1 to 1 or more precisely 1·03 rouble=1 yuan. We shall later show that this exchange rate greatly overvalued the rouble,[6] and we are inclined to think that it was probably only for the sake of the then much needed Soviet support of its industrialisation programme that Peking had kept silent on this highly unfavourable exchange rate. It was not until 1957, when the Soviet Union introduced the tourist rouble-dollar rate,[7] and when the Eastern European countries established the non-commercial exchange rates between their currencies and the rouble, that Peking began to seek adjustments of the unfavourable rouble-yuan rate of 1 to 1. We believe that it was either toward the end of 1957, or at the beginning of 1958, that the rouble value of the yuan was appreciated from 1 rouble to the new foreign trade rouble rate of 2 roubles=1 yuan. Apparently at the same time, a non-commercial exchange rate of 6 roubles=1 yuan was also introduced.[8] The doubling of the rouble value of the yuan at the new foreign trade exchange rate, together with the introduction of the non-commercial rate, has corrected to some extent the overvaluation of the rouble at the old rouble-yuan rate, and made it less embarrassing for Peking to begin to publish the adjusted rouble-yuan rate along with the exchange rates between the yuan and other currencies.

---

[4] See, for example, United Nations, *World Economic Survey 1957*, p. 222. The precise rate used there is 1·04 rouble = 1 yuan.

[5] The Communist term "non-commercial exchange rate" refers to the exchange rate which applies to foreign exchange transactions outside the "foreign trade" category, such as tourist spendings, expenditures of diplomatic missions and international cultural activities, etc. *Chugoku Seijikeizai Sōran (Political and Economic Views on Present Day China)* (Tokyo: Ajia Seikei Gakkai [The Association for Asian Political-Economic Studies], 1960 edition), p. 590.

[6] See this paper, *post*, p. 199.

[7] The tourist rate of 10 roubles = 1 dollar, as compared with the commercial rate of 4 roubles = 1 dollar, was introduced by Moscow on April 1, 1957.

[8] *Chūgoku Seijikeizai Sōran*, 1960 edition, p. 590.

The adjusted rouble-yuan exchange rate was effective until January 1, 1961, when Moscow revalued the rouble.

To support the above story, we submit the following information and argument:

(1) Peking's Foreign Trade Minister, Yeh Chi-chuang, in his often-quoted speech of July 11, 1957, implied that the "internal conversion rate" between the rouble and the yuan (*i.e.*, the foreign trade rouble-yuan rate) had been kept unchanged from April 19, 1950, up to that time.[9] What was that exchange rate and how was it actually set in 1950? The yuan has no gold content to be used as a basis for setting exchange rate with the rouble. The absence of adequate statistical apparatus and data in China at that time made it difficult to compute the relative domestic purchasing power of the two currencies. The most practical way to work out a rouble-yuan rate at that time would seem to be the derivation of a cross rate from the then prevailing rouble-dollar rate and yuan-dollar rate. This indeed was the case. On April 19, 1950, the official Peking quotation for the dollar was 39,000 old yuan (equivalent to 3·9 new yuan) to the dollar,[10] and the then official rouble-dollar rate was 4 roubles=1 dollar. These rates would give a rouble-yuan rate of 1 rouble=0·975 new yuan, or 1·026 rouble=1 new yuan. This deviation and its application to Sino-Soviet trade is also confirmed in Soviet sources.[11] Obviously under this situation an exchange rate of 2 roubles=1 yuan would be unacceptable to the Russians. Thus we believe the rouble-yuan rate set in 1950 was approximately 1 to 1 and this rate had been effective from April 1950 to July 1957, as stated by Yeh Chi-chuang.

(2) Peking has officially announced that Sino-Soviet trade in 1956 amounted to 5·8 billion yuan; the Soviet official figure for Sino-Soviet trade in 1956 was 5·989 billion roubles. These two figures give an implicit exchange rate of 1·03 rouble=1 yuan.

It has been pointed out that recent Soviet sources are unequivocal in stating that prior to January 1, 1961, the foreign trade exchange rate was 1·00 rouble=1·00 yuan, instead of 1·03 rouble=1 yuan.[12] However,

9 *Hsin-hua Pan-yueh-kan* (*New China Semi-Monthly*), No. 16, 1957, p. 93.
10 *Jen-min Shou-tse 1951* (*People's Handbook 1951*) Shanghai: Ta Kung Pao, section Shen, pp. 23–24.
11 See Alexander Eckstein, "Sino-Soviet Economic Relations: A Reappraisal" (July 1961, unpublished), p. 34 and note 40. The Soviet source referred to by Eckstein is A. A. Netrusov, *The Economic Relations of China with Foreign Countries* (in Russian) (Moscow: 1958), pp. 82–83.
12 Oleg Hoeffding, "Research on Communist China's Foreign Trade: Comments on three papers by Shu-hsin Chou, Robert F. Dernberger and Feng-hwa Mah," Santa Monica: The RAND Corporation (P-2689), January 1963, pp. 8–9. The Soviet source referred to by Hoeffding is I. P. Aizenberg, *Valiutnaia Sistema SSSR* (*The Soviet Currency System*) (Moscow, ? 1962), p. 149.

Communist Chinese sources have reported that, in computing the prices of imported equipment, the exchange rate used (presumably as of 1958) was 1 rouble=0·95 yuan.[13] Thus we still believe the 1 to 1 rate was a round figure, not the precise rate. For it would be difficult to explain why the decimal figure was used in Communist China if the rate was precisely 1 to 1.

(3) To our knowledge the earliest Communist Chinese publications referring to the exchange rate of 2 roubles=1 yuan appeared late in 1957. An article in the October 1957 issue of the *Academic Monthly* (*Hsueh-shu Yueh-kan*) states that "The exchange rate between the people's currency and the rouble is approximately 1 to 2, that is, 1 yuan is roughly equal to 2 roubles." [14] In its December 1957 issue (*Chi-hua Ching-chi*) *Planned Economy* published a table showing the conversion rates between the yuan and several foreign currencies, including the rouble. The rouble-yuan rate given there was 2 roubles=1 yuan. How-ever, the footnotes to that table explained explicitly that this rouble-yuan rate was not the official exchange rate at the time. It was "derived from relevant data" at the request of readers, and "the table is meant for general reference only." [15] These two sources have made it clear that the conversion rate of 2 roubles=1 yuan was not the official exchange rate at the end of 1957. They seem to suggest that during the last few months of 1957, Peking was making new calculations of the rouble-yuan rate in preparation for an official adjustment of the old rate. By that time the rouble-yuan rate had been pegged at 1 rouble=1 yuan for nearly eight years. It is likely that the relative changes of domestic prices in Russia and in Communist China had made the rate more and more unfavourable to the yuan, and an appreciation of the rouble value of the yuan had become more and more desirable to Communist China. Peking certainly was aware that during the first part of 1957, the Eastern European countries had all introduced "non-commercial exchange rates" for the obvious reason of offsetting somewhat the overvaluation of the rouble *vis-à-vis* their currencies. Very likely the new rouble-yuan exchange rate of 2 roubles=1 yuan was adopted at the beginning of 1958. Later we shall show that the appreciation of the rouble value of the yuan from 1 to 2 roubles also made the new rouble-yuan rate con-sistent with the foreign trade exchange rates of Eastern European countries.

13 See joint article by Tung Shu-ping, Li Tien-to, Shao Hsi-kuei, Hsu Hsiu-ching and Li Yao-chu in *Jen-min Tien-yeh* (*People's Power Industry*), No. 1, 1958, p. 14.
14 Yu Jui-hsiang, Cheng Hsi-yuan and Lu Chun-ken, "On the Problem of the Nature and Function of People's Currency," *Hsueh-shu Yueh-kan* (*Academic Monthly*), No. 10, 1957, p. 55.
15 *Chi-hua Ching-chi* (*Planned Economy*), No. 12, December 9, 1957, p. 29.

COMPARISON OF THE ROUBLE-YUAN RATE WITH OTHER COMMUNIST EXCHANGE RATES

The establishment of a general non-commercial exchange rate system early in 1957 by the Eastern European countries was a concerted action. These countries have selected a standard market basket of about 75 commodities and services for this purpose. The non-commercial rates were computed bilaterally on the basis of the relative domestic prices of the items in the basket in each pair of countries. Thus, generally speaking, the non-commercial exchange rates are nearer to the relative domestic purchasing power of the currencies involved than are the foreign trade exchange rates. Tables 1 and 2 show the official " foreign trade " and " non-commercial " exchange rates, respectively, of the Communist countries. When these tables are read horizontally, the figures in each line give the equivalent units of other Communist currencies. For example, in Table 1 one can read horizontally along the second line to find that 1 yuan is equal to 2 Russian roubles or 3·4 Bulgarian leva, etc. In these two tables, the exchange rates involving the yuan are the Bank of China quotations of July 1, 1959. All the other rates are given by the respective national banks in 1960. We believe the foreign trade exchange rates involving the yuan were all adjusted rates adopted at the beginning of 1958. The other exchange rates in these tables had practically unchanged from early 1957 to the end of 1960.

It can be seen from Tables 1 and 2 that the foreign trade exchange rates are consistent with one another, but that the non-commercial rates are not always consistent. In the latter case, however, the differences between the non-commercial rates and the rates concerted from them are not large, usually below 10 per cent.

Although these non-commercial exchange rates do not accurately represent the purchasing power parity of the currencies involved, they are nevertheless nearer to the latter than are the foreign trade exchange rates. If we compute the ratio of the non-commercial exchange rate to the foreign trade exchange rate for each of these countries, the results would roughly indicate whether at the foreign trade exchange rate the value of a particular country's currency is overvalued or undervalued. From Tables 1 and 2 it is easy to see that except for the Soviet rouble and the Communist Chinese yuan, the currency of each of the other Communist countries is overvalued in some cases and undervalued in some other cases. It is interesting to find that in all the cases the yuan is undervalued, and that except in the case of the rouble-zloty rate, the rouble is always overvalued. This finding is presented in Tables 3 and 4. In these two tables, if the ratio of non-commercial rate to foreign trade rate (all expressed in terms of foreign currency units to one unit of

Table 1. Foreign Trade Exchange Rates of Communist Countries as of 1960

National Currency (1 unit is equal to)	Russian rouble	Communist Chinese yuan	Bulgarian leva	Czechoslovakian crown	E. German DM	Hungarian forint	Polish zloty
Russian rouble		0·5000	1·7000	1·8000	0·5556	2·9350	1·4962
Communist Chinese yuan	2·0000		3·4000	—	1·1112	5·8700	8·9775
Albanian lek	0·0800	0·0400	0·1360	0·1440	0·0444	0·2348	0·1496
Bulgarian leva	0·5882	0·2940		1·0588	0·3268	1·7262	1·7198
Czechoslovakian crown	0·5556	0·2770	0·9445		0·3087	1·6305	1·2899
East German DM	1·8000	0·8990	3·0600	3·2394		5·2798	3·9196
Hungarian forint	0·3410	0·1700	0·5797	0·6133	0·1894		1·0687
Polish zloty	1·0000	0·5000	1·7000	1·8000	0·5556	2·9350	
Rumanian lei	0·6667	0·3330	1·1333	1·2000	0·3704	1·9565	1·5425

Sources: (1) *Chūgoku Seijikeizai Sōran*, 1960 edition, p. 590.
(2) Frederic L. Pryor, *The Communist Foreign Trade System*, Appendix B, p. 241, and primary data in Professor Pryor's files.

Note: — indicates not available.

Table 2. Non-Commercial Exchange Rates of Communist Countries as of 1960

National Currency (1 unit is equal to)	Russian rouble	Communist Chinese yuan	Bulgarian leva	Czechoslovakian crown	E. German DM	Hungarian forint	Polish zloty
Russian rouble		0·1667	0·8900	1·1600	0·3876	1·4000	1·4962
Communist Chinese yuan	6·0000		5·3400	6·9589	2·3020	8·4000	8·9775
Albanian lek	0·1000	—	0·0890	0·1160	0·0444	0·1400	0·1496
Bulgarian leva	1·1240	0·1873		1·2791	0·4357	1·5730	1·7198
Czechoslovakian crown	0·8621	0·1437	0·7818		0·3276	1·2067	1·2899
East German DM	2·5800	0·4344	2·2950	3·0521		3·7323	3·9196
Hungarian forint	0·7143	0·1190	0·6357	0·8287	0·2697		1·0687
Polish zloty	0·6684	0·1111	0·5800	0·7733	0·2544	0·9333	
Rumanian lei	1·0309	—	0·9175	—	0·3996	1·4433	1·5425

Sources and note: same as Table 1.

national currency) is less than unity, the national currency is undervalued at the foreign trade exchange rate, if the ratio is greater than unity, the national currency is overvalued at the foreign trade exchange rate.

It is to be recalled that, before 1958, the rouble-yuan exchange rate was 1 to 1, and there were no non-commercial exchange rates among the Communist countries. Thus, during the years before 1958, the under-valuation of the yuan *vis-à-vis* other Communist currencies was more serious than is shown in these tables. It seems clear that the losses incurred by Communist China in her international transactions at the old rouble-yuan exchange rate during 1950-57 must have been very heavy indeed.

Table 3. Ratios of Non-Commercial Exchange Rate to Foreign Trade Exchange Rate, Communist China

Foreign Currencies (1 unit is equal to)	Foreign trade rate (yuan)	Non-Commercial rate (yuan)	ratio (N.C. rate/F.T. rate)
Russian rouble	0·5000	0·1667	0·33
Bulgarian leva	0·2940	0·1873	0·64
Czechoslovakian crown	0·2770	0·1437	0·52
East German DM	0·8990	0·4344	0·48
Hungarian forint	0·1700	0·1190	0·72
Polish zloty	0·5000	0·1111	0·22

Source: Tables 1 and 2.
Note: F.T. rate=Foreign trade rate. N.C. rate=Non-Commercial rate.

Table 4 further shows that while the ruble is overvalued relative to all other Communist currencies except the Polish zloty, the extent of overvaluation of the rouble is greatest in the rouble-yuan exchange rate. Does this reflect to some extent the intra-*bloc* politico-economic relation-ship at the time?

Table 4. Ratios of Non-Commercial Exchange Rate to Foreign Trade Exchange Rate, The Soviet Union

Foreign Currencies (1 unit is equal to)	Foreign trade rate (rouble)	Non-Commercial rate (rouble)	ratio (N.C. rate/F.T. rate)
Communist Chinese yuan	2·0000	6·0000	3·00
Albanian lek	0·0800	0·1000	1·25
Bulgarian leva	0·5882	1·1240	1·91
Czechoslovakian crown	0·5556	0·8621	1·55
East German DM	1·8000	2·5800	1·43
Hungarian forint	0·3410	0·7143	2·09
Polish zloty	1·0000	0·6684	0·67
Rumanian lei	0·6667	1·0309	1·55

Source and note: Same as Table 3.

THE ROUBLE-YUAN EXCHANGE RATE SINCE 1961

The Soviet Union revalued the rouble on January 1, 1961. Internally, one new rouble is equal to ten old roubles. Externally, however, one new rouble is defined as equivalent to $1·11, instead of 1 new rouble= 10 old roubles=$2·50 at the old foreign trade exchange rate. In other words, externally, one new rouble equals only 4·44 old roubles. This amounts to a 55 per cent. devaluation of the external value of the rouble. Soviet sources have claimed that this new rouble-dollar exchange rate was based on the relative purchasing power of the two currencies for various groups of goods and services, and it approximates the average purchasing power parity " for the national product as a whole." [16]

After the Soviet currency revaluation, the exchange rates between the new rouble and the other Communist currencies were all recalculated accordingly.[17] Two conversion rates were used in the recalculation: In computing the non-commercial exchange rates, 1 new rouble=10 old roubles; in working out the foreign trade exchange rates, 1 new rouble= 4·44 old roubles. Table 5 shows the exchange rates between the new rouble and the other Communist currencies since January 1, 1961.

Table 5. Exchange Rates of Communist Countries, 1961

Foreign Currencies (1 unit is equal to)	Foreign trade rate (new rouble)	Non-commercial 'rate (new rouble)
Communist Chinese yuan	0·4500	0·6000
Albanian lek	0·0180	0·0100
Bulgarian leva	0·1323	0·1124
Czechoslovakian crown	0·1250	0·0862
East German DM	0·4050	0·2580
Hungarian forint	0·0767	0·0714
Polish zloty	0·2250	0·0667
Rumanian lei	0·1500	0·1031

Sources: (1) *Chūgoku Seijikeizai Sōran*, 1960 edition, p. 590.
(2) Frederic L. Pryor, *The Communist Foreign Trade System*, Appendix B, p. 241.
(3) *Shih-chieh Chi-hsi Nien-chien, 1961 (World Knowledge Yearbook, 1961)* (Peking: World Knowledge Publishing House), p. 1323.

The 1961 adjustment of exchange rates has probably corrected the overvaluation of the external value of the rouble. From Table 5 it can be seen that for the majority of the Communist counties, the foreign trade exchange rate is now closer to the non-commercial exchange rate. Poland again is an exception. The zloty is now even more overvalued than before in relation to the rouble. Table 5 also shows that among the eight

16 I. P. Aizenberg, *Valiutnaia Sistema SSSR*, Moscow, 1962, p. 143 *et seq.* Taken from Oleg Hoeffding, *op. cit* (RAND P-2689), p. 11.
17 The foreign trade exchange rates and the non-commercial exchange rates between other Communist countries are not influenced by the rouble revaluation.

Communist countries listed there, only the Sino-Soviet non-commercial exchange rate is still higher than the corresponding foreign trade exchange rate. This indicates that even after the 1961 rouble revaluation, the foreign trade rouble-yuan rate still overvalued the rouble.

AN ESTIMATE OF THE ROUBLE-YUAN PURCHASING POWER PARITY

In order to test our earlier hypothesis that the effective rouble-yuan rate during 1950–57 (or during 1950–60, for that matter) greatly overvalued the rouble, and to gauge the extent of correction of this overvaluation made by the 1961 adjustment, we attempt in this section to compute the " purchasing power parity " rouble-yuan rate for the early 1950s. Because the concept of purchasing power parity itself is vague, because the computation is very sensitive to the sample and weights used, and also because the available data are inadequate, our estimate is necessarily only an approximation.

The procedure of our computation is briefly outlined in the Appendix to this article. Dictated by the availability of data, our estimate is admittedly a patchwork. The commodity sample used in the computation is determined by what domestic prices and foreign trade values are available. For the producer goods in our sample, we compared the Chinese wholesale prices at the beginning of 1952 with the Soviet wholesale prices for 1950. For the consumer goods in our sample, we used the Chinese retail prices at the beginning of 1952 to compare with the Soviet retail prices for 1950. This is because convenient sources of Soviet retail prices for producer goods, and Soviet wholesale prices for consumer goods, for the early 1950s, are not available. These two different years' prices are used here, also out of necessity. The system of weights is derived from the 1955 rouble value of the itemised Chinese imports from and exports to Russia. The year 1955 is the first for which detailed value data on Sino-Soviet trade is available. To use value weights of later years would give greater distortions to our estimate, because of the changes of commodity structure in Communist Chinese-Soviet trade. A list of commodities (or commodity groups) included in our sample, and the steps of our computation, are summarised in Tables 6 and 7. For Communist China's imports from Russia, our weighted average price ratio is 0·85 rouble/yuan. For Communist China's exports to Russia, the weighted average price ratio is 13·45 rouble/yuan. In 1955, the relative importance of imports and exports in total Sino-Soviet trade value is 53·76 per cent. for Chinese imports and 46·24 per cent. for Chinese exports.[18] Using these relative values as weights, we average the two price ratios and arrive at the estimated rate of 6·68 rouble/yuan.

[18] For sources, see Appendix.

This estimated " purchasing power parity " rate of 6·68 rouble=1 yuan is reasonably close to the non-commercial exchange rate of 6 roubles=1 yuan introduced at the beginning of 1958.

The limitations of our estimate are as follows:

(1) In Communist China, prices were generally reduced from 1950 to 1951 but remained fairly stable from 1952 to 1955. In the Soviet Union there were no significant price changes during 1950–1954. New prices were introduced in 1955 in Russia. Thus our " purchasing power parity " rate seems to be more valid for 1952–54 than for the other years. Since Chinese prices were higher in 1950–51 than in later years, the rouble value of the yuan ought to be smaller than 6·68 rouble/yuan before January 1952. After 1955, the rouble value of the yuan might also be lower than our computed rate, because, since 1955, Soviet prices seemed to be lower than the previous years.

(2) Quality differences of the commodities may influence our estimated rates, too. The comparability of the producer goods in our sample is relatively good, because detailed specifications for many of them are available in the price data. For consumer goods, the quality differences are likely to be greater, and we suspect that because of the relatively inferior qualities of many Chinese commodities, the computed Chinese export price ratio, and hence the " purchasing power parity " rate, probably has an upward bias.

(3) The use of retail prices for consumer goods may also cause some upward bias for the Chinese export price ratio, and hence also for the " purchasing power parity " rate, because in the Chinese domestic market, the retailer's mark-up over and above the wholesale prices is relatively small.

(4) Machinery and the complete sets of equipment, which took about one third of Communist China's imports in the early 1950s, cannot be included in our computation of price ratios. However, this weakness in our computation perhaps would not lead to additional upward bias, because the price ratios for machinery are not likely to be lower than the computed price ratio for all imports, 0·85 rouble/yuan.

If one takes a conservative attitude, and assumes that, because of the above factors, our computed rouble-yuan rate of 6·68 roubles=1 yuan is upward biased by roughly 30 per cent., then even if we discount the calculated rouble-yuan rate by 30 per cent., the resultant rate would still be well above 4 roubles=1 yuan, which indicates that the earlier official foreign trade exchange rate of either 1 rouble=1 yuan or 2 roubles= 1 yuan, had substantially overvalued the rouble. Judging from the non-commercial rate of 6 roubles=1 yuan introduced in 1958, perhaps the degree of upward bias in our estimated " purchasing power parity " rate is not too large.

FINAL REMARKS

Although the purpose of this paper is to present the findings of our empirical study of the rouble-yuan exchange rate, it may nevertheless be in order to indicate some of the implications of our findings:

(1) To the extent that the effect of the overvaluation of the rouble at the foreign trade rouble-yuan rate was not completely offset by price manoeuvres in the Communist Chinese-Soviet trade negotiations, the Soviet Union took advantage of Communist China in trading with it at this exchange rate.

(2) It must be borne in mind that foreign trade and loan figures, converted from rouble to yuan values at the foreign trade exchange rate, are not comparable with the various measurements of the domestic economy in terms of yuan, because this procedure would inevitably exaggerate the importance of the foreign sector.[19]

Table 6. *Domestic Price Ratios of Communist China's Imports from the U.S.S.R.*

Commodity and Soviet Code	1955 value weight (%)	Average price ratio (rouble/yuan)	Number of prices compared	Weighted price ratio (rouble/yuan)
Electrotechnical equipment (111)	4·31	1·03	13	4·45
Ball and roller bearings (17300)	1·84	1·17	7	2·15
Petroleum products (22)	23·88	0·40	6	9·53
Ferroalloys (261)	4·00	0·78	3	3·12
Rolled iron and steel (264)	42·46	0·91	32	38·43
Pipes (266)	9·82	0·78	4	7·64
Metal products (268)	1·59	1·46	40	2·32
Rolled non-ferrous metals (272)	3·73	1·11	4	4·13
Copper and Aluminium in bars, coils & scrap (292)	0·03	2·36	2	0·07
Dyes, varnishes, paints & tanning materials (31)	1·52	1·44	6	2·19
Timber and cellulose-paper products (50)	5·83	0·98	6	5·73
Medicines, sanitary and hygienic articles, perfumes and cosmetics (96)	0·98	5·22	3	5·12
Total	100·00		126	84·88

Sources and notes : see Appendix.

[19] See Kang Chao, " Yuan-Dollar Price Ratios in Communist China and the United States," in *Two Studies on Mainland China's Economy* (The University of Michigan Center for Chinese Studies, *Occasional Papers*, No. 2), July 1963, p. 19.

(3) The use of unrealistic exchange rates suggests that the official Communist Chinese foreign trade returns in terms of yuan present a distorted picture. If more realistic foreign exchange rates are used, then the total volume, regional distribution, and other related aspects (such as the rate of annual increase or decrease) of Communist China's foreign trade would all appear different from what one can read from the official Communist claims.[20]

Table 7. *Domestic Price Ratios of Communist China's Exports to the U.S.S.R.*

Commodity and Soviet Code	1955 value weight (%)	Average price ratio (rouble/yuan)	Number of prices compared	Weighted price ratio (rouble/yuan)
Coal, hard (200)	1·98	3·59	2	7·10
Pig iron (26000)	10·40	2·91	2	30·30
Non-ferrous metals and alloys (270)	22·29	4·28	10	95·42
Chemical products (30)	2·59	1·15	21	2·98
Building materials (40)	2·51	4·72	8	11·84
Rope, fish nets, technical cloth and other materials (592)	1·77	14·91	3	26·40
Meat and dairy products, animal fats & eggs (80)	29·03	17·63	5	511·89
Products of the flour milling industry (820)	17·46	29·65	2	517·60
Vegetables, fruits, berries & produce (83)	5·95	11·04	3	64·70
Outer garments and under clothing (91)	6·02	12·51	2	75·33
Total	100·00		58	1344·56

Sources and notes : see Appendix.

APPENDIX

Sources and Notes to Tables 6 and 7

Notes:

(a) The commodity classification system of Soviet foreign trade statistics is used here. The Soviet Code number (immediately following the name of each commodity group) is given in the tables to facilitate identification and checking.

[20] For more detailed discussion of this and related problems, see Kang Chao, *op. cit.*, in *Two Studies on Mainland China's Economy* (The University of Michigan Center for Chinese Studies, *Occasional Papers*, No. 2), pp. 16–25; Feng-hwa Mah, " Some Problems in the Study of Communist China's Foreign Trade " (a paper prepared for the First Research Conference of the Social Science Research Council Committee on the Economy of China, Berkeley, California, January 31–February 2, 1963. Unpublished). Section II, pp. 4–14.

A code number with more digits refers to a narrower commodity group. A code number with few digits refers to a broader commodity group.

(b) Within each commodity group, the average price ratio is the arithmetic mean of the rouble/yuan price ratios of the individual commodities in that group. Between commodity groups, the average price ratio for each group is weighted by the relative importance of the 1955 import (or export) value of that group. The computation formula is $\Sigma \left(\dfrac{Ps}{Pc} \bullet \dfrac{V}{\Sigma V} \right)$

where Ps=Soviet price, Pc=Communist Chinese price, $\dfrac{Ps}{Pc}$=average price ratio of a commodity group, and V=actual import (or export) value of that commodity group in 1955.

(c) For Communist China's imports, the covered commodities account for 16·90 per cent. of the total value of Communist China's imports from Russia in 1955. For Communist China's exports, the included commodities represent 48·55 per cent. of the total value of Chinese exports to Russia in that year.

Sources:

(a) For producer goods: The Chinese prices are from *Kung-yeh Chi-tsai (Industrial Equipment and Material)*, January 1952. The Russian prices are from N. M. Kaplan and W. L. White, *A Comparison of 1950 Wholesale Prices in Soviet and American Industry* (Santa Monica: The RAND Corporation (RM-1443), May 1, 1955).

(b) For consumer goods: The Chinese prices are the market retail prices quoted in *Ta Kung Pao*, January 3, 1952. The Russian prices are taken from E. S. Wainstein, *A Comparison of Soviet and United States Retail Food Prices for 1950* (Santa Monica: The RAND Corporation (RM-1294), July 13, 1954), and E. S. Wainstein, *A Comparison of Soviet and United States Retail Prices for Manufactured Goods and Services in 1950* (Santa Monica: The RAND Corporation (RM-1606), January 5, 1956).

(c) The 1955 value weights are computed from *Vneshniaia Torgovlia SSSR za 1956 god—Statisticheskii Obzor (Foreign Trade of the USSR in 1956—Statistical Summary)* (Moscow: 1958), pp. 121, 127.

List of Contributors

Kang Chao is Assistant Professor of Economics at the University of Michigan. He has published several articles on industrial production and prices of Communist China, and is at present engaged in research on the construction industry in Communist China.

Audrey Donnithorne is Lecturer in Chinese Economic Studies at University College, London.

Charles Hoffmann is Associate Professor of Economics and Acting Chairman of the Department of Economics at the State University of New York.

William Hollister is Research Associate at the University of California, Berkeley. He has spent many years in research on the economy of Communist China and is author of *China's Gross National Product and Social Accounts—1950-1957*.

Ronald Hsia, Ph.D., is Senior Lecturer in Economics, University of Hong Kong, and visiting Lecturer, London School of Economics. He was formerly associated with Harvard University, Massachusetts Institute of Technology and the RAND Corporation. He is the author of *Price Control in Communist China* (1953), *Economic Planning in Communist China* (1955), and *Government Acquisition of Agricultural Output in Mainland China* (1958).

Fred C. Hung is Acting Director of the Economic Research Center University of Hawaii.

Leslie T. C. Kuo, who got his Ph.D. in Agricultural Economics at Cornell, was an officer of the Food and Agriculture Organisation (FAO) of the United Nations for eleven years. He has been Chief of the Oriental Project, National Agricultural Library, United States Department of Agriculture, Washington, D.C., since 1960.

Choh-Ming Li, author of *Economic Development of Communist China*, is now Vice-Chancellor of the Chinese University of Hong Kong.

Feng-hwa Mah is Assistant Professor of Economics at the University of Washington and a member of the Far Eastern and Russian Institute at the University.

Peter Schran studied economics and sociology at the Free University of Berlin, and economics and Chinese at the University of California, Berkeley. He is now Assistant Professor of Economics at Yale University.

Franz Schurmann is Associate Professor of Sociology and History at the University of California, Berkeley. He is author of two forthcoming volumes, *Ideology and Organization in Communist China* and *Industrial Management in Communist China*.

Yuan-li Wu, Professor of International Business at the University of San Francisco and Research Associate of the Hoover Institution, Stanford University, is the author of *An Economic Survey of Communist China* and *Economic Development and the use of Energy Resources in Communist China*.